ALSO BY BRAD BALUKJIAN

The Wax Pack: On the Open Road in
Search of Baseball's Afterlife

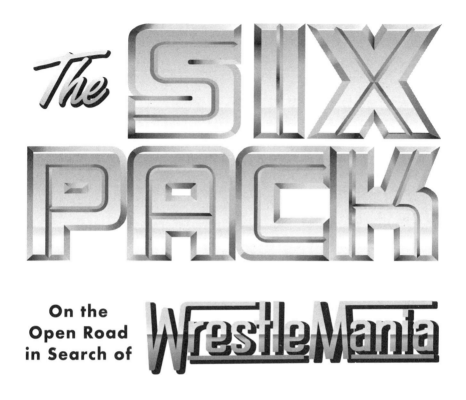

The SIX PACK

On the Open Road in Search of WrestleMania

BRAD BALUKJIAN

hachette
BOOKS

New York

Hachette Books
Hachette Book Group
1290 Avenue of the Americas
New York, NY 10104
HachetteBooks.com
Twitter.com/HachetteBooks
Instagram.com/HachetteBooks

First Edition: April 2024

Published by Hachette Books, an imprint of Hachette Book Group, Inc. The Hachette Books name and logo is a trademark of the Hachette Book Group.

The Hachette Speakers Bureau provides a wide range of authors for speaking events. To find out more, go to hachettespeakersbureau.com or email HachetteSpeakers@hbgusa.com.

Books by Hachette Books may be purchased in bulk for business, educational, or promotional use. For information, please contact your local bookseller or Hachette Book Group Special Markets Department at: special.markets@hbgusa.com.

The publisher is not responsible for websites (or their content) that are not owned by the publisher.

Library of Congress Control Number: 2023951551

ISBNs: 9780306831553 (hardcover); 9780306831577 (ebook)

Printed in the United States of America

LSC-C

Printing 1, 2024

My dad never liked wrestling. He still doesn't. So it speaks volumes about the kind of dad he is that he took me to so many live events at the Providence Civic Center when I was a kid. He sat there and endured the spectacle while I turned heads with my shrill screams from the nosebleed seats. It was real to me, dammit, and so too was my dad's love.

Thank you, Dad.

Want to go on an adventure?

—Bianca Offers, the author's niece, age 3

A student said, "Master, I am reaching for the light—please help me!"
Yunmen replied, "Forget the light; give me the reaching!"

—Zen koan

)

CONTENTS

AUTHOR'S NOTE

THERE ARE SECTIONS OF THIS BOOK IN WHICH I HAVE ALTERED OR COM-pressed the chronology to create a more streamlined narrative. Quotes are accurate, having been tape-recorded or documented contemporaneously in my notebooks. I did clean up some of the "ums" and "uhs" for the reader's enjoyment. Some names have been changed, but there are no composite characters.

This book focuses on a specific period in wrestling history, namely the 1970s and 1980s, a time when almost all of the featured performers were men. As such, I use the term "the Boys" to collectively refer to wrestlers of the era, a term they used for themselves. I am glad to see that women now comprise a significant portion of wrestling rosters, and their general exclusion here is simply the result of the period that I am covering.

KAYFABE GLOSSARY

Angle: An ongoing, episodic storyline between wrestlers.

Babyface: A "good guy" wrestler; a fan favorite.

Blade: To cut one's forehead with a concealed razor blade during a match to create real blood flow, adding to the drama.

Blow-off: The culmination of a program in which one wrestler, usually the babyface, prevails.

Boys: Wrestlers referred to collectively.

Bump: A fall on the ring canvas.

Clean: Describes a match that ends without any outside interference or illegal activity.

Finish: The ending of a match.

Heat: Negative crowd reaction, usually directed at a heel; also friction between wrestlers.

Heel: A "bad guy" wrestler, or villain.

Highspot: A particularly acrobatic or "high-risk" move, often some aerial maneuver.

Job (noun): The loss of a match.

Job (verb): To lose a match.

Jobber: A wrestler who consistently loses matches to more marquee talent.

Lock-up: When two wrestlers grab each other by the collar and elbow in the middle of the ring to start a match.

Mark: A fan who thinks wrestling is legitimate sport.

Office: The employees of the wrestling organization, namely the bookers and agents (not the wrestlers).

Pop: Positive crowd reaction.

Program: An ongoing feud between two wrestlers in which they tour around, wrestling each other night after night.

Promo: Short monologue-style interview in which a wrestler discusses an upcoming match.

Push: Winning a series of matches, usually entailing elevation toward the main event.

Put over: To lose to one's opponent or to praise another wrestler.

Road: The lifestyle of long travel with few breaks that defined pro wrestling in the 1970s and 1980s.

Screw job: To deviate from the script, such that one wrestler loses unexpectedly.

Sell: To act injured or hurt as part of the planned sequence of a match.

Shoot: An event or incident that is "real" because it is not planned or staged as part of the show; a screw job is an example of a shoot.

Smart: Someone who knows that wrestling is predetermined entertainment rather than legitimate athletic competition.

Spot: A move executed in a match.

Stiff: A move (usually a punch or a kick) that lands especially hard, blurring the line between reality and fiction.

Valet: Someone who accompanies a wrestler to the ring, usually a woman.

Work: An event or incident that is planned and staged as part of the show.

Worker: A wrestler.

PART I
THE ENTRANCE

PROLOGUE

2005, Fayetteville, Georgia

THE IRON SHEIK JUST THREATENED TO KILL ME.

To be fair, he's giving me choices:

"I'll shoot you with my .38 Magnum, stab you with my Bowie knife, or just break your fucking leg," he spits, his voice coarse.

At age sixty-three, the ropes of muscle in his neck and shoulders remain thick. His head sinks into a cement-mixer chest, his handlebar mustache still meticulously curled but now flecked with gray. The very same man whose action figure I once smacked against Hulk Hogan in elaborate matches on my bedroom floor is now swaddled in front of me in a plaid blanket, the fabric concealing an eggplant-colored left ankle and two poorly replaced knees. The ankle is so bad that he takes every step on the side of his foot to minimize the pain.

A Dallas Cowboys wool hat covers his iconic bald head, his scalp pocked with scars from years of cutting himself with razor blades during matches, a practice known as *blading* in the parlance of professional wrestling (they don't use blood capsules). Toward the back of its lunar surface lies a particularly deep crevice, marking the spot where a crazed fan in South Africa hit him in the head with a blackjack.

"The people have to pay to see the head," he is fond of saying. Outside of showering, his head is always covered with a hat or durag representing some sports team or wrestling event given to him by a promoter or fan. You never pay for clothes when you're a household name.

At the height of professional wrestling's boom in the 1980s, the Iron Sheik was my hero. He appeared in Cyndi Lauper music videos, starred in Toyota commercials, and was literally a cartoon (part of the ensemble cast of *Hulk Hogan's Rock 'n' Wrestling*). Hailing from Tehran, Iran, he was the ultimate bad guy, or *heel*, marching to the ring waving a flag of Ayatollah Khomeini, shouting "Iran Number One!" and playing off every Middle Eastern stereotype at a time when such jingoism ran rampant.

But few knew that he really *was* from Iran, born Hossein Khosrow Vaziri (he goes by "Khos"), and that his life *before* becoming the Iron Sheik was just as full of controversy. Even his birthday is a dispute—his passport says March 15 while his driver's license says September 9; the small town where he was born, Damghan, didn't keep reliable records. Growing up before the country's Islamic Revolution, Khos had only one dream—to be the greatest amateur wrestler Iran had ever seen. At age fourteen he went to a brothel to get the number 90 tattooed on his right forearm, representing the weight, in kilograms, of his hero, Olympic gold medalist wrestler Gholamreza Takhti. He eschewed any carnal delights, dedicating himself to training and prayer. For forty consecutive Fridays he rode a bus two hours each way to worship at a Shia mosque. He enlisted in the Iranian army and, given his prowess on the wrestling mat, was recruited to be a bodyguard for Shah Mohammad Reza Pahlavi's wife Farah.

But right now all of that is a distant memory as I stand in his living room facing the most surreal multiple-choice question of my young life: How do I want to die? At the hands of my hero, no less?

I scan the living room, which is tastefully decorated thanks to his wife of thirty years, Caryl. There are two couches and a plush chair located toward the center of the room, and in the adjoining dining room I spy a chandelier, china cabinet, and, on the wall, a framed wedding photo—Caryl with a short, mod, seventies hairstyle and Khos in his pre–Iron Sheik days, svelte, sans mustache, with a mane of thinning black hair.

I am positioned several paces away from Khos, and although he is as mobile as an anvil, I don't feel particularly good about making a run for it.

My left hand tightens around my notebook while my right clenches a pencil. My heart thumps as I look down at the floor, not wanting to acknowledge my idol's eyes. There have been plenty of tense moments over the past couple months—driving him to a roach motel to buy drugs, hearing him rant and scream at Caryl for no good reason—but death threats are new. My mission, to work with him on writing a book about his life, now seems compromised.

Apparently Iron Sheiks also don't take kindly to fact-checking. Moments ago, following a trademark out-of-the-blue, pec-slapping, mustache-twirling rant about how he is the only wrestler to come out of the Middle East and become a star in the US, I had calmly stated, "Well, Khos, there was someone else. General Adnan from Iraq."

The moment my words reached his eardrums, his dark brown eyes turned a shade darker. It's a look that had become all too familiar. Not only had I contradicted the former World Wrestling Federation (WWF) champion, I had invoked the name of the country that had fought a bloody nine-year war against his native Iran.

I was right, of course, that General Adnan (real name: Adnan Alkaissy) is from Iraq; he had been a childhood friend of Saddam Hussein and played the role of evil henchman to Sgt. Slaughter during the Desert Storm war in 1991 (ironically, Khos played Slaughter's *other* henchman under the name Colonel Mustafa, but I don't dare pile on).

To Khos, I am unnecessarily putting him down, letting facts get in the way of a perfectly good *promo*.

Just as I am leaning toward the .38 Magnum for my fate (the quickest option), I look up and see some of the crimson starting to drain from his face, the adrenaline rush subsiding.

"Brad baba" (he calls everyone "baba"), "why do you say that? Why don't you put me over?" His accent is thick and his English choppy, inspiring many imitations from fans and fellow wrestlers alike.

In the lexicon of "Kayfabe," pronounced ˈkāˌfāb, *putting someone over* means allowing your opponent to win a match, or more generally, showing them support. (Kayfabe is the all-encompassing name given to wrestling's bizarre and unique set of customs, language, and overall culture. The term's origin is a mystery—some believe it to be bastardized Pig Latin for "fake." Indeed, such manipulation of words created the foundation for the

carny language that wrestlers use to communicate with each other, invert-
ing words and adding syllables.) In order for a wrestling match to work,
you have to, well, *work*, which is Kayfabe for cooperating, and is the opposite of a *shoot*, which would be a legitimate fight. For the last thirty-three
years, Khos has been working so well that his grip on reality has become
somewhat tenuous. At the moment, I am shooting (*but what about General
Adnan?*) when I should be working.

But it wasn't always like this. A couple months prior, when I had arrived
in this suburb of Atlanta to start work on his biography, Khos had greeted
me at the airport with a big smile, flashing a set of gleaming, gap-ridden
teeth and saying, "Excellent, Brad baba, we're going to make million, million dollars together."

So what went wrong?

*   *   *

WITHOUT A DOUBT, PROFESSIONAL WRESTLING AND I ARE UNLIKELY BEDFEL-
lows. A product of private schools and upper-middle-class rearing in the
outskirts of Providence, Rhode Island (to be fair, everything in Rhode
Island is technically in the outskirts of Providence), I shouldn't be a fan of
such lowbrow entertainment, such *trash*.

"You like that stuff?" they would ask. "How? It's so fake!"

And that was my own parents talking.

But to timorous, scrawny, six-year-old me, wrestling was the ultimate
outlet, a world where I could be strong and fearless, where I could let my
bottled-up anger loose and still not hurt anyone because it was all done with
a wink and a nod. When my mother saw me practicing the figure-four leg-
lock on my younger sister, Lauren, she grew concerned and called my aunt.

"Don't worry about it," Aunt Rom replied, putting me forever in her debt.
"Brad's such a shy kid, it's a good outlet for him!"

Watch any Balukjian home video from the 1980s and you will witness the
product of Aunt Rom's counsel. Buck-toothed and gangly, one minute I'm
perched in the corner silently paging through the world atlas, and the next
I'm in the face of the camera, finger-pointing, shouting to an imaginary
opponent, "I'm the best, I'm the champion, you've got nothing!" My dad's
irritated baritone undercuts my high-pitched rant—"Brad, I can't see your
sister!"—but this is no matter; I have morphed into Exciting Balukjian, my

good guy or *babyface* persona, and have declared war on all the heels in the dressing room.

Social critic Roland Barthes once called wrestling "a spectacle of excess," and for an insecure kid with headgear and a stutter, that excess gave me something to look forward to every Saturday morning when I plopped in front of the TV to watch Hulk Hogan, "Macho Man" Randy Savage, and the Iron Sheik grapple in sweaty make-believe.

The Iron Sheik, whose entire gimmick was predicated on xenophobia, was my favorite. I was drawn to him not because I was unpatriotic—I proudly pledged allegiance every day at Henry Barnard Elementary School—but because the Iron Sheik was the guy *nobody* cheered for (I was always about the underdogs), and he had a really cool handlebar mustache and curly-toed elf boots (these things matter when you're six!). While some of the other heels like "Rowdy" Roddy Piper or Jake "The Snake" Roberts got cheers for being cool antiheroes, the Iron Sheik was universally disliked. How could you cheer for a man whose tag-team partner, Nikolai Volkoff, demanded that the crowd stand and respect his singing of the Soviet national anthem at the height of the Cold War?

Wrestling dominated my childhood and adolescence. A friend who won backstage passes invited me to meet a few wrestlers before a show at the Providence Civic Center, and Jake "The Snake" Roberts and Hillbilly Jim loomed like redwood trees as I watched them sign autographs. I marveled at my proximity to these men who until that moment seemed to only exist in the flattened realm of my TV screen. They were real, and yet they were still theatrical, Jake with his python-emblazoned neon-green tights and Jim with his overalls and beard the size of a porcupine.

In the seventh grade I hit an all-time low of social capital as classmates mocked my stutter and demonstrated the type of assholery that only seventh graders are capable of. But I never fought back, never stood up for myself; instead I went home, plugged in my wrestling VHS tapes, and escaped. My mom cried when I taped *Saturday Night's Main Event* over one of her episodes of *All My Children*.

Whatever aggression wasn't taken out through wrestling was channeled into my schoolwork. When final exams rolled around in high school, I posted a sign on my bedroom door that read "The War Room" and told my parents to hold any phone calls from my friends (by this time, I had some).

I staged study sessions that would make the most ascetic German tear up with pride, marathons of rewriting notes with such pressure that the paper felt like Braille. And when the last exam was done, it was back to the VCR to escape to the land of the bodyslam.

*   *   *

MUCH TO MY PARENTS' CHAGRIN, I NEVER GREW OUT OF WRESTLING. WHEN the internet emerged, I signed up for my first ever email address: IrSheik55@aol.com (yes, it will bounce back now). I was in college when I had, or rather *created*, the opportunity to meet the Iron Sheik for the first time. By the late 1990s, I knew that, like so many of his brethren, the Sheik had fallen on hard times. Brandishing headlocks doesn't make for a very transferable skill, and once the spotlight faded, the Sheik's generation of wrestlers had little to fall back on, with no retirement plan from the WWF and no union to support them (they were classified as independent contractors). Knowing this, I did a little googling and ingratiated myself to the Iron Sheik's agent, a pasty, prematurely bald, part-massage-therapist, part-wrestling-promoter, all-weird-dude named Eric Simms who lived with his parents in suburban New Jersey. I endured a weekend of riding roller coasters and eating taffy in Wildwood, New Jersey, along with my childhood friend Cristian (who I duped into coming with promises of a "coastal vacation"), while also indulging Eric's ribald humor, all to get in his good graces for a chance to meet my hero.

It worked.

In July 2001, I drove from Rhode Island down to the Secaucus Expo Center in New Jersey to join Eric's crew of Sheik-wranglers at a weekend toy and collectible show. I had heard through internet whispers that the Sheik had become quite the loose cannon in his later years, and that it took a small army to control him. But I had no idea what was coming.

Outside the convention hall at nine in the morning, my childhood dream came true.

"What's your name, baba?" the Sheik asked me, his eyes bright. He was sitting in the front seat of a blue Oldsmobile, dragging on a cigarette with two empty Molson Ices at his feet. An American eagle durag covered his head. He wore a WWF T-shirt, his old wrestling pants (with IRAN in giant letters down one side), and his trademark pointy-toed boots.

His hand was thick and rough, but he squeezed mine gently the way wrestlers do (in Kayfabe, a limp handshake was a signal that you were in on the con). The owner of the Oldsmobile, a vulgar little nineteen-year-old burnout named Zeke, retrieved more Molsons from the trunk, causing the Sheik to perk up. Another member of the crew, Steve, was a fifty-year-old ex-army chef who aspired to promote wrestling with Zeke.

"Hey, Sheik, check out my last name," Steve said, passing him his driver's license.

The Sheik hesitated, then took the ID and stared hard.

"I'm sorry, I can't read. What does it say?" he asked in his thick accent, slightly embarrassed.

"It says Stallone!" Steve proclaimed, proud.

The Sheik's eyes narrowed and then crinkled as his face broke into a huge grin.

"Sylvester Stallone is an American star, just like the Iron Sheik," he said, beaming.

The Sheik labored to his feet, and I was surprised to see that I looked down on him by a couple inches (his billing at six feet was clearly charitable). It was time to get inside to start signing autographs. Hampered by a twice-injured ankle (once in the ring, once in a car crash) that never healed properly and two bad knees, the Sheik limped toward the arena with me at his side, peppering him with everything I knew about his career. I couldn't contain the fanboy inside.

With each accolade that I listed (Amateur Athletic Union [AAU] gold medalist in 1971, WWF Champion in 1983 . . .) his smile grew wider.

"You are intelligent American. You know the Iron Sheik is the real world champion, not that Hollywood blond, guitar-playing faggot Hulk Hogan," he said.

Once we were seated at his autograph table, the Sheik was in full performance mode. A boy no older than eight and his dad approached the table looking for a Polaroid and an autograph.

"It's the Iron Sheik, Iron Sheik!" the boy squealed. "We saw you at WrestleMania!" The Sheik pulled himself out of his chair, stepping on the side of his left foot to avoid putting too much weight on his busted ankle, and put a keffiyeh on the boy's head, handing him a replica championship belt to drape over his shoulder. The Sheik burst into character, raising a palm

to the heavens and exclaiming "Yo Allah, yo Mohammad!" as Eric Simms
eagerly snapped a Polaroid. Lowering himself gingerly back into his chair,
he scrawled something in Farsi on an old picture of himself holding the
WWF championship belt.

"That means 'God is great,'" he told the boy, whose eyes never retreated
back into their sockets during the three-minute encounter.

I saw the perfect opportunity to further pump my hero's ego.

"See, Sheik, even the younger generation knows you," I said.

"Exact-a-ly!" he replied with a huge grin. "You are intelligent American,"
he repeated. "Older generation know me, your generation know me, young
generation know me."

I nodded and smiled. He signed one of the eight-by-tens for me, inscrib-
ing it in all caps "TO MY BEST FRIEND BRAD, 2001, GOOD LUCK," which
still hangs on my apartment wall (although I have a feeling he had many
"best friends" in 2001, considering we had just met).

For the next couple of hours I lived my dream, sitting at the Sheik's
side and spelling out names like "John" and "Mike" for him as he signed
autographs and shook hands. For a few extra bucks, the Sheik would actually put fans in his finishing hold, the camel clutch, a move that involves
mounting your opponent from behind. I couldn't resist the opportunity
and gleefully lay on my stomach on the filthy cement floor while the Sheik
straddled me, picked up my shoulders in one effortless heave, and hooked
my arms behind his knees. He completed the move by interlocking his
fingers around my chin and pulling up. Even with this kid-gloves version
of the hold (he kept his weight forward on his toes, never leaning back),
I could feel his raw strength as he cinched the move in. The pressure was
considerable. I quickly submitted.

A few minutes later the Sheik turned to me, handed me a keffiyeh, and
said, "Brad baba, do me a favor, get the keys from Zeke, wrap a few beers in
this, put it in your bag, and bring it inside."

It was the first sign of the Sheik's dark side. Always an obedient rule fol-
lower, I was reluctant to smuggle booze in, but it was the Iron Sheik, for
Christ's sake—the Iron Sheik!—and I returned a few minutes later as
requested. No bottle opener was necessary; with a flick of his cigarette
lighter the cap was gone, and a few gulps after that, so too was the Molson Ice.

After the show I ended up back in the Sheik's room at the Holiday Inn huddled with Zeke and Steve, where almost twelve hours later I would finally pass out for about three hours of sleep. In the interim, my dystopian Make-A-Wish took some more colorful turns: Zeke produced a bundle of marijuana, which the Sheik called his "green medicine" (as opposed to the "white medicine," cocaine); they took turns "shotgunning" as one inhaled as deeply as possible and then blew the smoke directly into the other's open mouth. When Zeke started pressuring me to join the festivities, the Sheik (undoubtedly the world's most unlikely D.A.R.E. officer) intervened: "Don't force him to do it. Brad is intelligent young American, he doesn't want to smoke the medicine, he doesn't have to," he said, before offering that if Zeke knew of any local sources for cocaine or crack, he knew how to cook it. At three in the morning, a munchies-induced trip to a twenty-four-hour diner turned into a personal appearance, as the Sheik paid for the meal by signing a stack of eight-by-ten photos he had brought with him (clearly not the first time he had done this) and left messages on answering machines for a gaggle of drunk college kids.

But the night also laid the groundwork for the future: when Zeke and Steve left for dinner with Eric around seven thirty, I seized the opportunity for some one-on-one time. Following a half-hour shower, the Sheik emerged from the small bathroom in a skimpy white towel and stood in front of the mirror, flexing his pecs, brushing his mustache, and squirting Obsession cologne ("Muslim men, we must smell good, must be clean for the people, to show respect") directly in his face. This was one of the few times I would ever see him without some kind of hat or head covering, a bit like seeing Darth Vader sans helmet. With both ears exposed, I noticed the right one was gnarled and covered with hardened cartilage, the cauliflower remnants of his amateur wrestling days. He was in a great mood, clean and high.

"What a beautiful day, thank you God, thank you Jesus, ya Mohammad," he said, taking a seat on the bed, a bowling ball gut spilling over the edge of the towel. I found it a bit odd that this Shia Muslim interchanged deities at will, but who was I to question the Iron Sheik?

I had prepared a book tribute, a collection of articles and email testimonials recapping his career. He seemed genuinely touched when I handed it to him, his dark brown eyes twinkling. He took the book and softly flipped through the pages, saying, "Wow, God bless you, thank you," in a gentle voice.

Looking through the book, he began sharing stories of his life in wrestling, describing a culture of great fame but also a sordid underworld of deceit and deception. He talked about doing "A to the Z" (the Sheik is known for adding unnecessary articles to his speech) drugs with his fellow wrestlers, of going over to Hulk Hogan's apartment to learn how to inject steroids into his ass a few years before Hogan would begin telling kids to "train, say their prayers, and eat their vitamins."

The wheels were spinning in my head, and despite having only one journalism class under my belt, I vowed to myself that one day I would write a book about him.

*   *   *

OVER THE NEXT FEW YEARS, I SET UP WHAT FELT LIKE AN IDEAL LIFE. I landed in Santa Barbara, California, after college, met my two best friends, Adam and Jesse, and fell in love with a coworker named Melissa who I assumed would be my future wife and the mother of my children. I quickly turned an unpaid internship at my dream company, *Islands* magazine (my major in college was island biogeography), into a full-time job as a research editor (fact-checker), and in my early twenties I was brimming with self-confidence.

Every now and then I'd pick up the phone and call the Sheik, who quickly learned to recognize my voice:

"Khos!"

"Brad Belushi! [This is the closest he would ever get to Balukjian.] How are you?" he would reply.

The conversations were invariably short and superficial, Khos having little use for small talk. I planted the seed of writing a book, and the idea sprouted in Khos's mind—while his body was broken and his wrestling career long gone, he wanted his legacy to be preserved for time immemorial. And who better to write it than his number one fan?

When *Islands* got bought out by a much larger company and Melissa decided to move to Los Angeles for culinary school, I sensed the timing was right to tell the Sheik's story and quit my job, convinced my dream life could get dreamier yet. I was riding high, too young and dumb to know any better.

*   *   *

2005

FAYETTEVILLE, POPULATION 12,944, IS A BLEND OF OLD SOUTH AND MODERN corporate—Starbucks and Target mixed with twenty-eight Baptist churches and a courthouse that dates back to 1825—located about twenty miles south of Atlanta. Margaret Mitchell spent a good deal of time in Fayette County while doing research for *Gone with the Wind.*

With lots of open space and wooded glens, Fayetteville's newer housing complexes sprawl over many acres of bright foliage, with names like Foxhall Farms and Woodsong Estates. At the end of a cul-de-sac aptly named Fairway Overlook, in a housing development inaptly named the River's Edge, I arrive at a one-level ranch home with a trimmed front lawn and rows of flowers. An old Cadillac with a badly flat tire slumps in the driveway.

Behind those walls, I find Khos stuck in a simple life of retirement. His wife, Caryl, works as a travel agent at Carlson Wagonlit, bringing in a steady but modest income to make ends meet; he receives $650 per month from the government in disability and the occasional royalty check from the WWE (the name changed from WWF to WWE in 2002).

Down the hall, Khos's room is a shrine to expired fame that smells of cigarettes and cologne. Half-empty Gatorade bottles, a retainer, an Iron Sheik keychain, and other tchotchkes spill across a tabletop. The walls are a gallery of family photos of Caryl and his three daughters, Marissa, Tanya, and Nikki, along with a framed photo of Khos and Cyndi Lauper. In a corner leans a six-foot pole wrapped in red-white-and-blue duct tape that he uses as a cane. Several storage containers around the room are labeled in shaky handwriting: "Carol foto" and "Wreslin."

Extending into the center of the room lies a twin bed with eight layers of sheets and blankets, the mattress nothing more than a 1.5-inch slab of plywood mounted on cinderblocks, essentially the mat of a wrestling ring. A poster of a snarling Iron Sheik hangs on the wall above the bed, his head and chest drenched with sweat, turning one of his adversaries over into the Boston crab submission hold.

"The face tells the story," Khos is fond of saying, to describe the myriad ways pro wrestlers sell their emotions to the audience.

I have big plans for his biography. We'll retrace his career, reunite with his old amateur wrestling coach Alan Rice, who took him in when he defected to the US and couldn't speak a word of English; climb in a ring together so he can train me on basic pro wrestling moves, the magician taking me behind the curtain; track down his old nemesis Hulk Hogan and resolve the real bad blood still lingering between the two. But a couple weeks after showing up in Fayetteville, I begin to have serious doubts. Many days when I call him up, he says he is sick and doesn't have the energy to talk. Those days I do come over he seems more interested in watching *Friends* and Rachael Ray than going down memory lane.

The only times he perks up are when he has his medicine. Khos's drug issues have been well documented, all the way back to his arrest with his in-ring foe "Hacksaw" Jim Duggan in 1987, but when I was back home in California, I had no idea how much they had taken control of his life. He badgers me for money, claiming more flat tires than there are wheels on his car, and when I push back and tell him I suspect the money is for drugs, he gets enraged and defensive.

"You don't want to help your friend? You break my heart. I ask for thirty dollars, twenty dollars, not ten thousand. What the fuck? You want to be a cheap motherfucker like that, fine. The medicine, it is from the God, from the Mother Nature. Don't tell me the drugs are bad, the drugs are going to kill me. If you are my friend, and I am broke, then you help me out!" he blurts, before ranting in even bluer language about how Caryl spent all his money.

"I make all the money, I take my shirt off all over the world, coast to coast, make $10,000 a week, and she spends it all. She shop too much," he says.

Khos's perception of reality can't be further from the truth. As soon as any money comes in, whether it's WWE royalties from a new action figure or, most recently, a $33,000 settlement from a car accident, it goes right to his addiction. When he is "on" and willing to talk, every work session turns into a promo, every other word "motherfucker."

"My medicine give me energy," he says.

"Thank you God, thank you Jesus, I hope you take care of me and Brad Belushi, make him like Iron Sheik more than when he was six years old," he says.

While his abuse of marijuana is problematic, it is smoking crack that really upends things. In one of my lowest moments, he directs me to the side parking lot of a motel where he meets his dealer. I wait in the driver's seat of my Honda Accord, my eyes darting back and forth, watching my childhood idol hobble to the back door.

In between the haze of successive highs, Khos has moments of sobering clarity and profound sadness, a window into his mental state. His incredible physical pain (his knees, ankle, and shoulder are wrecked from years in the ring) is compounded by the unfathomable emotional pain of having lost his oldest daughter, Marissa, two years prior. By all accounts a charming, affable woman (I never met her), she was murdered at twenty-seven years old by a crazed suitor she had met only weeks earlier. There are days when I come over to Khos's house on Fairway Overlook and find him on the couch, covered in blankets and near tears, recovering from the nightmares that have become all too common.

"I had a dream we were at the Hall of Fame, and Hulk Hogan comes into the locker room and he says, 'Sheiky baby, I'm sorry about your Marissa.' I say, 'Why didn't you call me?' He says, 'Because I didn't have your number' or some bullshit. And I say, 'OK, I forgive you.'"

Marissa's death broke an already broken man. A few months before her death, she had come to him asking if he would train her to be a WWE wrestler, to follow in her father's footsteps. He told her, "OK, I'll teach you, but you have to stop hanging around bad friends, and no drinking, you have to be serious, go to church, go in the gym, and I can take you to Mr. [Vince] McMahon [CEO of the WWE] and introduce you." But she never got that chance.

In these dark moments with Khos, two things give me hope that I can make our project work: One is Caryl. Born Caryl Peterson, she is an outgoing, loquacious woman from Minnesota with a big smile and a sharp laugh. In 1975, when she was a student at Normandale Community College in Bloomington, Minnesota, she met Khos at a bar called The Left Guard.

"He had these massive muscles and a full head of dark, black hair and thick eyebrows. He was gorgeous. His English was heavily accented. You had to listen carefully. He loved to watch *Sesame Street* to learn English," she tells me.

That man is now a distant memory.

Her short, straight blond hair reaches a little past her chin, and her voice carries like a stiff Midwestern breeze.

"Khos loves kids. He was the most generous, kind man, nothing like this guy now," she says.

During the two months I spend with Khos, Caryl is my confidante. She goes out of her way to make me feel at home even though she barely knows me. She does her best to help me, to try to get Khos to work with me, but she can't get him to do much of anything, let alone work on a book. She tries being sweet; she tries being aggressive; none of it works.

"He hides from the public. He cut off ties with all his old friends. He doesn't want to go out, I think because he is ashamed. I think he is embarrassed. He didn't used to be this way. He was so generous and polite, that's the man I married. He's depressed," she tells me.

I'm there in Khos's living room when he gets the call from Howard Finkel telling him he will be inducted into the WWE Hall of Fame. When we attend the induction ceremony in Los Angeles in April (during which I get to meet Vince McMahon), rather than hang out in the hotel with his old friends (fellow household names Hulk Hogan, "Rowdy" Roddy Piper, and Nikolai Volkoff were among the other inductees), Khos chooses to ride with me in my Rent-A-Wreck to pick up Caryl from her friend's house. We drive mostly in silence, stopping to get a bucket of fried chicken for the ride home.

At the ceremony itself, Khos delights the audience, immediately launching into a wrestling promo in his induction speech, earning chants of "Sheik! Sheik!" from the adoring crowd. But it's the Iron Sheik talking, not Khosrow Vaziri. Although the event is supposed to be a shoot (out of character), the line between fact and fiction has been blurred for so long that not even the WWE knows what is real—in their introductory video, they say that Khos represented Iran in the 1968 Olympics.

Not true.

The other thing that boosts my hopes is that I know this is not the same man who had bravely come to the US and charted a new life for himself. There are signs of that Khos in the archive of material he fastidiously saved and organized from his career—numerous hotel stationery pads with detailed notes from his matches; planners with each of his wrestling payoffs documented; spiral notebooks full of line after line of practice as he taught himself English: "Hello, how are you?" and "The popcorn here is better than in Minneapolis."

But at some point, the myth had become the reality, and Khosrow Vaziri had become the Iron Sheik. But when? And how? It is a question that starts to consume me.

The more time I spend with Khos, the more I realize I can no longer ignore the other question that has been nipping at my conscience ever since I arrived: Do I even *like* my hero anymore? I had been told so many stories by other wrestlers about his bad behavior. Yet I find myself constantly rationalizing it, blaming it on everything but the man himself.

By now I am complicit in his self-destruction, lending money that I'm sure goes to drugs, driving him to crack motels. I can no longer claim innocence; whatever stain is on Khos is now on me as well.

PART II
THE LOCK-UP

OPENING MATCH

BACK ON THE ROAD

In the early eighties, and certainly before then, it was viewed as a six pack and a blow job.

—WWE promoter Vince McMahon on the professional
wrestling business

2022

WHAT HAPPENS IN ELKO, NEVADA, STAYS IN ELKO, NEVADA. AND A LOT can happen in Elko.

A quick search of the Nevada Brothel Directory (yes, that's a thing) turns up four establishments in this town of twenty-odd thousand with names like Inez's DD Bar and Sue's Fantasy Club. Almost a mile into the sky, Elko has the road atlas's largest font size in the long, desolate stretch between Reno and Salt Lake City. The promise of literal gold continues to lure newcomers, and despite that industry's notorious cycle of booms and busts, the town's population has grown steadily in the decennial census since 1890.

As I pull onto Idaho Street, a strip alive with bars, motels, and western-themed trinket shops, a series of bad ideas flashes through my mind. But I've learned a few things in the years since my last book-writing adventure, *The Wax Pack*, which began with me passed out in a grove of ice plants along the freeway in Visalia, California. I would probably not be in Elko if it wasn't for that latent bildungsroman in which I ~~stalked~~ searched for all the players in a single pack of 1986 Topps baseball cards that had been sealed for twenty-nine years (and yes, the stick of gum inside tasted exactly how you might expect). What began as a simple "where are they now?" concept evolved into an unexpected meditation on growing up, both for me and for the ex-players I wrote about.

Since then, my T years (my twenties and thirties) have yielded to the F years (forties and fifties), and with it some forced humility—suddenly jumping on the ice without a proper warmup for my beer league hockey game leads to a yearlong glute strain, and a couple evening drinks reliably produces a jackhammer in my head the next morning. No, there will be no brothels, no shots, no ice-plant mattresses this time around.

It's Sunday, and I'm at the start of a sixty-two-day road trip that will span 12,525 miles, thirty-three states, 154 cups of coffee, and one island territory. Setting out earlier in the day amid an apocalyptic rainstorm in the Bay Area (it *never* rains in June), I established only two rules for this journey—no eating in the car (I recently upgraded to an electric-blue 2012 Ford Fusion, having finally retired the 2002 Honda Accord from *The Wax Pack* odyssey), and staying only in roadside motels, given their kitschy, underdog status.

By the time I cross the Nevada state line there are already crumbs strewn about the floor of the car, so as I cruise Idaho Street looking for lodging, I remain steadfast in my commitment to affordable mediocrity.

The outstretched teal-and-red wings of a Thunderbird spreading above a sign of the eponymous motel provide just what I am looking for, and $62.70 later, I push open the dented door of Room 205 (hinting at the things that can happen in Elko) to discover an ashtray with three butts. I grab my backpack, head out, and find a table for two at the nearby restaurant Toki Ona.

My dinner companion is eight inches tall, made of rubber, and stained with blotches of red and black paint, the scars of past bouts—the very same Iron Sheik action figure I clutched as a six-year-old in Rhode Island. While I nudge through a plate of limp green beans and maroon spaghetti that tastes like tin, the pair seated to my left catches my eye.

They are a father and son from Reno here on a fishing trip, headed to a reservoir sixty miles north where they can "stick the pole in, wait, and have a beer." The father is wearing glasses and an "Army Strong" T-shirt, and the son, pink-faced and burly, could be close to my age. I explain the journey I've just begun, and then reach across the table for my companion.

"Do you know who this is?" I ask, holding up my date.

A smile creeps across the son's face as he takes the Iron Sheik into his hands, his eyes sparkling with nostalgia.

"Sure I do—that's the Iron Sheik!" he says.

Almost thirty-nine years since he won the WWF championship, in a restaurant in a town where no one wants to be found, complete strangers still recognize the Iron Sheik.

Before leaving, the father turns to me and says, "We just want to say, it's really impressive what you're doing."

So what am I doing?

*   *   *

FOLLOWING THE DEATH THREAT FROM THE IRON SHEIK IN HIS LIVING ROOM IN 2005, I packed my things and retreated to California, waking up from my dream-turned-nightmare and accepting that the book was not to be. Breaking up with your childhood hero is no small thing, but I did my best to get over it.

I moved to the San Francisco Bay Area to get my PhD in entomology and settled down to teach at Merritt College in Oakland. I always kept an eye on the Sheik from a distance, checking the internet headlines, shaking my head as his popularity soared thanks to drug-addled rants on YouTube and Howard Stern, appearances that reeked of exploitation. And yet despite all I had been through with him, I believed that under the layers of addiction, Khosrow Vaziri was still there somewhere inside.

I could never shake the feeling of unfinished business. When I wrote *The Wax Pack*, it got me thinking about my original book idea and that twenty-four-year-old who had returned to California.

And then I realized: it's time for a new mission. While the prospect of an Iron Sheik biography is long gone, what gets me reaching for my notebook and back on the road is wanting a deeper understanding of this cultural phenomenon called pro wrestling—where did it come from, why is it so popular, and most importantly, just how real was its impact on the personal lives of its participants? I want to seek out truth in a world predicated on illusion—where did fiction end and fact begin?

Before the Iron Sheik's era, wrestling had experienced surges of popularity, but it wasn't until the 1980s that it joined mainstream pop culture, eventually evolving into the multibillion-dollar enterprise it is today. It turns out that the Sheik was at the center of that transition, beginning with the day after Christmas, 1983, when he defeated six-year-incumbent Bob Backlund to become WWF world champion. The 24,592 fans jammed into New York City's Madison Square Garden (and adjoining Felt Forum) watched in shock and horror as the "evil foreigner" won, but their dismay would be short-lived: the following month, in the same building, the ultimate patriot, Hulk Hogan, split the atom and defeated the Sheik to take the championship back for the USA. Within a year, celebrities Cyndi Lauper and Mr. T would get involved in storylines, launching the inaugural "WrestleMania" and bringing wrestling into the spotlight.

Given the importance of that card in Madison Square Garden on December 26, 1983, I decide to make the wrestlers who performed on that show the focal point for my exploration. Of the twenty-six men who were there, sixteen are still alive. Of those survivors, I have chosen six to track down, which seems a manageable number: "Mr. USA" Tony Atlas (real name: Anthony White), Tito Santana (Merced Solis), Sgt. Slaughter (Bob Remus), the Masked Superstar (Bill Eadie), Jose Luis Rivera (Marcelino Rivera), and if all breaks right, a reunion with the Iron Sheik. Given that Hulk Hogan (Terry Bollea) became champion a month later and carried the WWF to new heights, I decide to pursue him as well.

I want to understand the people behind the characters. Where does Hulk Hogan end and Terry Bollea begin? What is the cost of playing fictional characters nonstop for decades, to both the men behind the characters and the people they love?

Wrestlers from this time were the world's most committed method actors, forced to stay in character twenty-four seven by an industry that for so long refused to openly acknowledge that their craft was entertainment, not sport. While living the illusion, they had to deal with the stress of the most frenetic and unsustainable schedule of any profession, beyond the rigors of even a rock star's life. At the height of the WWF's boom in the 1980s, the company put on more than nine hundred live events per year, with three different troupes of wrestlers touring year-round. They were literally and figuratively going a hundred miles per hour, drinking six packs while trying to maintain them. There was no off-season, no rest, and perhaps most notably for the wrestlers' well-being, no union, health insurance, or benefits. If you got hurt, you were out of work. It's no wonder that so many wrestlers became addicted to a cornucopia of drugs—steroids to get big, cocaine and alcohol to keep the party going after the matches, painkillers and muscle relaxers to go to sleep.

No such investigation would be complete without a look at the wizard behind the curtain, WWE founder and CEO Vince McMahon Junior (technically Vincent K. McMahon), a third-generation promoter (he bought the company from his dad, Vince McMahon Senior, or Vincent J.) with a quintessential American story and a crypt's worth of skeletons in his closet. Khos once told me, "Vince is the Caesar of the Rome. He is the master, he is the genius. He can do whatever he wants." Backstage, people even referred to Vince as "Emperor" or "Caesar." No one deserves more credit for hauling wrestling from the sidelines of pop culture than Vince, whose meteoric rise could not have been possible without the Sheik and friends. But how exactly did Vince make that happen?

As a former fact-checker with a double life as a scientist and journalist, my job is to disentangle reality from the rat's nest of exaggeration and outright deception, to seek truth in a world of make-believe. I have my work cut out for me. Of all the subjects in which to launch a pursuit of truth, professional wrestling is perhaps the most unlikely—there is little written record (sports media didn't cover it given that its outcomes were predetermined), and for most of its hundred-year history its leaders refused to acknowledge that it was an exhibition. Truth in wrestling was avoided at all costs in order to preserve the illusion, and so I expect the Six Packers' (my preferred term for my quarry) command of it to be questionable. Wrestlers from that era are also notorious for having faulty memories—in their recollection, every show was sold out, packed to the rafters.

I have a plan, but no guarantees. A few of the Six Packers have agreed to meet, while my attempts to contact others have gone unanswered, which will force me to get creative. If all goes well, the journey will end where it all began, back with Khos in Fayetteville, Georgia.

But first I must time travel to that event in late December 1983, when the Iron Sheik changed wrestling history forever.

CHAMPIONSHIP WRESTLING

Madison Square Garden
Monday, December 26, 1983

Tonight's Official Line-up

Main Event...For the World Wrestling Federation Heavyweight Championship,
One Fall, One-Hour Time Limit

BOB BACKLUND   -VS-   **THE IRON SHEIK**
Princeton, Minnesota...234 lbs.   Iran...247 lbs.
(WWF CHAMPION)   (CHALLENGER)

- -

JIMMY "SUPERFLY" SNUKA   -VS-   **THE MAGNIFICENT MURACO**
Fiji Islands...250 lbs.   Sunset Beach, Hawaii...257 lbs.
&   &
BUDDY "NATURE BOY" ROGERS   **CAPTAIN LOU ALBANO**
New Jersey...225 lbs.   Carmel, New York...305 lbs.

- -

THE MASKED SUPERSTAR   -VS-   **IVAN PUTSKI**
Atlanta...269 lbs.   Krakow, Poland...235 lbs.

- -

TONY "MR. U.S.A." ATLAS   -VS-   **THE WILD SAMOANS**
Roanoke, Virginia...260 lbs.   Combined Weight...877 lbs.
&
ROCKY JOHNSON
Washington, D.C....250 lbs.
&
S.D. JONES
Philadelphia, Pennsylvania...245 lbs.

- -

SGT. SLAUGHTER   -VS-   **CHIEF JAY STRONGBOW**
South Carolina...296 lbs.   Pawhuska, Oklahoma...258 lbs.

- -

IVAN KOLOFF   -VS-   **TITO SANTANA**
Russia...255 lbs.   Tocula, Mexico...242 lbs.

- -

Plus other All-Star bouts, featuring Iron Mike Sharpe, Butcher Vachon, The Invaders,
Jose Luis Rivera and Rene Goulet.

TV Wrestling:
WOR-9 Saturdays 10 a.m.
Saturdays Midnight

MATCH 2

THE IRON SHEIK VS. KHOSROW VAZIRI

December 26, 1983

C ARYL VAZIRI GETS JUST WHAT SHE WANTED FOR CHRISTMAS THIS YEAR— her husband at home.

Year after year Khos has had to work Christmas Day, one of the biggest days of the year for the wrestling industry, when the kids are off from school, families are together, and a trip to the matches makes for an ideal holiday outing.

But this year, Khos's new employer, the WWF, gives everyone the week before Christmas off, a rare respite in their grueling schedule. Vince McMahon is gearing up for the biggest year of his life, and wants his soldiers well rested.

The front-page headline of this morning's *Atlanta Constitution* reads "Arctic Blast Brings Georgia Coldest December, Kills 7." As Caryl and Khos scramble to pack their bags outside their spacious apartment in the suburb of College Park, Caryl is shocked to see her own breath.

I left Minnesota to get out of this cold! she thinks. It's so cold that water pipes have burst at the airport.

But no deep freeze is going to stop Khos from his date with destiny.

They fly to Pittsburgh, where Khos had left his blue Chevy Monte Carlo before the break. He's a nervous wreck the whole flight, fidgeting, stroking his mustache, every muscle pulsing with energy. For the past week, he's been home, running laps at the local high school track, drilling through calisthenics in the backyard, and doing rep after rep of exercises with his *meels*, the seventy-five-pound Persian clubs that he first learned to twirl as a teenager in Tehran. He's treasured this time off from the Road. When his three young daughters Marissa, Tanya, and Nikki climb on his legs and roll around with him on the living room floor, he's reminded of why he puts his body through such torture.

After only a few months in the WWF, the Iron Sheik is getting top billing on professional wrestling's most prestigious marquee: the main event at Madison Square Garden, challenging Bob Backlund for the crown he has held for nearly six years. Backlund, like Khos, has an impressive amateur wrestling background, having been an NCAA Division II National Champion at North Dakota State University. Unlike Khos, he doesn't really have a gimmick—his wrestling persona is simply Bob Backlund, the All-American babyface.

Although Khos's boss, Vince McMahon Senior, has not yet told him the outcome of the match, Khos knows there's a possibility that he may win the title tonight. At the last TV taping, they shot an *angle*, or storyline, where he injured Backlund's neck and back, providing the audience with some context and explanation should the evil Iron Sheik emerge victorious at Madison Square Garden. Khos thinks winning the championship is such a probability that he's asked Caryl to come with him on this trip, which she never does. In the script, the Iron Sheik has threatened to take the belt back to Iran to present to Ayatollah Khomeini.

Caryl is proud of her husband and thrilled to get away for a couple days to New York City. It's been hard, so hard, these past eight years since they married, moving with him from Minneapolis to Dallas back to Minneapolis to Vancouver to Blaine back to Minneapolis to West Haven to Charlotte to Baton Rouge and finally to Atlanta. They have never made much money, and with three more mouths to feed and Khos gone most of the year, the burden has fallen hardest on her. But she is Midwest tough, second oldest of seven kids, an assertive go-getter who was a surrogate parent to her younger siblings in Bloomington, Minnesota. She has built her life around their family, letting go of her plan to be a nurse and following Khos which-ever way the capricious winds of the wrestling industry blow its captive band of nomads.

The Road is a cruel master. When Khos comes home irritable and hyped up from all the travel, or when the drugs and partying start taking an obvious toll, Caryl keeps the sails up, the ship pointed straight ahead. It wasn't her choice for her husband to morph into a snarling, bald-headed, anti-American bad guy, to watch as fans turned fantasy into reality, filling their Monte Carlo gas tank with sugar and slashing its tires. Some of them even called in death threats to the Boston Garden, leading promoter Vince McMahon Senior to pull Khos from the show, telling him to stay in his hotel room.

No matter how hard it gets, she made a vow on March 21, 1976, to stay with him for better and for worse. And Midwesterners don't break their vows.

The cold bites at their faces even harder when they land in Pittsburgh. Caryl thinks about the girls back at home who are staying with a neighbor. The couple makes the six-hour drive across most of the state of Pennsylvania, stopping at a Perkins for lunch, and arrive in plenty of time before the start of the eight o'clock show.

When they arrive in Midtown Manhattan, crawling through traffic, fans recognize Khos through the driver's side window.

"Hey, that's the Iron Sheik!" they yell.

The taunts and jeers soon escalate to tossing all manner of debris, even eggs and tomatoes. They pelt the Monte Carlo as Khos pulls into the safety of the underground parking garage. Caryl and Khos ride the elevator up to the backstage area and then part ways, Caryl with a security guard to her ringside seat and Khos to the locker room.

Vince McMahon Senior calls Khos and Bob Backlund together in the bathroom, the place where the industry's most sacred meetings are held, and gives them the plan for their match: about twelve minutes in, the Iron Sheik will put Backlund in his finishing move, the camel clutch, further straining Backlund's "injured" neck and back. Overcome with pain but too proud to quit, Backlund will remain in the hold until his manager, Arnold Skaaland, throws in a white towel, signaling submission. The Iron Sheik will become the ninth WWF champion in the company's twenty-one-year history.

For Backlund, who has known about this for weeks, it's simply the sealing of his fate. He is legitimately bummed, having grown into the skin of his virtuous role model character so much that he struggles to distinguish between the performer and the real Bob Backlund. But if he has to lose the championship after these six long years, he's happy to do the honors for a man he respects, a fellow amateur wrestling champion. It was Backlund who came up with the match's end or *finish*, allowing him to save face by not actually submitting, but putting Khos over strong by implying that the camel clutch is such a devastating move that Skaaland will have no other choice than to throw in the towel.

Khos is overjoyed but remains focused. He thanks Backlund, showing his appreciation by presenting him with a pair of his *meels*, and then leaves to warm up for his match.

He looks around the locker room and allows himself just a moment to reflect on the long road that led here. Growing up in Tehran, all he ever wanted out of life was to be a champion wrestler like his hero, Olympian Gholamreza Takhti. It's happening later than he expected, at age forty-one, in a foreign country and through a form of wrestling that he didn't even know existed as a youth, but his dream is about to come true.

He sees his buddy Tony Atlas, who he once pulled from a car wreck in Ohio after the driver of the car, fellow babyface Tommy Rich, had swerved off the road. Khos and wrestler/booker Ole Anderson, who were heels, were driving behind them; when they saw Rich's car crash, Khos said, "Pull over, we have to help them!" Ole, forever dyed in the wool of Kayfabe, said, "You can't, they're babyfaces!"

Tito Santana, who Khos wrestled in this very building in 1979, walks by and says hello. Khos also sees his good friend Bob Remus, who was developing the character of Sgt. Slaughter in the Kansas City territory at the same time that Khos was learning how to be the Iron Sheik. The two heels made road trips together, Bob's wife, Diane, cooking them many a prematch meal, and they grew so close that Khos named his third child after Bob's daughter Nicole. Khos would come over to Bob's house an hour early just so he could sit with Nicole and read picture books to her, the two of them learning English together.

The first match goes on, with Puerto Rican Jose Luis Rivera getting a *push* (being strongly promoted) against veteran Rene Goulet of France.

Khos is on sixth out of nine total matches. Vince Senior likes putting the main event in the middle of the card so they can announce the next month's lineup afterward and then take intermission, giving fans a chance to buy tickets at the box office.

Khos secludes himself in a corner of the locker room and does a series of neck bridges, a layer of sweat now gleaming on his bald head. He talks to no one, including Backlund, who he won't see again until he gets to the ring.

The last match before the main event ends in a double disqualification: the Masked Superstar, played by Khos's friend Bill Eadie, vs. "Polish Power" Ivan Putski. Eadie was on Khos's first tour to Japan in 1974, well before the Iron Sheik character had been invented, when Khos had a full head of hair and wrestled under his real name.

The time has come. During the ring introductions, Backlund stands stoically in the corner wearing an American flag ring jacket. His red hair is buzzed short, part of his new look that he is convinced will reinvent his stale persona, and he is wearing a singlet instead of the traditional wrestling trunks.

In the opposite corner, the Iron Sheik paces, his brown robe hanging open to reveal a protruding gut with improbable washboard abs. He wears a red-and-white keffiyeh secured with an agal, and his manager "Ayatollah" Fred Blassie, an American who in the storyline has sold out to the riches of the Middle East, is wearing his own purple keffiyeh. Playing the heel manager role perfectly, Blassie points to the sky and chants "Bali Bali!," nonsense supposedly approximating some Farsi exclamation of faith. The crowd boos the Sheik vociferously; although Backlund's popularity has been waning in recent months, the announcement of his name draws cheers and a "U-S-A! U-S-A!" chant.

The match is bigger than Bob Backlund vs. The Iron Sheik. It's the United States vs. Iran. Freedom vs. Oppression.

Good vs. Evil.

*   *   *

IF YOU LISTEN CAREFULLY TO MANY OF THE IRON SHEIK'S INTERVIEWS FROM that time, this supposedly bad, bad man is actually quite polite. He typically begins with a preamble in Farsi, in which he greets his fellow Iranians, saying that everyone knows that Iranians are some of the best *pahlavans* (champion wrestlers) in the world. When he transitions to English, he extols the virtues of Iran as a proud nation, then goes on to some generic criticism of his opponent. But other than drawing the distinction of being a foreigner, there is actually little "evil" about the character. To the American masses of the time, being from Iran is enough to make him the object of their scorn.

All that matters to them is that on November 4, 1979, more than 150 Iranian college students, whipped into a frenzy by Ayatollah Khomeini, had taken sixty-three Americans hostage at the US embassy in Tehran, and that they had been held captive for 444 days.

What they don't know is why.

For professional wrestling's purposes, it is fine to leave it at that. But in reality, the Iranian hostage crisis was the culmination of decades of Iranian frustration with America's meddling in their affairs, and more broadly, centuries of interference from outside nations.

In his interviews, the Iron Sheik calls Iran the "oldest country in the world," which is true, as it has more or less been an independent country for the past three thousand years. In the fifth century BCE, the Persian Empire was home to sixty million of the world's one hundred million people (Iran has always been the name for the country; Europeans named it "Persia"). It was one of the world's great ancient civilizations; look no further than the spectacular ruins of Persepolis. And it had a long history before the prophet Mohammad walked the earth, when many Iranians practiced a religion called Zoroastrianism.

Iran is now a Muslim country, having first been invaded by Arabs in the seventh century CE. It is the second-largest country by land area and population in the Middle East and one of the few majority-Shia Muslim nations (greater than 90 percent of the people are Shiites).

For most of their shared history, the US and Iran were friends, if not quite tag-team partners; just a year before the 1979 hostage crisis, fifty thousand Americans were living in Iran, and in December of 1977, President Carter called the country "an island of stability in one of the more troubled regions of the world." The two nations shared mutual admiration dating back to America's inception, when the Founding Fathers revered the accomplishments of ancient Iran. By the same token, Iranians were impressed with Americans' spirit of resistance and independence and refusal to be ruled by the British.

In the early nineteenth century, they found a common foe in Britain, but America had the advantage of its geographic isolation. Iran, on the other hand, provided Britain with a strategic route to India, while another great power, Russia, sought influence for passage to the Persian Gulf. Iran went to war with Britain in 1841 and again in 1856, with Britain swallowing up the country's mineral and railway rights. But nothing shaped the direction of the region's geopolitics more than cash-strapped Shah Muzaffar al-Din's decision in 1901 to give the British exclusive oil-drilling rights almost anywhere in Iran for the next sixty years.

Through the end of World War II, Iran remained a pawn on the global stage, having sold off control of its resources and bouncing between British and Russian influence. Iran looked to the US for support, baffled that their fellow anti-imperialist country would not be more of an ally, but the US was wary of upsetting Britain, their key friend. Iran had theoretically become the world's first Muslim democracy in 1906, when a national parliament, the Majles, was formed and drafted a constitution. Iran was also clearly a theocracy, ruled by five ayatollahs who had the power to overrule the will of the Majles, and a king, the shah.

On September 16, 1941, Mohammad Reza Pahlavi ascended the throne at the age of twenty-two. Western-educated and fluent in both English and French, the new shah set out to build a partnership with the US and to build up Iran's military might. He was tantalized by weaponry. Throughout his reign he struggled to reconcile his deep-seated need to be liked with his obsession for power and control. One day he would employ Khosrow Vaziri.

*   *   *

THERE IS A WORD IN FARSI, *JAVANMARDI*, WHICH ROUGHLY TRANSLATES TO A notion of chivalry, ethics, and humility, that dates back to antediluvian times, well before the advent of Islam.

Before the match between the Sheik and Backlund even starts, Sheik sneak-attacks him, charging forward and walloping the side of Backlund's neck with a right fist. Not very *Javanmardi*. Right away they're telling a story, the Sheik ignoring the rules and trying to further injure Backlund's already sore neck.

The Sheik flexes his thick chest and poses to the crowd, showing off the physique he first built in Iran in houses of strength called *zurkhanehs*. In ancient Iran, a class of warriors practiced a brand of martial arts in these houses, imbued with the spirit of *Javanmardi*.

The *zurkhaneh* tradition persists to this day, with five hundred such buildings remaining in the country. At its center is an octagonal pit seventy-five to one hundred centimeters deep, with a top layer of clay overlaying ash, dried straw, and crushed tumbleweeds. Participants remove their shoes, wash their hands, and then duck their heads under a low ceiling to enter the pit as a forced gesture of respect. For the next sixty to ninety minutes they move through a ritual of exercises, including forms of calisthenics, dance, wrestling, and exercises with *meels*, all to the beat of a large wooden drum called a *zarb*.

A young Khosrow Vaziri spent much of his youth in such *zurkhanehs* in Tehran, training with other young men (women were not and are still not allowed to participate). Khos brought those lessons of humility and respect with him wherever he went, forever mindful of the spirit of *Javanmardi*. It's why he was so strict and disciplined with his daughters growing up, drilling in lessons of manners and propriety, imploring them to always look their best. It's why simple routines of showering and dressing turn into legendary hours-long grooming rituals with Khos; "cleanliness is next to godliness," he often says.

About eleven minutes into the match, just as Vince McMahon Senior had instructed in the bathroom beforehand, the Sheik pulls Backlund up by the shoulders, wrenches his arms behind his knees, sits on his back, and pulls hard on his chin, applying the dreaded camel clutch.

"Pull on it, pull on it!" screams Ayatollah Blassie from ringside.

The Sheik nods his head vigorously, rivers of sweat pouring off his bald head under the bright ring lights. Backlund's face is a mask of pain.

Suddenly a white towel flies into the ring. Referee Dick Kroll looks at it, pauses for just the right amount of time, and then signals for the bell to end the match.

The Iron Sheik is WWF champion.

The crowd is in shock. Caryl, sitting at ringside, jumps to her feet, cheering for her husband. Ayatollah Blassie wraps the title belt around the Iron Sheik's waist with such excitement that he puts it on upside down. Bob Backlund, vanquished after 2,135 days as champion, writhes on the mat in faux agony, *selling* his injured neck and back.

Little kids are in tears, confused at what has just transpired. A ripple of shock courses through the building. Caryl realizes she might want to tamp down her enthusiasm, as no one can understand why this fetching young blond is over the moon about the evil Iranian becoming champion. Confusion could quickly turn to violence.

Before leaving the ring, the Iron Sheik grabs the microphone and screams to the crowd, "Iran number one!" as the boos rain down.

*   *   *

KHOSROW VAZIRI WAS BORN IN 1942 IN THE TOWN OF DAMGHAN, SOME 215 miles northeast of Tehran. He was named after Khosrow I, an Iranian king who ruled from 531 to 579 CE and was considered a patron of arts and scholarship.

Khos was one of four children born to Ghassem and Mariam Vaziri, who farmed pistachios, grapes, peaches, and cantaloupes. Despite the country's oil wealth and its royal family's obscene lifestyle, the masses in Iran suffered from great poverty. The Vaziri family had no electricity, using kerosene lamps at night and sometimes sleeping next to a charcoal pit to stay warm. Life got a bit easier when they moved to the big city of Tehran when Khos was five. They were still far from wealthy, finding a home on the poorer southern side of the city, but Ghassem worked in their family bathhouse where people came for massages and spa treatments, and for the first time, the family had modern amenities.

Khos was a mediocre student but found his calling on the wrestling mat. Beginning in seventh grade, weighing 125 pounds, he began learning the craft of freestyle and Greco-Roman wrestling. Wrestling had soared in popularity thanks to the accomplishments of Khos's hero Takhti, twelve years his senior, who also came from humble roots. As a child in southern Tehran, Takhti's family had been thrown out on the streets when his father, an ice maker, was unable to cover his debts. Takhti never forgot what it felt like to have nothing.

After Takhti won the gold medal in freestyle wrestling for Iran at the 1956 Olympics in Melbourne, Australia, he used every bit of his fame, fortune, and celebrity to give back to the people. He couldn't stand to see such suffering across Iran while the shah built a personal fortune and amassed a war chest that was beyond ludicrous.

The shah tightened his grip on the people following a CIA-backed coup of Prime Minister Mohammad Mosaddeq in August 1953. Mossadeq was enormously popular, stirring a movement toward Iranian autonomy. In 1951 he took back control of the country's oil from Britain, creating the National Iranian Oil Company (the same year, he was named *Time* magazine's "Man of the Year"). The move enraged Britain, who embargoed Iranian oil, crippling its economy, and worried the US, who feared that Iran would turn to the Soviet Union for support. Fear of communism underlay almost every American foreign policy decision of the time, and the situation in Iran was no different.

In a desperate move called Operation Ajax, President Eisenhower authorized a coup to remove Mossadeq from power, giving the shah complete control. The CIA funded strongmen and thugs from the *zurkhanehs* of southern Tehran to riot and to frame Mossadeq as a communist sympathizer. He was arrested for treason and put under house arrest until his death. With the opposition silenced, the shah solidified his dictatorship while building a close friendship with the US. He imposed martial law, created a secret police force called SAVAK, and shuttered newspapers and political parties. Iran became one of the US's favorite customers for weaponry—by 1976, Iran was spending as much on its military as China, and a third of the US's international arms sales went to Iran.

All the while, the Iranian people suffered. Unemployment soared. Their best chance at societal reform and upward mobility had been snuffed by the shah and his best friend, the United States. Iranians' antipathy toward America was deepening. One day it would erupt.

Amid this backdrop of totalitarianism, Takhti emerged as a folk hero for his willingness to challenge the shah. When the Buin Zahra earthquake killed eleven thousand people in 1962, he took to the streets to personally solicit and deliver donations to those left homeless. He turned down all opportunities to capitalize on his fame, from movie roles to endorsements, preferring to focus on helping others, embodying *Javanmardi*. When he refused to attend a state event in March 1964, the shah suspended his salary from his railroad job and banned him from wrestling, even from coaching. Rich with the people's love but poor in his bank account and exiled from the sport he so loved, Takhti's heart was broken.

While Takhti's career was declining, Khos's was on the rise. His one and only concern in life was becoming a wrestling champion just like his hero, and as he developed into a young man, he even began to physically resemble Takhti. At the age of twenty (the Iranian school system was much different from the American one), Khos flunked twelfth grade at Farahmand High School; his highest marks were in physical education and "discipline," while his worst classes were math and physics. It mattered little to Khos, however, since he saw his future on the mat, not in books. He would ride a donkey ninety minutes into the Alburz Mountains to run at high altitudes, punishing his body, building it up. Once back in town, he'd down glasses of apple or carrot juice.

He enlisted in the army for two years, where he excelled in wrestling competitions, and then found work as an assistant cameraman for Iranian National Television. When he wasn't at the TV station, he was in the local *zurhkhanehs*, chasing his dream. He maintained a strict training regimen, following the Muslim protocol of avoiding all alcohol and praying five times per day. He impressed enough to be named to the national Greco-Roman wrestling team from 1966 to 1968, placing second in the 87-kilogram weight class at the European Championships in 1966 and 1967. As a standout "state wrestler," he was even recruited to act as a bodyguard for the shah's wife, Farah Pahlavi, and her retinue when they would travel to the cities of Persepolis and Shiraz.

Although he dutifully fulfilled the role of bodyguard, Khos had little interest in politics. He befriended Takhti, who lived near him on the south side of Tehran, but steered clear of his friend's rabble-rousing, knowing how dangerous such dissent could be. That fear was only cemented on January 7, 1968, when Takhti was found dead in a hotel room from an alleged suicide.

The country was in absolute shock, refusing to believe that their hero, a devout Muslim, would take his own life. Immediate suspicion was cast on SAVAK, the shah's secret police. Thousands of people poured into the streets, including Khos, who can be seen in archival footage wailing at the funeral procession. To this day, Takhti's visage decorates restaurants and shops in Tehran, and people continue to debate his cause of death. Although he did leave a note with a will, the mystery may never be solved. When I reach

Takhti's nephew, Ali Dehestani, on the phone to ask about the situation, he replies, "We're his family, and we don't even know."

He adds, "One tidbit you may not know is that my grandfather hired an investigator after his [Takhti's] death, and he [the investigator] ended up getting murdered."

Khos was heartbroken. Every Friday he went to the cemetery where Takhti was buried to pay his respects. He gave wrestling for Iran one last shot, trying out for the 1968 Olympic team. But he placed third and didn't make the cut.

"I'm done with this place," Khos thought. "If Iran isn't good enough for Takhti, it's not good enough for me." He had met a friendly American coach named Alan Rice from Minnesota at an international competition who had said to look him up if he ever came to the US.

In late fall of 1969, unable to speak more than a couple words of English, Khos bought a one-way plane ticket to New York, which then connected to Minneapolis. His goal: find Alan Rice.

Alan Rice had no idea what was coming.

*   *   *

2022

I LEAN MY FOREHEAD TOWARD THE TEMPERATURE SCANNER. THE WOMAN behind the desk watches her screen, gives a nod of approval, and then prints out a visitor's badge to stick on my shirt.

I'm at Discovery Village at Naples, a retirement home on the east side of the Florida city that itself feels like a resort for seniors. Natural light pours into the airy, tiled lobby, centered around a grand piano. The newish, $40 million development sits on 6.9 acres and has an outdoor pool with a putting green, an ice cream parlor, a bar/lounge, a spa/salon, and a movie theater.

Back in 2005, one of my dreams was for Khos and me to track down Alan Rice together, to find the man arguably most responsible for his eventual success.

Alan, now ninety-four, is still alive, although he's apparently become a bit of a recluse since moving down to Florida. I was able to reach him on the phone and was delighted to hear that he sounded both lucid and enthusiastic.

A fake plant sits atop a small shelf just outside his apartment door, decorated with four small American flags, perhaps some Fourth of July leftovers. I knock, and after a long pause and some shuffling, a small, stout man with uncombed gray hair answers.

"I'm so sorry, I lay down for a few minutes and fell asleep," Alan says, offering a soft handshake and entry to the dimly lit space.

He's wearing a blue National Wrestling Hall of Fame T-shirt and sweatpants, his feet bare.

"I've been having trouble with my balance lately," he says as I help him walk to his white recliner positioned in front of a flat-screen TV. The apartment is slightly cluttered, papers strewn across a desk and the floor, with a bookshelf holding some of his old wrestling awards.

Once upon a time, this man was a wildly successful stockbroker, a national champion amateur wrestler, and an Olympian (he competed for the US at the same Olympics where Takhti won the gold medal). He is the godfather of Greco-Roman wrestling in the US, a style of grappling in which holds below the waist are prohibited. While freestyle and folkstyle (high school and collegiate) incorporate takedowns aimed at the legs, Greco-Roman emphasizes upper body strength and various suplexes and throws. Alan specialized in Greco-Roman and imparted his knowledge through the founding of the Minnesota Wrestling Club in the early 1960s. He welcomed amateurs to train for free with him at the University of Minnesota, quickly turning the state into a breeding ground of the country's finest Greco-Roman competitors. In 1968, the year before Khos arrived in the US, Alan's club represented three of the ten slots on the Greco-Roman Olympic team; by 1976 it was up to six of ten.

"How are you doing, Alan? Do you have family around here that visit you?" I ask, glancing at a printout of the scheduled activities for the week at Discovery Village. Boredom seems impossible here.

"Well, not family, but friends," he says in a slightly nasal voice. He has a polite, exacting manner to him, a sense of propriety from a different time.

"Do you have kids?" I ask.

Deadpan, he replies: "My common answer to that is—not yet."

Although his humor is still intact, things have been hard lately. His two nieces and nephews live far away, and in the past year, he suddenly lost his wife. Ever since she passed, he's had a hard time getting excited about anything.

"We just had a movie here about a place called the Iguazu Falls," he says, referencing a recent screening in Discovery Village's movie theater.

I wonder where this is heading.

"It's the largest waterfall in the world in terms of the quantity of water. It's fed by three rivers, and the world championships were held in Argentina the year I was elected to be coach of the US team. And I wanted to be sure to take the team to places they might want to go as tourists," he explains.

Day after day sitting in his white recliner, with his wife gone, Alan finds himself thinking more and more about all the international experiences he had with the young wrestlers he once coached.

Which is why I'm here.

"Tell me about Khosrow Vaziri," I say.

His eyes light up.

"To the best of my recollection, I was living in Minnesota. One night, I got a phone call from some official at the airport in Minneapolis. And he says, 'There's a guy here that doesn't speak English. He says he knows you. His name is something like Khosrow. Do you know him? Does this mean anything?'"

Khos had apparently boarded a plane in New York with nothing but Alan Rice's name in his pocket. His plan consisted of repeating the words "Alan Rice" to everyone in the Minneapolis airport until someone took mercy on him and offered to help.

"They put him in a taxi and sent him to my home," Alan continues. "I put him up in my basement, and I forgot that the basement was kind of cold. It was a Minnesota winter. The fireplace wasn't working too well."

When Alan came to check on him the next morning, he saw that Khos had moved the entire bed next to the fireplace. So much for the luxury of the United States—this was more like sleeping next to the charcoal pit in Damghan.

But Khos was fiercely determined to make this new life work. Alan immediately found him more permanent lodging in his old fraternity house at the University of Minnesota, and in exchange for all the help, Khos signed on as one of his assistant coaches at the wrestling club. Alan was always on the lookout for a competitive edge and found it in recruiting foreign wrestlers to show his Americans their unorthodox techniques. He had brought in the entire Polish team, a Romanian named Ion Baciu, and now Khosrow Vaziri. Since Alan had put on some weight and was no longer able to effectively demonstrate Greco-Roman holds, he turned to Khos as his proxy, a twenty-seven-year-old beast weighing 190 pounds with a body cast in iron. He put Alan's students through the paces, instilling an edge and a confidence they had been lacking.

In 1972, when Alan was named head coach of the US Greco-Roman team for the Olympics in Munich, he took Khos along as one of his assistants.

Khos's Olympic dream had come true. He may have been on the sidelines wearing the colors of a country eight thousand miles away from his own, but he had made it. He never could have imagined that a decade later, 24,592 Americans in Madison Square Garden would be calling for his head.

Before leaving, I have Alan film a short video for Khos that I plan on sharing with him in Atlanta when I see him in a couple weeks.

Alan keeps his message short and sweet, referring to Khos in a way that speaks volumes to how he saw him more as a peer: "Well, keep it up, Khosrow. I'm glad to hear you're still alive. Not many of our old teammates are."

*   *   *

PAT MARCY WAS ONE OF THOSE STUDENTS WHO BENEFITTED FROM KHOS'S training. He knew Khos years before the Iron Sheik was invented, and that is the Khos he chooses to remember.

"He represented a paradigm shift for us. We'd never really had a Middle Eastern guy that was big and strong and talked like that. He would show us stuff, and it was his mystique as much as his technique. We just followed him and believed in him because he was cool, man," Pat says, pressing down on the gas and zipping us toward downtown Minneapolis in his white BMW.

When I pronounce Khosrow "Cause-row," he quickly points out that the correct pronunciation in Farsi is "Cose-row," the "c" a guttural sound almost like an "r" in French.

One year away from retirement, Pat's taken some time out of his schedule as a sales rep for Beacon Building Materials to show me the room at the University of Minnesota where Khos trained the Minnesota Wrestling Club for Alan Rice, a space known as "the Dungeon." Pat is short and slight (he wrestled in the 150-pound weight class at the 1976 Olympics), with a trimmed white beard and thin hair.

The university straddles the Mississippi River near downtown. I have an address for the first place Khos lived after leaving the fraternity house, and Pat indulges me to check it out on the way. Within a year of arriving in Minneapolis, Khos met a woman named Carol (not the same woman as Caryl, his current wife) whom he may have married in order to be able to stay in the US, and they lived here together (they divorced after only about a year). Pat pulls up next to a bleak fifties-era tan brick building with weeds sprouting on the front lawn and the number 904 in faded black lettering. The front door is locked, and hanging in the window of the first-floor apartment adjacent to the front door is a white bedsheet with "KEEP OUT" written in bright red. We heed the command.

A few minutes later we're in Dinkytown, a lively neighborhood full of bars and restaurants that surround the university. We park behind Bierman Field Athletic Building, home to the Dungeon. It's still standing.

Every day in the late afternoon Pat would come here to train. After getting off his welding day job, Khos would be waiting for him with a unique routine of exercises. They hit it off instantly.

"He was such a likable person, just a fun guy. I mean we partied. Work hard, play hard," he says.

Following practice, they would often hit the bars around Dinkytown. Although the conventional narrative says that Khos didn't touch alcohol or drugs until after he became a pro wrestler, he in fact let his guard down when he came to the US. He was still a proud Muslim, but far away from Iran's stifling culture, he allowed himself to indulge in the Western lifestyle in moderation.

"Land O'Lakes Inc. Center for Excellence" reads the lettering atop the expansive glass-paned entrance of Bierman. Just inside, a high-ceilinged lobby with giant electronic video boards welcomes us to the training facility, which hosts the university's wrestling, track, basketball, and cross-country programs. The Dungeon has long been replaced by a state-of-the-art practice facility with multiple wrestling mats, abundant natural light, and a second-floor overlook where the coaching staff has their offices.

The Dungeon is in the older wing of the building, down some flights of stairs. Without an appointment or any official reason to be there, Pat and I seem out of luck until we bump into a short, muscled athlete who looks to be about college age. He turns out to be a fifth-year wrestler named Brayton Lee.

"You're one of the better guys!" Pat says to him. He still keeps up on the wrestlers, and Brayton seems delighted to be recognized.

Brayton uses his card to open up a passage to the stairwell, and we come to a door simply marked "Wrestling Room."

Inside is a bare room stripped to its concrete base with low ceilings and fluorescent lights. Several pillars, once padded, break up the floor plan. A few cords, wires, and left-behind trophies lie along one wall. It is, indeed, a dungeon.

"There was like two inches of water down here for a long time," Brayton explains. A flood forced a complete stripping of the room, and with the new fancy facility upstairs, there's no rush to renovate this space.

Pat stands quietly and takes it all in, thinking back to all the hours spent here with Khos almost fifty years ago. It's clear what a profound effect Khos had on him as a young man in the way he speaks of him, with admiration bordering on awe.

"He was in my corner; he was so supportive. I couldn't have gotten where I got without him. He somehow instilled confidence in me," he says. Only a few years older than his pupils, Khos could do everything they could do. He was relentless, showing them a move or throw and then having them practice it over and over again until they got it right. He brought an intensity to everything he did, every movement, every expression, an intensity that seemed almost cultural, as if the Americans needed someone to toughen them up. There was a brutality there, controlled but always evident. It was just what the group needed to elevate their game.

Before meeting Khos, Pat didn't think he had a shot at making it on the biggest stages. He ended up competing on the Olympic team in 1976 and in three world championships.

Looking around the dungeon, I can picture a young Khos with his square jaw and searing intensity pushing these young men to their limits. At his heart, he is a teacher, supremely gifted but wanting to give back, a devotee of discipline and hard work and the dividends they pay. It's the Khos I met that day in 2001 who instantly took me in and inspired me to want to learn more about his background, before the drugs took over.

I thank Pat for showing me this place. It's a reminder of why I still keep a photo of the Iron Sheik on my apartment wall.

*   *   *

OVER HIS DECADES-LONG CAREER, THE IRON SHEIK ROUTINELY WENT ON CAMera and claimed to have won a gold medal representing Iran in the 1968 Olympics. He repeated it so many times that many of the people in the wrestling business started to think it was true, that it was a shoot. But if the camera ever zoomed in on the medal he wore around his neck in those interviews, it would show that it reads "1971 USA Amateur Athletic Union 180.5 lbs."

It is the ultimate irony that Khos's Olympic gold medal for Iran was complete fiction, but in reality, he was a national champion for the red, white, and blue.

Winning the gold medal was especially sweet for Khos after having to swallow the runner-up pill at the national championships in 1970 in Minneapolis. That year, competing in the 220-pound weight class (technically weights between 198 and 220 pounds), he tied gold medal winner Jim Duschen in the tourney's final match. Since Duschen had more points overall in the tournament, he took home the gold.

"Khosrow was very physical, very competitive. We were constantly fighting for position, to be able to lock up and throw. I don't think there was a takedown the whole match," Duschen recalls to me during a brief stop in Hendersonville, Nevada.

For the first few years in Minneapolis, Khos struggled financially while excelling on the wrestling mat. Despite winning championships and bringing out the best in Pat Marcy and others, he didn't even have a high school diploma and barely made a living as a welder. He would tell friends, "In Iran, we were paid [to be wrestlers], but here you can bring your gold medal to the grocery store and they won't give you one banana."

He did his best to learn the language, taking ESL classes at North Community High School, bingeing *Sesame Street,* and filling notebook after notebook with English phrases (he eventually passed an equivalency exam to earn his high school diploma).

One day Alan Rice brought Khos and his wrestlers over to a TV studio where promoter Verne Gagne was taping his American Wrestling

Association (AWA) wrestling show. Outside the building Khos saw the professional wrestlers get out of their Cadillacs and Mercedes, and his eyes got big. In the ring, what they did looked ridiculous—this wasn't wrestling; this was a show. In some ways it had more in common with the dancing and other rituals practiced in the *zurkhanehs* back home than it did with amateur wrestling. But amateur wrestlers didn't drive Cadillacs.

Khos begged Alan to put a word in with Verne to see if there might be a spot for him in one of his famed training camps. Although Khos didn't speak the language well and would clearly have a hard time adjusting to the showmanship of the pro game, Verne always respected amateur champions, having been one himself, and decided to give the green Iranian a chance. When the next camp rolled around in late 1972, Khos joined a "who's who" of future star wrestlers, including "Nature Boy" Ric Flair, Ken Patera, "Jumping" Jim Brunzell, and Greg Gagne. For about six weeks Khos learned to fall in a hard ring stained with goose shit in a barn on Lake Riley, the temperatures regularly in the single digits. The physical conditioning, which broke several other students, was the easy part for Khos. It was the "pro" aspects that were challenging for him—all his life he had trained to be a killer on the wrestling mat, and now he had to learn how to lose on purpose, often to guys who could never beat him in a real contest. On top of that, the most successful wrestlers were great on the microphone, using colorful language and charisma to get over even if their actual wrestling skills were mediocre.

"I think pro wrestling was extremely hard for Khosrow to learn, because he had been taught all his life about aggressive shooting, as far as Greco-Roman wrestling. I think he was the last one of the group to really feel comfortable in terms of working with other people and being comfortable in the ring," says Jim Brunzell, who I met with during my time in Minneapolis.

For the first three and a half years of his pro career, Khos wrestled under his real name, or as "Ali Vaziri" (Ali is one of his brothers' names and is much simpler for Americans to pronounce than Khosrow), a clean-cut babyface from Iran who often wrestled the preliminary matches. Khos pitched in wherever he was needed, setting up the ring, driving the ring truck, even refereeing. It was a hard life of long travel with low pay in brutally cold weather, as the AWA stretched across the Midwest from

Minnesota to Wyoming and Montana. One example from his journals: "June 15, 1975, Green Bay, wrestled Paul Perschmann, Food $25, Room $10, Gas $20, Paid $100."

Khos was a sponge, soaking up whatever he could from the Boys when they were willing to share and help him. Ray Stevens, Don Muraco, and Nick Bockwinkel taught him the psychology of pro wrestling, how to best engage the audience. But others took advantage of his naïveté. During training camp, veteran wrestler Billy Robinson slammed his knee into Khos's thigh during practice, a blatant cheap shot to humble him.

"Guys took advantage of him. They'd kick him in the stomach, hit him in the head," Brunzell says.

By 1976, Khos was getting desperate trying to make ends meet. One of his students, a three-time Olympian named Dan Chandler, had recently found work as a tree trimmer. Khos asked if he could get him a job.

"You don't want to be a tree trimmer," Dan replied.

At the 1976 Summer Olympics in Montreal, Khos accompanied the wrestling team once again, but this time watched from the stands with Verne Gagne and his wife, Mary. While eating at a French restaurant, Khos turned to the couple.

"Coach, I'm not getting over. I don't want to be a babyface anymore. I want to turn heel," the typically reserved Khos said.

Verne seemed reluctant. Heels were ring generals who had to generate heat. How could this mild-mannered, handsome Iranian turn heel?

Mary had an idea: "Khosrow, why don't you embrace your heritage and become a sheik?" There was already a well-known heel named The Sheik, a Syrian American named Ed Farhat, so to distinguish himself, Khos could become "The Iron Sheik," since "your body is like iron," Mary said.

Khos smiled. For the first time in a long time, he could see a future.

* * *

CARYL PETERSON DIDN'T FEEL LIKE GOING OUT.

She was studying to be a nurse at Normandale Community College, working on a paper comparing the American and Russian medical systems. Her friend wanted to go to the Left Guard, a popular bar in Bloomington founded by a couple of Green Bay Packers and frequented by football players. Caryl, twenty-one, reluctantly agreed to go. She was standing off to the side when a tall, dark Iranian man with limited English approached and asked if he could buy her a drink. She said no, thank you, I've already got one, but he persisted until she finally relented to a dance.

Khos was smitten. He loved American women, especially blondes. Caryl was intrigued, drawn to his accent, sinewy build, and dashing looks, but she was in no hurry to find someone or settle down.

They exchanged phone numbers, and then Khos called. And called. And called. He applied the same intensity to his courtship of Caryl that he did on the wrestling mat. It was a bit much, sure, but Caryl loved the attention, how he doted on her, always so polite and chivalrous. *Javanmardi.* While she was in no rush, there was a twelve-year age gap, and Khos was anxious to marry and start a family.

Only a few months after meeting, Khos proposed to her as they soared over the city in a gondola at the Minnesota State Fair. He gave her a beautiful turquoise gold ring, and they wed on March 21, 1976. Khos wrestled a matinee show that afternoon (it was a Sunday), then showered and raced to the Lutheran church in Edina for the service. The audience was a mishmash of amateur and pro wrestlers and Caryl's friends and family, who undoubtedly wondered what their little girl had gotten herself into.

Caryl thought nothing of pro wrestling before she met Khos, and their union didn't change her opinion much. It was his job and his passion, but she personally didn't see the appeal. Her main concern was that he not get hurt, a very real worry considering Khos's inhuman tolerance for pain and aversion to doctors. Before they met, he once broke his ankle in the ring and rather than have it treated, he taped it up and kept wrestling.

It took many, many years for Khos to admit to Caryl that his profession was a work, that it was staged. He was from the old school of Kayfabe. When Verne Gagne finally revealed wrestling's secrets toward the end of training camp, he told Khos and the others: "Don't smarten up anyone, not even your wife!"

Five months after their wedding, Caryl gave birth to a beautiful baby daughter named Marissa; two years later came Tanya, and in 1979, their third daughter Nikki. While Khos would have loved to have a boy, he loved his daughters dearly, and it broke his heart to have to be away from home so often. He wrote Caryl as often as possible, on hotel stationery, postcards, whatever he could get his hands on. The handwriting changed from letter to letter as he enlisted the help of other wrestlers to write in English and dictated what he wanted to say, each letter signed "Khosrow" in his distinct chicken-scratch cursive. In a series of missives from an extended overseas tour in 1977—Papua New Guinea, Australia, New Zealand, and elsewhere—he discussed the possibility of buying a house when he returned and emphasized how hard he was working to support the family, with baby Marissa always front of mind.

As an example, a letter dated 10/8/77 from Melbourne, Australia, began, "To my darling wife Caryl," and said, "Honey I love you and Marissa very much more than anything in the world and I miss you both very much. Honey you know and God knows how much I love you and Marissa and I never give up even when I'm hurting and I'm sick. I'm doing it all for you and Marissa's future."

When Khos transformed into the Iron Sheik character, Caryl was sad to say the least about her husband's new look—the bald head and handlebar mustache wasn't what she had signed up for—but she understood it gave him his best chance of success. He had new wrestling trunks made, emblazoned with the silhouette of a camel, along with the infamous pointed boots, also decorated with camels.

It took years of experimentation—he tried other ring names, like Muhammad Farouk and the Great Hossein Arab, and his home country ranged from Iran to Saudi Arabia to Lebanon. His country of origin mattered little to wrestling fans, who saw that region of the world as one monolith hostile to the US. Few noticed or cared that Iranians were not Arabs, or that relations between the US and Iran had been historically friendly.

While Khos tinkered with his gimmick, the world turned in a way that put him suddenly in the crosshairs of America. Resentment in Iran toward Americans had been simmering ever since the CIA-backed coup to overthrow Mohammad Mossadeq in 1953, but erupted into a screaming boil when the US admitted the shah for medical tests (he was dying from cancer) on October 22, 1979. Earlier in the year the shah had been exiled during the Islamic Revolution, which deposed the monarch and replaced him with cleric Ayatollah Khomeini, a populist who promised to bring reform to Iran. Rather than work with the new regime, the US shunned Khomeini. When they admitted the disgraced ex-king for treatment, the Iranians had had enough. The US was now the Great Satan.

The hostage crisis began a couple of weeks later.

All of this happened while Khos was performing in the WWF, wearing his keffiyeh and agal and declaring war on America. Suddenly he was the most despised wrestler on the roster, creating genuine fear for his safety. Fans called in death threats. Caryl was terrified. Just eight years prior, her husband was winning a gold medal for the United States, and now Americans wanted him dead, having no clue that this cartoonish heel was actually one of them (he had his citizenship by then) with no affection for the shah or ayatollah.

The myth was now all too real.

*   *   *

THE IRON SHEIK WOULD NOT BE WWF CHAMPION FOR LONG. HULK HOGAN was waiting in the wings, and the Sheik's victory was simply a transitional device to get the championship from one babyface (Backlund) to another (Hogan). The WWF was built around babyface champions, and Hogan was the anointed one to carry the company into its nationwide expansion.

My mission is to find the other guys who were there the night the Iron Sheik started it all, witnesses to history.

But before I meet the rest of the Six Packers, I need to know what it feels like to be one of them, if only for a day.

I've enrolled in a one-day training class in New Jersey.

Exciting Balukjian is about to make his comeback.

MATCH 3

EXCITING BALUKJIAN VS. BRAD BALUKJIAN

It's real.

—Me

T HE DREAMS THAT END IN THE WWE BEGIN HERE, IN A MUGGY GRAY grotto tacked on to the back of Gene's Deli & Convenience Store in Lake Hiawatha, New Jersey.

Mo is the first to arrive, dangling a gallon water jug from his thick fingers and placing it next to one of the four-tiered sets of bleachers surrounding the ring. He's in his late twenties or early thirties, short and solidly built, wearing a black hoodie, black shorts, and a backward hat, a thick black beard adding gravitas to his baby face. He climbs the steps, wipes the soles of his black sneakers on the apron to show respect to the ring, and eases himself through the ropes.

A few minutes later, Jason Flambers explodes through the side door, fresh from a trip to Israel and wearing a Ramah Day Camp lanyard. Unlike Mo, he's slight with a sunken chest and alert eyes, his gray T-shirt hanging off pointy shoulders.

He practically skips into the training center shouting "whoo!" and then calls out to Mo, who's pacing around the ring.

"You missed a good show last weekend!" he yells.

Mo gives a slight nod, but he's already in the zone. He has a ring to get ready.

On TV, the ring looks like a trampoline, an adult funhouse where combatants flip and flop to the delight of the belief-suspending audience. But in reality, the mat is a half-inch slab of hard foam supported by eighteen-foot wooden planks overlaying a metal frame. A central spring differentiates a wrestling ring from its much stiffer boxing cousin, providing some give when a body part collides with its surface and producing a crashing sound that magnifies the violence. The ropes, far from the rubber bands they appear to be on TV, consist of steel cable wrapped in garden hose and covered with colorful duct tape.

Mo stalks each of the ring's four corners with a tool to crank the turnbuckles, and then pulls on the ropes to make sure they're sufficiently taut. His job as manager of a local convenience store may pay the bills, but this testosterone cosplay every Monday, Tuesday, Thursday, and Saturday night is what gets him through his shifts. With the ropes tightened, he starts on one side of the ring and takes off, bowling across the canvas in four long strides, reaching toward the ropes on the other side. Just before he hits them, he turns 180 degrees and sinks his ample backside into the ropes until the steel cable within coils and slingshots him back across. He crisscrosses the ring over and over, always in four strides, the sound of his feet echoing up the twenty-foot rafters. Hitting the ropes is an essential part of every wrestler's toolbox and perhaps the most obvious tell of wrestling's choreographed nature (why would anyone run into ropes, turn around, and run straight back into their adversary in an actual fight?).

Two large industrial fans strain to blast humidity from the den, and a rack of old free weights and bench presses are scattered along the room's periphery. A sign that reads "East Coast Professional Wrestling School" (ECPW) adorns the black cinderblock walls in bright pink letters.

When Jason finds out that I'm a writer, his enthusiasm grows. He examines me with an avian tilt of the head, volunteering his backstory:

"I've been doing this about six months," he says as I sprawl on the foam mats surrounding the ring, waking up my own muscles wound tight from the three-thousand-mile drive across the country.

"I was studying theater at a local college and then COVID hit. I rediscovered wrestling with some friends, and thought, 'What can I do? I'm not the most fit—I could be a referee!' And I'm sure you know this, but the referee is important to the match, he has to kind of guide the guys."

I picture Mo rolling his eyes somewhere in the ring behind me.

I do, in fact, know the importance of the referee, for I played this role in my only prior foray into pro wrestling, an ill-fated one-off at a New England Wrestling Alliance show in a parking lot in the summer of 1998 (broadcast on public access TV and forever immortalized via VHS). While my friends were off at the beach, I was being greeted with a "this ref sucks!" chant by a surly Rhode Island crowd that didn't appreciate my 130-pound build and lack of zebra-striped shirt.

I explain to Jason that before I get face-to-face with the wrestlers of my past, I need to know what it feels like to bounce off the ropes and to get slammed on the canvas. I imagine legendary ring announcer Howard Finkel's booming voice announcing my entrance: *Coming down the aisle . . . hailing from Greenville, Rhode Island . . . weighing 170 pounds—Exciting Balukjian!*

In the Six Packers' era of the seventies and eighties, I would have had no such chance to sneak behind the curtain. At that time, promoters went to great lengths to protect their trade secrets, publicly insisting that every punch and kick connected. Wrestling lore is full of stories of football players and so-called tough guys getting ligaments stretched and noses bloodied by promoters' enforcers during tryouts, sending them home with the lesson that *rasslin'* was real.

Lucky for me, the curtain has long been lifted.

"Most of the guys that are coming in are young guys looking to make this a full-time gig," explains Gino "Mr. Italy" Caruso, the founder, owner, and trainer of ECPW who has graciously allowed me to attend this practice. While the class trickles in and warms up, Mr. Italy (his wrestling gimmick before hanging up the tights in 2000) sits behind a desk in his upstairs office scrawling in two legal pads crammed full of phone numbers, names, and notes. Those pads are Gino's Google Drive; his office, free of electronics, is illuminated by a single light bulb and is wired with a landline.

"Maybe they were college athletes, but now that's done. They still want to continue, to be involved in something physical. And there's also some guys in their mid- or late thirties. They know it's not going to be a full-time gig. But it's something they can do on the weekends to make some extra money. And you're getting that kick in front of a crowd."

Although the WWE is the biggest game in wrestling, a network of small independent promotions like ECPW create a farm system where wrestlers can break in and where fans can still go to a show for ten dollars. The company runs seventy to eighty shows per year, generally in the New Jersey/New York/Pennsylvania area, but sometimes stretching from Maine down to Mississippi.

For $3,000, Gino provides full-service training, which takes about six months. There's the physical part, learning how to fall and to create a sequence of moves that tell a story, but also the equally important character development, the aspect of wrestling that gets the audience to emotionally invest. It is this emotional participation that sets wrestling apart as a unique form of entertainment—the fans' reactions can literally change the script. A wrestler presented as a babyface gets booed mercilessly by the fans, and suddenly he has a change of heart, transforming into a heel.

Gino explains the character development process:

"We sit down for an interview, and I get your background to get an idea of what you're about. We make sure you're going to be OK mentally because there's some guys that it just isn't for them. We create the illusion of violence, but it's physical. You're gonna get bumps and bruises. It's gonna hurt."

While most don't make it, Gino has several success stories: Nunzio, Deuce 'n Domino, and Luke Gallows all spent time training here before going on to work for the WWE.

This is Gino's livelihood. This is his life. The former pro football player with a torn rotator cuff and a degree in animal science has been doing this since 1987, and at fifty-eight, he even wrestled a couple weeks ago.

If my career can last one day, I'll have made it.

When I had first asked Gino about participating in the training myself, his lips parted slightly to reveal a set of small teeth as he considered my unusual request.

"If you want to get in there, it's up to you," he said with a glint in his eyes.

*   *   *

LET'S GET THE FOUR-LETTER F-WORD OUT OF THE WAY RIGHT NOW.

You know the one. It has forever dogged pro wrestling and still dogs it to this day.

It's a word I refuse to use simply because it is too crass, too disrespectful to a profession that has such value as both social commentary and art form. Mark Cuban's hair color is fake; the Christmas tree in your aunt Patty's living room is fake; pro wrestling may be a lot of things—loosely scripted, yes; broadly choreographed, sure—but it is not fake. If your eyebrows are now raised, you're probably not alone—many still dismiss pro wrestling as too corny for anything but the fringes. (And yet, there have always been many fans in the closet—when asked what she would miss most about Washington when leaving the White House, Bess Truman said "wrestling on Thursday night.") While its supporters compare it to ballet, that association would draw a snort from polite society. So why does wrestling have such a hard time getting respect?

As Freud would suggest, let's go back to its childhood.

Wrestling writ large has existed since our species' origin, across cultures and continents, the appeal of controlled violence both innate and obvious. One of the oldest works of literature, *The Epic of Gilgamesh* (2150–1400 BCE), features a bout between Gilgamesh and Enkidu in Mesopotamia. But what we call professional wrestling is the early twentieth-century Frankenstein creation of three existing styles of wrestling—catch-as-catch-can, Greco-Roman, and collar-and-elbow—accented with elements of martial arts and football.

The Irish brought their upright, collar-and-elbow brand to the US in the 1830s and '40s, in which the victor was the first to throw his opponent to the ground for a "fall" (a word that persists to this day as a synonym for a pinfall or submission). The less restrained "catch" style arrived from the English county of Lancashire in the later part of the nineteenth century, and was often featured alongside bouts of Greco-Roman wrestling, which arrived in the US in 1875 and was practiced at the first Olympic Games in 1896 (and still is).

Between the end of the Civil War and about 1930, pro wrestling gradually evolved, accumulating various mutations along the way. As immigrant communities flocked to young cities and urbanized, the legitimate sport found a home in the saloons and bars where gambling ran rampant. But with money on the line, sports were vulnerable to shenanigans, perhaps none more so than wrestling, which was easily fixed with no equipment, a single official, and only two competitors.

Questions about wrestling's legitimacy were already commonplace in the 1870s. Newspaper accounts of a November 1873 match between Colonel James McLaughlin and John McMahon (no relation to Vince), in which McMahon prevailed despite giving away forty pounds, reported extensive betting on the outcome of the match and explicitly stated that the match was legitimate. That qualifier alone suggests the cloud of suspicion already hanging over the sport.

In those pioneer days, there was no centralized wrestling promotion, no regulating authority. Championships were routinely invented and forgotten, and matches often took place outdoors on grass or on canvas-covered hard floors. While some bouts were held in sports venues or bars, others became a regular attraction as part of the "athletic shows" at touring carnivals, in which a wrestler in the troupe challenged a local from the audience, who was often a plant cut in on the receipts.

Little by little, modern pro wrestling emerged. Around 1900, matches began taking place in a ring with ropes and the first *tag team* (two on two) matches were booked; by 1905, an estimated 90 percent of all matches were fixed. Looking at the historical record, the legitimate contests were likely those that stand out for their length, such as the longest match on record, a nine-hour-and-thirty-five-minute affair between William Muldoon and "Professor" William Miller. The star grapplers of the day had such snoozy monikers as Frank Gotch, Dan McLeod, and Tom Jenkins, but the first gimmick wrestlers played on ethnic stereotypes and xenophobia, such as Yusuf "The Terrible Turk" Ismail, who claimed to be a Turkish sultan and wore flowing robes and a fez to the ring.

By the end of World War I, it was clear to promoters that legitimate wrestling matches were too, well, *boring* to generate much revenue. And so with dollar signs in their eyes, they pumped up the entertainment aspects of the industry. One impresario in particular, Jack Curley, helped establish Madison Square Garden as the seat of wrestling's power, crowning a unified world champion in Joe Stecher in a 1920 bout that drew ten thousand fans and a $75,000 gate (about $1.16 million in 2022 dollars). Curley also ushered in rule changes to improve the audience experience, such as shortening matches through time limits and implementing single-fall matches (versus two-out-of-three). He was soon followed by a group that raised the bar even further, the Gold Dust Trio of new world champion Ed "Strangler" Lewis, trainer-booker Joe "Toots" Mondt, and Lewis's manager, Billy Sandow. (Even in pro wrestling's infancy, identity was tinkered with: Lewis's real name was Robert Friedrich and Sandow was born Wilhelm Baumann, changing his last name to Sandow to mimic German strongman Eugen Sandow.) The Trio completed pro wrestling's transformation from sport to entertainment, creating an itinerant band of performers who toured the country repeating the same matches in different towns, with combatants paired off for series of matches that culminated in a decisive winner. Emphasis was placed on creating finishes that maximized drama, such as count-outs and disqualifications that avoided declaring a clear-cut victor but drove interest in the return bouts. Ostensibly enemies, wrestlers learned how to cooperate to drive interest in the match, devising series of moves that incorporated football (for example, the flying tackle), amateur wrestling (the suplex), catch-as-catch-can (the armbar), and straight-up brawling (the simple punch and kick).

In short, wrestling discovered storytelling.

But the Gold Dust Trio's reign was short-lived, brought to an end by an infamous double-cross that would cast the die for wrestling tradition until our story picks up again in the 1970s.

Six-feet-six, 260-pound Wayne Munn (with the imaginative nickname "Big"), a former football player at the University of Nebraska, was tapped as the next champion in line after Strangler Lewis for his irrefutable charisma and awesome presence. Unlike previous champions, Munn had no real background in amateur wrestling and was not known to be able to handle himself in an actual fight. After winning the belt from Lewis on January 8, 1925, Munn entered the ring against Stanislaus Zbyszko on April 15 in Philadelphia, fully expecting to win as had been arranged. But the cunning Zbyszko had other ideas. He deviated from the script and pinned Munn (multiple times, in fact) to exact revenge on promoter Sandow. Lesson learned—for the next fifty years, promoters almost always kept the world championship on someone who could protect himself if things got too real.

Following the double-cross, the Gold Dust Trio lost their grip on power, and wrestling settled into a territorial system of regional promotions that would endure for fifty years. Gimmick matches became more common, such as "midget" wrestling, and the morality play motif was fully established, with "a Manichean system of rule-abiding good guys ('babyfaces' or 'faces') and despicable villains who resorted to tactics not according to Hoyle ('heels')," as historian Scott Beekman writes in *Ringside*, his excellent history of pro wrestling. He goes on: "Although no hard rules existed for determining personas, promoters usually pushed handsome or former college star wrestlers as clean-wrestling faces, while older, fatter, or foreign-born wrestlers often became heels."

The seeds of the Iron Sheik and Hulk Hogan had been planted.

*   *   *

DESPITE WHAT WRESTLERS MAY CLAIM, MOST FANS HAVE ALWAYS KNOWN THAT wrestling is more spectacle than sport, even in the 1970s and 1980s when promoters insisted otherwise.

"It's possible that the illusion at the heart of wrestling was not that fans believed wrestling was real, but that *wrestlers believed that fans believed it*," writes Abraham Josephine Riesman in her 2023 Vince McMahon biography, *Ringmaster*.

Convinced that the business would tank if they acknowledged the truth, wrestling promoters fiercely guarded the alternate reality of Kayfabe. The world was divided into *smarts*, those in on the trade secrets, and *marks*, the rubes who bought tickets and believed in Santa Claus.

The wrestlers, or *Boys*, may have underestimated their fans.

"Every one of them [groupies who slept with wrestlers] knew it wasn't real, and every one of them pretended around the wrestlers that they thought it was," says Dave Meltzer in Riesman's book. Meltzer has written and edited the wrestling industry's leading publication, *The Wrestling Observer Newsletter*, since 1982.

The real-vs.-fake paradigm captivated audiences who, much like the spectators at a magic show, were fascinated by how the tricks were pulled off. Even if most people knew what they were watching was staged, they loved losing themselves in the drama playing out in the ring. Look no further for evidence of this than the many fans at wrestling shows who walk around the arena wearing replica championship belts, as if they too are part of the show.

"The audience has to buy in to what they're seeing, unconsciously or consciously," says CarrieLynn Reinhard, professor of communication arts and sciences at Dominican University in River Forest, Illinois, and the president of the Professional Wrestling Studies Association, an academic think tank that analyzes wrestling.

"I think as you get older, and you develop your imaginative literacy, you're able to buy into it easier if you're emotionally connecting with the wrestlers. I wouldn't be a *Star Wars* fan if I was not buying into the Force and the Jedi and the Rebellion and the Empire. I know they're not real. But there's something in them that connects with me. And I think that's really no different than Kayfabe, all these fictional realities humanity has been creating, possibly since the beginning of humanity," she says.

An entire lexicon developed that many old-school wrestlers use to this day, and that can be wildly entertaining to adopt in your own life.

First a quick primer (if you need a reminder throughout the book, flip to the first few pages for a glossary): A *babyface* and a *heel* are paired together on tour in a *program*, in which they wrestle each other night after night, often with roughly the same match. Sometimes they will work a particular storyline, or *angle*, that raises the emotional stakes, like when "Macho Man" Randy Savage accused Hulk Hogan of trying to steal his valet, Miss Elizabeth. In a match, the heel tries to generate negative audience reaction, or *heat*, while the face tries to elicit positive reactions, or *pops*. The match itself consists of a series of moves, or *spots*, culminating in an ending or *finish* in which one person, usually the babyface, wins, or *goes over* via a pinfall (both shoulders down for the referee's three-count) or submission, while the loser *jobs*. If the fall is done without any outside interference or use of an illegal weapon (e.g., a folding chair), it is said to be *clean*. In order for the match to work and for the audience to invest emotionally, the recipient of a given move or hold must *sell*, using body language and facials to convey the illusion of being in agony. The more *over* a wrestler is, the more likely he is to win several matches or even the championship, getting a *push*.

We could all use a little Kayfabe in our lives. Imagine how fun it would be if the moment you step through the doors at work, the lights dim and your entrance music hits. Or try working this vocabulary into your daily routine: Put over your partner clean when they are feeling low and you will become the ultimate babyface; leave your dirty dishes in the sink, however, and you will get tons of heat and might even end up on the couch as the finish. The good news is identity can change on a dime—perform some act of kindness in the morning and your heel turn will be over, your babyface status restored. You might even get a pop, and if you're lucky, a push where you won't have to do any jobs for a long while.

*   *   *

I WILL NEVER BE MISTAKEN FOR A PROFESSIONAL WRESTLER.

While the rest of the ECPW class gears up, I search for a place to change, filing past a rack of metal folding chairs bent and dinged from someone's skull in a recent match. I duck into the bathroom to change and am greeted by two dirty bright blue socks discarded on the floor. On the peeling walls hangs a single piece of art, a painting of Jesus kneeling down to comfort a crowd of children.

I don't wear briefs in daily life, self-conscious as I am about my chicken legs, so there's no way I'm about to don a pair of wrestling tights. I emerge wearing baggy mesh shorts and a highlighter-green quick-dry T-shirt and find my place among the pupils: "Big Bad" Blake, a four-hundred-pound behemoth engrossed in his cell phone; "Dr. Venkman," with a mad scientist gimmick; "Corazon," a masked Latino; Connor, on only his second day of training; CJ, accompanied by an older woman who may be his mother; the aforementioned ref Jason Flambers; and Mo, who has now transformed into his persona "Sami Nasir," and in true method actor form, goes by "Sami" for the remainder of the session. My presence draws some sideways glances, but mostly the Boys tease and goof around like any other day.

Sami, Jason, Connor, and I get in the ring to begin practice.

The very first thing you learn in professional wresting is the forward roll. This seems easy enough, reminding me of my gymnastics classes at age five: squat low, plant both fists on the mat in front of me, put the top of my head on the mat, and use my fists to propel myself forward in the air, the momentum carrying me over to end where I started, ready for the next roll.

I quickly realize I peaked at five.

While I complete the forward roll, when I go to plant my feet, I fall back and crash on my side on a very stiff mat, my equilibrium destroyed, my head spinning. The next one is slightly better, but when I try to stand up I see black squiggles and lose my footing, eliciting a chuckle from the others.

We mercifully move on to rolls on our sides, and this I'm a little better at, having done a half dozen jiujitsu classes many years ago. I take a couple steps and hurl my body forward, planting the back of my left arm and shoulder on the mat to absorb the impact, my momentum carrying me forward to my feet.

"The reason why we have you focus on rolls on your left side is we work everything on the left side in wrestling," Sami says.

I've watched thousands of matches in my life without realizing that every move is done to the left side, from headlocks to armbars to wristlocks. Always working the left side helps with timing and reduces the guesswork in positioning.

The irony of people describing wrestling as "scripted" is that there is no script, at least for the wrestling portion (modern WWE now employs writers to tightly script promos and skits). Instead, the two wrestlers only know the finish and the approximate time of the match and then call the various spots on the fly, whispering to each other.

Sami directs us to try just such a series of spots to start a match: he and I circle each other like two predators, then lunge forward to *lock up*, a vestige from wrestling's collar-and-elbow origins. We grab each other's trapezius muscles with our left hands and our opposing elbows with our right hands, our arms extended, simulating a tussle for positioning.

"OK, now throw my left arm off your neck and grab a side headlock," he instructs.

I do as I'm told, clamping my toothpick bicep tight around his head. He flails his arms in pretend agony, momentarily surprising me.

"Loosen up, loosen up!" he yells as I realize he might not be pretending.

"Stand more upright so the crowd can see," he says, his arm wrapped around my waist.

He signals a reversal by grabbing for my hand, my cue to release the headlock while he applies a wristlock on me.

My turn to sell.

He lightly holds my left wrist, bending my hand forward, the palm toward me, and I instinctively start grimacing. In reality, he's being so gentle.

So far we've exchanged a few holds, but to really know what it feels like to be a pro wrestler, I have to experience the most fundamental part of any match: taking a *bump*.

A bump is the act of hitting the mat, which doesn't hurt too badly—if you know how to land properly, with your knees bent, arms outstretched, and palms down, so that your hands, feet, and mid-back all hit the mat at the same time while you exhale, distributing the impact and making a loud noise as the canvas slams against its metal frame. Clearly, bumps add up—many wrestlers have had knee and hip replacements from the repeated pounding—but what does a single bump feel like?

Sami and I begin a new sequence, locking up, but this time he throws my left arm off his trap and turns 180 degrees while reaching for my head with both hands and dropping to a knee. We're about to execute the "snap mare," which creates the illusion of one wrestler being so strong that he is able to reach up and flip his opponent forward simply by pulling on his neck, slamming him down to the canvas. I am the bump taker here, but in reality I am doing all the work. When Sami drops down, I plant my hands on his shoulder and throw my body forward, much like a forward roll, somersaulting down on my back to complete the bump. He does little more than cradle my head while "wrenching" me forward.

It's the simplest of moves, and yet as we set it up, I'm momentarily frozen by the idea of throwing myself into the abyss, hoping to land just right on wood backed by steel.

Here we go. I tuck my chin and jump up. My landing provides an immediate and painful lesson.

I don't tuck my chin quite enough. Too much of my upper back and the back of my head hit the mat when landing. I remember to exhale to keep my wind, but I'm seeing a couple stars as I wobble up to my feet and feel the impact lingering.

The next drill is to hit the ropes, running from one side of the ring to the other just as Sami had make look so easy while warming up. Each time I lean into them, the steel cable wrapped in tape digs into my back just below the shoulder blade, shooting me off to the other side. The next morning I wake up with raspberries below my armpits from the repeated collisions.

I'm sweating hard now, my breath short, my body aching from bumps and rope burn.

"Normally we don't run the ropes until after the first day, but you're only here one day, so we wanted you to get a feel for everything we can," Gino says with a little smirk.

I nod, panting, and look over at CJ, the one-month veteran dressed in all blue with a durag covering his head.

"What do you think?" he asks.

"It's tough. It's real," I reply, bent over and breathing hard.

I've passed the test. He smiles big and offers me a fist bump.

I bail out of the ring to catch my breath and cool down. At the start of the session I had dreams of jumping off the top rope. Now I have no such desire. I grab a seat in the bleachers and watch as Dr. Venkman and Corazon practice a full eight-minute match, complete with Jason prancing around pantomiming as referee.

Matches have a traditional blueprint, beginning with the wrestler entrances, which these days come complete with blaring music and pyrotechnics. The heels snarl at the fans, sometimes directly antagonizing them ("shut up!" is a common taunt) while the babyfaces give out high fives and pose or gesture, seeking approval. Once the bell rings, the two clash at center stage in a lock-up and initiate their first series of spots. After some early jockeying, the heel usually establishes control (the heel leads the match, calling out each spot) and crescendoes with a series of *highspots*, a fast-paced series of maneuvers such as a dropkick or flying forearm off the ropes. Just as the babyface appears beaten, the crowd ratchets up the noise, spurring an incredible comeback that culminates with a finish in which justice typically prevails, sending everyone home happy. The whole thing is a remarkable exercise in improvisation requiring a real-time reading of the audience to work within the parameters of a loose script.

Dr. Venkman, the heel, clearly has more charisma than his masked opponent, Corazon. They're both in full dress rehearsal—if they botch the timing of a move, they take counsel from Gino, the veteran sage leaning on the ropes at ringside, and try again. Venkman, pasty and of average size with a plain face and short haircut, transforms into his evil alter ego, cackling to an imaginary audience and yelling "now I will use the power of science!" before executing his next move. Comedy is another ingredient in the wrestling elixir, which Venkman implements as he climbs to the middle rope, exclaiming "witness the power of physics!" and then remembering that he is a cowardly heel, says "too high" and moves down a rung to the bottom rope.

Their match is fast-paced and all action, highspot after highspot. This kind of "flippy" wrestling is au courant, much to the chagrin of old-school purists who consider it to be glorified gymnastics and who long for the days when a more sedate pace allowed the wrestlers to better "tell a story."

Wrestling has undoubtedly come to resemble stunt work, with larger, more spectacular leaps and falls in and out of the ring. The old "steel chair to the head" spot looks mundane compared to the backflips off of ladders crashing through tables that frequent today's matches. Watching that level of risk-taking has become one of the pillars of modern wrestling's appeal.

"Wrestlers are essentially live action superheroes, because a lot of them in their performance seem to be able to do things with their body that other humans cannot, including a lot of them taking a lot of physical pain," says Professor Reinhard.

When you jump backward off a ladder and land on top of another human crashing through a table, it's going to hurt, no matter how well you know how to fall. Wrestling fans admire the performers' commitment to their craft and willingness to endure pain just to entertain them. While no one wants wrestlers to get seriously hurt, there is a desire to see limits get tested, to explore what is possible. That boundary-seeking, living in that liminal zone between fake and real, myth and reality, is the key—has always been the key—to wrestling's popularity. Even as a kid I was aware that what I was watching was not true sport, and yet I scrutinized each spot, looking for the one that might have been "more real" than the others, impressed by any move that made me say, *That* had to hurt."

When the WWF's Linda McMahon (Vince's wife) testified to the Pennsylvania House of Representatives in 1987 that wrestling was an exhibition and not a sport (in order to avoid paying costly fees to the State Athletic Commission), it effectively ended Kayfabe, a moment that many predicted would spell the end of pro wrestling. Once those in charge openly admitted to wrestling's true nature, the fans would turn away, refusing to watch a "fake sport."

But the opposite happened.

Thirty-five years later, wrestling is alive and well. If anything, pulling back the curtain and breaking the fourth wall has increased wrestling's popularity, lengthening the time we spend in that liminal zone between work and shoot. Wrestlers will more often let "real life" seep into the show, so that some backstage conflict that gets reported on the internet suddenly is written into a storyline. In a full-circle moment, today's wrestlers' ring names are often real or real-adjacent—today's most popular stars are not Iron Sheiks or Ultimate Warriors; they are "Roman Reigns" and "Cody Rhodes," a callback to the origins of the art form in the early twentieth century. Today heelish behavior is often cheered, babyfaces booed. The marks are all smart.

Since it's time for Exciting Balukjian to morph back into Brad, I watch the end of the Dr. Venkman vs. Corazon rehearsal and quietly slip out into the warm New Jersey night, satisfied with my initiation into the wrestling brotherhood.

I turn the Ford Fusion northeast and set the GPS for Maine. I have a date with Tony Atlas, the first of the Six Packers.

And man, does he have a story to tell.

PART III
THE HIGHSPOTS

MATCH 4

MR. USA TONY ATLAS VS. ANTHONY WHITE

1989

Tony Atlas is cold.

Teeth-chattering, soul-rattling, breath-catching cold, the kind of cold that makes your skin feel like it's on fire.

He's been wearing the same sweatsuit since fall and hasn't bathed in months. His black hair, short but thick, obscures the myriad sores covering his scalp.

For dinner, he dives into a dumpster behind a fast-food restaurant to scavenge pieces of hamburger and fries. The only way he can get warm is when he gets ahold of a glass pipe and takes a long drag, the freebase cocaine rushing into his system, an instant wave of warmth and energy that curbs the hunger pangs.

He's just been kicked out of the latest flophouse, owned by a woman named Shirley, who let junkies stay there and cook their product in exchange for a hit. Tony, sick and tired of the grip of addiction, had flushed three and a half grams of the house supply down Shirley's toilet, sparking a riot. Five of his fellow squatters attacked, livid that $120 of street value had just entered the Lewiston, Maine, sewage system.

But if there's one thing Tony knows, has always known, will always know, it's how to fight. Even in an altered state, his arms, twenty-three inches around at their peak, flexed with rage and his fists rained down like ham hocks as he fought off the squatters.

It took a visit from the police to keep Tony from annihilating his five assailants. Once things settled, Shirley said he had to leave.

With nowhere to go and desperate for warmth, Tony hugs himself under a bench in Kennedy Park, a nine-acre rectangle dusted with snow and named for JFK after he stopped there on the campaign trail in 1960. The twin cities of Lewiston and Auburn lie on either side of the Androscoggin River. Hydro-powered textile mills sprang up during the mid-1800s, and by 1865 Auburn was producing six hundred thousand pairs of shoes, earning it the title of "Shoe Capital of the World."

Later this week Tony will defend his International Championship Wrestling (ICW) heavyweight championship in front of several hundred fans, who would be flabbergasted to know that this six-foot-three, 260-pound colossus is homeless. The ICW, struggling to stay afloat, is a far cry from the marquee at Madison Square Garden where less than a decade earlier he had pinned Hulk Hogan, *the* Hulk Hogan, the last time the Hulkster had been pinned cleanly.

Tony squeezes his massive forearms, part of the physique that once earned him the title of Mr. USA 1979, and closes his eyes. Maine may seem to be an unlikely place for a self-described Black hillbilly from 1950s western Virginia, but when the ICW called, he was pleasantly surprised by the progressiveness of the local community. Shortly after arriving, he saw a white woman and a Black man walking down the street and thought, "Oh, they're gonna hang him." But the locals just said, "We aren't about that up here."

As welcoming as Maine can be, there's no getting around the gelid winters. He reaches up with an exposed hand and rubs the dent in the middle of his forehead, a permanent reminder of the day Anthony White died and Tony Atlas was born.

Anthony White was born one of nine children on April 23, 1954, in Clifton Forge, Virginia, and soon moved four miles down the road to Low Moor. He was primarily raised by his mom, Beatrice James, and his grandmother. His father, Norris, absconded to Richmond with his triplet sisters and twin brother and sister when Beatrice James tired of his nonstop drinking and carousing (Norris claimed to have fathered thirty-six kids before meeting her; she shooed him out of town with her .38 revolver). She was a tough, hard-working woman who weighed more than three hundred pounds and who did everything she could to provide for her family. Every morning she was at work at the Hotel Roanoke by seven o'clock to work as a cook, and then after a brief break, she went to her second job as a maid until eleven at night.

The family was short on money but long on faith; with no indoor plumbing, Anthony and his brothers had to defecate in a bucket they kept under their bed, and without heat, they built fires in the kitchen stove just to stay warm.

As a toddler, Anthony would sit at the feet of his grandmother and her friends and fall asleep under their shoes, where he felt safe and secure. To this day, he craves the feeling of a woman's shoes on his face, smothering him, dominating him, even kicking him to inflict some pain. One of the strongest men in professional wrestling, a decorated bodybuilding champion with a physique carved from stone, he needs to have all that strength and power and white-hot rage subdued and contained. When the beast inside threatens to bolt out of its cage, he seeks out a woman to step on his face. Large tennis shoes are his favorite.

At age six, Anthony was walking behind a girl in Low Moor, admiring her shoes. As they crossed a bridge, he looked down and noticed that the creek bed, full of water only a few weeks before, had dried up. A boy named Spike, who was keen on the girl, walked up to Anthony.

"I want to push you," Spike said, without explanation.

"Well, you better not," Anthony replied, never one to shy away from a confrontation.

In the next instant, Anthony felt himself flailing as he fell ten feet from Spike's shove, landing with a thud on his head on the bone-dry ground. His face was immediately covered in blood as he somehow staggered home to his grandma, who clutched him and rocked him and prayed so hard her hands hurt. When Beatrice James came home late that night Anthony had gone into a coma, and when she rushed him to the hospital, the doctors said they weren't sure if he was going to make it.

"If he's gonna die, let him die in my arms," she told the doctors.

When he woke up, he was Tony Atlas. Beatrice James was worried his mind was never the same, but Tony was as determined as ever to get stronger, to get bigger, to become so powerful that the Spikes of the world could never hurt him again. He saw Steve Reeves in the movie *Hercules* and said, "I want to be like that."

The dream came true. He started boxing at age eight and by the sixth grade was wrestling in the 155-pound weight class. While other kids carried basketballs around town, Tony piled giant weights on his shoulders. He got in his first fight at age eleven, against a nineteen-year-old, and when one of the few white families in town stiffed him for some fieldwork he had done, Tony took on both of their sons, who were four years older, and won. When their father, a farmer named Redeye Hinton, saw Tony getting the best of his sons, he jumped off his tractor and stabbed Tony in the back with a pitchfork.

But Tony kept on coming. When his dad (who briefly returned when Tony was twelve) took him down to Scrappers Corner in Low Moor, an intersection where locals would fight (with money at stake), Tony took on all comers, boy or man.

"If you lose, I'm gonna give you a worse whippin' when you get home," his dad warned.

By the time Tony graduated from Patrick Henry High School in Roanoke in 1974, he stood six foot two and could bench press five hundred pounds.

The beast wasn't just out of the cage. He was bending its bars.

*   *   *

2022

WITH TEARS FOR FEARS' "HEAD OVER HEELS" BLASTING, I PUSH THE FORD Fusion almost eight hundred miles in a single day, by far the longest driving day of the trip. I travel many of the same roads that Tony Atlas traveled forty years ago, the roads he called home.

At age sixty-eight, Tony is still taking bumps. He's coming back from a match in Minneapolis for an independent promotion much like Gino Caruso's ECPW (he still wrestles regularly for Gino) and has set aside the next two days for me.

Not for free, however. When I got his phone number and called to set up an interview, I caught him on the road fighting with his GPS and we got disconnected. When he called back to hear me out, he said, "No freebies. I'm too old to do anything for free anymore."

I explained that what I was doing was journalism, not public relations, and that he was just one of several wrestlers I was interviewing. Paying your subjects can color the interaction, I explained.

"The WWE gave me the same song and dance," he replied, referring to a recent interview with them in which he demanded a fee.

I didn't like it, but I understood. Tony still has to make a living, and the only thing he has ever known is wrestling. He was, and still is, a corporation of one.

"You have to understand, all these guys you're meeting with, I'm different. I have to work for a living. My day starts at seven and ends at six," he said.

I agreed to pay him $1,000 for two days of his time, with the caveat that I would disclose the arrangement to you, the reader.

From there I couldn't get Tony off the phone. He took me on a wild ride through his life and career, a stream of self-help and regret and aphorisms that had my head spinning.

"Pro wrestling died in 1990," he said, "when Vince McMahon said it was entertainment. Back in the eighties, especially the seventies, about 50 percent of what we did was real."

The memory of Tony's words ring around my head as the blackness of the Road engulfs me and the heavens begin spitting rain somewhere around Massachusetts. I flit around my Spotify playlist to stay awake, blaring Styx's "Renegade" and AC/DC's "Dirty Deeds Done Dirt Cheap." When I finally pull into the greater Lewiston area around midnight, a roadside motel rejects me with a "No Vacancy" sign, forcing me into neighboring Auburn and the glitz of a Hilton Garden Inn. I gingerly walk into the lobby, my quads and hamstrings stiff, past a pool crammed with college kids showing off their cannonballs. My budget is now out the window as I crave any horizontal surface. I approach a beanpole with floppy hair at the front desk whose name tag reads "Niall." He's wearing a mint-green sweater and doing his calculus homework. The lobby smells like chlorine and cucumbers.

"The only rooms we have are junior suites for $316," he says apologetically.

"We have five weddings staying here," he explains.

Right, a Saturday at the start of summer in a town that depends on summer.

Back out into the night, into the Fusion. I briefly consider looking for the park bench in Kennedy Park that Tony once called home. It's warm enough, in the midfifties, and I brought a sleeping bag anticipating just such a dilemma.

My last shot is an eyesore called the Center Street Inn, whose front door is wide open but whose lobby looks like it was abandoned mid-renovation. I'm surprised to find a handwritten sign scrawled "No Vacancy" taped to the door.

I tap out, unfurl my sleeping bag, and zip up my black jacket in the driver's seat of the Fusion. I try to recline the seat but am immediately betrayed by my own research archive, boxes of paper pushing back. I lean back, the smell of my own body odor wafting to my nostrils, and shut my eyes, grateful that it's summer, thinking of Tony under that park bench down the street, at the height of winter.

*   *   *

TONY ATLAS DOESN'T SIT ON FURNITURE. HE CONSUMES IT.

Thighs parted and legs fully extended, he waits for me on the couch in the Hilton Garden Inn lobby the next evening. He's wearing a red hoodie, black swishy pants, and Converse sneakers, with a double-decker fanny pack wrapped around his waist and a gold chain with a large gold cross that dangles over his broad chest. His biceps are about the size of my waist, and although he stands only a few inches taller than me, I feel like a hug might snap me in two.

We shake hands, and his face lights up, his nostrils flaring like two caves, his wide-set eyes dark brown and warm with some age spots underneath, crested by faint eyebrows. A trimmed gray-white mustache and beard cover the lower part of his face, whiter on the chin, creeping halfway up his cheeks before petering out well before the margin of his small ears. His head is a large smooth dome, lines crossing the back of it just above his neck.

Everyone here knows Tony. When we grab a table in the lobby restaurant, the waitress comes by and asks, "Mr. Atlas, do you want anything?"

"I got the proclamation of the government here for work with kids. I know all the policemen, the fire department, I do benefits for the police. I'm a personal trainer right here at the YMCA," he explains to me.

He turns to the waitress, a gleam in his eye. He's on.

"Do you sell monkey vomit?" he asks.

"Not that I'm aware of," she replies with a laugh, as if she's heard this one from Tony before.

"You know I'm trouble, don't ya?" he says as she walks away to fill my order.

"What was that?" I ask, thoroughly confused.

"I go through the whole list: monkey vomit, camel snot, scab sandwich, pus on top," he says.

My face is blank.

"That's wrestling. I'm a seventies wrestler," he explains. The lyrics to children's gross-out songs were apparently wildly entertaining to the Boys in the seventies.

"You see, the guys that trained me was out of the fifties and sixties. When I broke into the business, what they do, they will take the young wrestlers and have them travel with the old wrestlers to teach them the ropes. So most of the stuff that I learned, I learned from the old-timers," he says with a thick but soothing Southern drawl, "wrestlers" pronounced "rasslers" and "fifties" "fiftus."

His hands fly in front of him as he talks, two rings on his right hand, one of them commemorating his 2006 WWE Hall of Fame induction. He's in his comfort zone, talking about himself.

"My only problem was I didn't listen to them until it was too late. I didn't listen to those guys," he says, some regret creeping into his powerful voice.

It's a refrain he'll come back to several times, the way he was pushed to the moon so young and just as suddenly came crashing back down.

The old-timers told him to save his money, but for a kid out of poverty who wore the same outfit to school every day because that's all his mom could afford, financial planning was the last thing on his mind. What he didn't spend on fancy things he gave away, generous to a fault, always wanting to help those in need because *he* was *them*. When promoters discovered him lifting weights at the YMCA in Roanoke, he was making sixty-five dollars a week washing dishes; in 1975, during his first week as a pro wrestler, he made $1,500 ($1,000 of it went to new suits and $500 was sent back home to Mom). Promoters from the Mid-Atlantic territory were smitten with his Adonis physique and weight-lifting prowess and agreed to pay *him* to train to be a wrestler, an unheard-of arrangement.

In his caramel complexion they saw gold. Black wrestlers were enormously popular with the largely Black audiences of the South, but promoters only made room for one star Black wrestler per territory, just as there was only room for one Latino babyface. Reflecting the geopolitics of the times, Asians, Russians, and Middle Easterners were considered heels, while Pacific Islanders and Africans were depicted as savages who grunted and groaned through their interviews.

"[Black star] Thunderbolt Patterson told me one time, you can't do what the white guys do and keep a job. Even if you're on top," Tony tells me.

Ric Flair, who went from fellow rookie in the Iron Sheik's training class to National Wrestling Alliance (NWA) champion in less than ten years, was a notorious hell-raiser who could get away with stripping down and shaking his penis like the blades of a helicopter in public, but not Tony Atlas or his tag-team partner, Rocky Johnson.

"S.D. Jones [another Black wrestler] knew he was never gonna be the top Black as long as I was around, or Rocky Johnson was around. He knew he was never gonna get that top spot, so S.D. and these guys underneath, they had to be the nicest, sweetest guys in the world," he explains.

He's at ease, bouncing from one subject to the next, never at a loss for words, his voice echoing around the lobby. The couple next to us, drinking Bud Lights and nibbling on a plate of broccoli and cauliflower, are stone silent, now part of Tony's audience.

How entrenched was the racism when Tony was breaking in?

"I didn't mess around too much down South. I was talking one time to [wrestler] George 'Two Ton' Harris. And he showed me his KKK card. I asked him, 'Why did you join the KKK?' And he said, 'It keeps me out of tickets.'"

He leans forward.

"So what does that tell you?" he asks.

This is not rhetorical. This is classic Tony, call-and-response, the teacher and the student.

"That the cops are all . . . " my voice trails off.

"Most of the cops were Klansmen," he finishes for me.

The locker room conversations of the 1970s would today make anyone shudder. Getting called a "nigger" was a daily occurrence, just as Latinos were "wetbacks," Irish were "micks," and those of Polish descent were "dumb Polacks." Tony never considered such racism malicious or even derogatory. It was just the way the guys talked. When Hulk Hogan had a PR crisis in recent years after his N-word-filled rant was caught on tape, Tony came to his rescue.

"Terry [Hulk's real name] likes me. You know why?" he asks.

This time I don't answer.

"I stood up for him. I went to his beach shop down in Florida. [A fan] told him, 'I came to meet one legend, and I'm meeting two.' And Hogan told the guy, 'I don't see Tony as a legend. I see him as my friend.'"

Racism was so deeply ingrained in wrestling culture that it was simply assumed that Black wrestlers would use head butts in their matches (because their skulls were "harder"). If a white wrestler tried to head butt a Black wrestler in the seventies and eighties, he immediately sold it as backfiring, his skull too soft for the cranium of his more "primitive" opponent.

My pasta carbonara appears, and after I take a few bites, Tony returns to his story of breaking into the business. He had a remarkable naïveté that was both sweet and stunning. A few months after his debut, he showed up at the County Hall auditorium in Charleston, South Carolina, where he was booked for a show. When he reached the front gate carrying his wrestling gear, the promoter, who had never worked with him before, assumed he was a fan and told him he had to buy a ticket. Tony complied, then was shocked to discover backstage that the rest of the Boys got in for free.

"No, we work here, Tony. We don't have to buy a ticket," one of them said to a room full of laughter.

A short time later, he was wrestling Two Ton Harris in Winston-Salem, North Carolina. Promoter George Scott pulled Tony aside and said, "I want you to shine out there tonight!" Tony was a rising star, while Harris was a veteran, and Tony was scheduled to go over, being built up for a program with Blackjack Mulligan. Harris would be selling for much of the match.

But for almost its entirety, Harris dominated, wiping the mat with Tony. Right before the fifteen-minute time limit expired, Tony caught him with two dropkicks and the sleeper hold, winning just before the bell. When he got back behind the curtain, Scott was furious.

"Kid, I told you to shine! You went out there and let Harris kick the crap out of you," he lamented.

"But, George," Tony protested, "I used about a half a bottle of baby oil before the match!"

Tony was on the fast track. His look was irrepressible, his charisma undeniable. Only a few wrestlers in the seventies had that cut body that steroids would make commonplace a decade later. He was unique, with the presentation of a strongman but the agility of a high flyer, mixing press slams with dropkicks and head scissors.

Before making him a champion, the Boys tested him, making sure he could handle himself in a real scrap. An old-timer named Swede Hanson, whose greeting for Tony was always "Hey, nigger!," invited him to his bar in Charlotte, North Carolina, called the Ringside.

"It was right at the beginning of desegregation. I was the first and only Black to go into that bar. So of course I got into a fight. I didn't go down. I didn't win, but I didn't lose," he says.

Having passed the crucible, the promoters deemed him worthy of carrying the Mid-Atlantic heavyweight championship only four years into his career. Less than a year later, he was on WWF TV, and shortly after that, wrestling in Madison Square Garden.

"We got so much money, we got so much fame, that it went to our heads. We figured we could do what we wanted without any consequences," he says.

"You know I never paid for a car until I got out of wrestling?"

The fact-checker in me wakes up.

"Well, you had to rent cars," I reply.

"I didn't have to pay for it! I was Tony Atlas."

"That's not true. Tony, you had to rent cars!" I argue back.

Yes, Tony admits, when the WWF started flying everywhere during their expansion in the mid-1980s, they had to pay for their rental cars. But before then, car dealerships would lend star wrestlers their vehicles for a year or one hundred thousand miles as free advertising. Tony went for a Lincoln, and later, a white Corvette.

The Boys were gods. They abused those cars, speeding, getting high, and driving drunk night after night.

"Ronnie Garvin, he would come up behind you and put his front bumper on your back bumper and push you down the highway at frickin' eighty miles per hour," Tony says.

"Were you ever worried about the drunk driving back then?" I ask.

"It never dawned on us. We were young kids, man. We thought we was invincible."

If they got pulled over, the cops almost always let them off, sometimes even asking for autographs.

Hotels were often discounted down to twenty-five dollars for the Boys.

"'Your money is no good here,' people would say. Free meals. A lot of perks. Clothes, women . . . " he says. It was so easy to get laid, one of the more entrepreneurial wrestlers, the Junkyard Dog, started charging groupies to have sex *with him*!

You would never know today from watching Tony putter around Auburn and Lewiston in his 2001 Pontiac Bonneville that this is a man who trained with Arnold Schwarzenegger, the man a young Snoop Dogg looked up to.

"When you introduce yourself to people who don't know you, do you introduce yourself as Anthony White or Tony Atlas?" I ask.

He pauses, then responds in a subdued tone.

"Anthony White don't exist no more. I became my own character. Anthony White disappeared before wrestling," he says.

"How so?"

"You see, in a Black neighborhood, there's nicknames. So when a *Ben-Hur* movie came out, everyone called me 'Ben-Hur.' When Steve Reeves played Hercules, everybody called me 'Hercules.'"

"You were a street fighter, right?"

"Every Black kid was a street fighter. The police didn't protect the Black neighborhood."

His friends started calling him "Argo" because every time the opportunity for a fight arose, Tony volunteered: "I'll go," he would say, sounding more like "Argo."

When he was in junior high, a bookish classmate started calling him Atlas.

"Why are you calling me Atlas?" Tony asked.

"Because Atlas is Black," the boy replied, providing a geography lesson about the Atlas Mountain range in Morocco along with some Greek mythology and the story of Atlas. Although he debuted in wrestling under his real name, Anthony White, it wasn't long before he shared this story with promoters, who quickly changed it to "Tony Atlas."

"Did you fight in the orphanage too?" I ask. I had read about the state of Virginia taking him away from his mom when he was twelve because she couldn't provide enough food. For the next three years, Tony lived at the Virginia Negro Baptist Children's Home.

"Oh yeah. You had to. Or you'd get it up the butt."

There's no monkey vomit or camel snot written on his face. He isn't joking.

"They would put their penis in you. They would rape you," he says.

"When the house mother fell asleep, things went on. A lot of kids got raped and abused in those orphanages."

Only Tony's immense physical strength saved him from meeting that fate. But the ordeal stoked the furnace deep within, the rage that just kept on growing into adulthood, that could only be quelled by the rubber sole of a woman's shoe. One time in the WWF, Tony cleared the whole Madison Square Garden locker room by waving around his .357 Magnum in a blind, inexplicable rage. The promoter, Vince McMahon Senior, called Atlas's best friend, S.D. Jones, who rushed to the arena with the antidote: a woman from the audience who was willing to step on his face.

I sit back in my chair and exhale, needing a break for the night.

"What time should I meet you tomorrow?" I ask.

"Well, I'll be at the Y tomorrow about eight. I'll get my workout first. Now, the first forty-five minutes I don't want to talk to you," he says. He hands me a guest pass for the gym and heads for the door.

*   *   *

THE YMCA IS TONY'S SANCTUARY. IT'S WHERE WRESTLING'S BRASS FIRST spotted him at age twenty down in Roanoke, and it's where he lived while training in Charlotte to become a pro wrestler. When he moved to Maine in 1989, the local Y, a three-story brick building built in 1922 in downtown Auburn, provided instant refuge.

He waves hello, giving me a loud "Hey, buddy" (sounding like *budday*), but true to his word, doesn't speak to me for the next hour. He's wearing a red hoodie over a gray muscle shirt and black sweatpants tucked into gray socks, earbuds shutting him off from the world. He lies under a bench press and warms up with nothing but the forty-five-pound bar, knocking out fifteen to twenty reps in his sleep. He adds two scuffed and chipped forty-five-pound plates for his next set, expelling lungfuls of air with each press, breathing into the burn. He adds weight and drops reps, sitting up to scribble in a notebook after each set, an orange pad with "Tony ATLAS Work Out 2022–" written in shaky black Sharpie on the cover. When the pandemic hit and Tony had to start lifting at home, he decided to start tracking his workouts, making sure he rotated among muscle groups in a sensible way. He moves from chest to shoulders to triceps, walking from machine to machine with the deliberation of someone in ski boots. He may be a bit stiff, but he's in much better shape than almost all of his contemporaries, many of whom need both hands and feet to count all their joint replacements and surgeries. He doesn't go too heavy anymore, having hurt his back squatting five hundred pounds a few years back.

It's an odd setup for a gym, divided into two cardio areas and a weight room, with radiators under window-mounted air conditioners and wood paneling around the windows. The architecture resembles an early twentieth-century office or even a private residence, with a boarded-up wood-paneled fireplace supporting a digital clock. The room starts to fill up as morning sunlight streams in, and I grab a corner by the mirror and self-consciously do a set of tricep kickbacks with twelve-pound dumbbells, wondering if Tony's watching. But he's in coach mode, walking over to a woman wearing a Bowdoin College T-shirt to spot her on a deep squat, waving hello and fist-bumping regulars and calling everyone "bruddha" to the backdrop of the Beastie Boys' "Fight for Your Right" on the club radio.

His bald head shines with a layer of sweat as he chugs a red Powerade and walks toward me.

"Want to know why I wouldn't talk to you during my workout?"

I do.

"Focus. What makes Tom Brady so great?" he asks, back in professor mode.

Then: "What makes a person go to the gym every day?"

"Wanting to be healthy and strong," I offer.

"You're not wrong, but you're looking at it from a physical aspect only. Think about it in a psychological form. Nobody do anything for nobody they don't like. So in order for you to work out, you have to first what?"

"Like yourself," I answer.

"Once you start liking yourself, you won't give a fuck what anyone else thinks," he says, moving on to other topics.

"People get angry over something so small. Why is that little thing so devastating to you? You know, you go through the whole day, there's twenty-four hours in the day. For twenty-three hours everything was beautiful for you, and for five minutes something went wrong. But all your focus is on that five minutes."

He grabs the bar for chest raises and looks at the digital clock on the mantle, one earbud in, the other dangling free. That childhood incident with Spike pushing him into the creek back in Low Moor still haunts him.

He lowers his voice, not wanting anyone else to hear, and I lean closer.

"In a way, I'm mentally challenged," he says.

"I was born in '54. I graduated in '74. How old is that? Twenty. I'm a slow learner, ever since that accident."

But whatever insecurities he has, the gym brings him back up.

"I like when all the kids challenge me," he says, referencing the twenty-somethings he coaches here.

"Not bad for a senior citizen. I'll be Atlas till I die. I go to these [wrestling] conventions and people say, 'Hey, Tony, you're still in good shape.' When I got elected to the Hall of Fame in 2006, the first words out of Vince's [McMahon's] mouth were 'Those fucking arms!'"

"Will you spot me on the bench press?" I ask. I'm curious what I can do with some help from a professional.

His eyes narrow, sizing up just how serious I am.

"OK, you gotta be serious though. Focus," he says, walking behind the rack as I lie across the bench. While I work out regularly, I don't lift weights much, and certainly have not used a bench press in many years. I know I can comfortably do several reps at 135 pounds, and so we begin there, Tony stacking a forty-five-pound plate on each side of the bar.

He helps with the lift-off, and I lower the weight down to my chest, closing my eyes.

"Piss and vinegar!" Tony bellows, guiding the bar up. "C'mon son, c'mon son, you're cooking now. Tom Brady, no pain!"

I snap my eyes open, startled by his sudden gruffness. This is a different Tony, no trace of playfulness, all business.

"Mmmmhmmm, go, no pain, people laugh and joke, not you. You're focused. You're an animal, a beast. Piss and vinegar!"

His words provide a surge of energy. My mind is locked in. I'm usually a skeptic for such mental exercises, but I've suspended all disbelief in this moment.

I rest in between sets, but don't speak, completely under Tony's spell. I hear him adding weight with each set, but don't ask how much.

On the last set I do one rep, unleashing a primal scream as I push the bar up, surprising myself with its intensity.

Tony sets the bar down and I spring up.

"How much was that?" I ask.

"205," he says. But he's not surprised.

"I was a weakling emotionally," he says. "People made fun of my butt, my nose. Called me names. 'Tony's retarded,' they would say."

"Focus," he tells me with a nod.

*   *   *

I CLIMB INTO THE FRONT SEAT OF TONY'S SILVER 2001 PONTIAC BONNEVILLE and we head to lunch. There's a water bottle and paper cup stuffed with a used napkin on the floor, and scraps of paper with notes are taped to the dash: "Legs, Back, Neck" reads one. "Call Water, Cable." "FedEx WWE." "11 A.M.—Dominic," a reminder for one of his YMCA clients.

"I'm taking you to this place that used to be a firehouse," he says. "It's called the Firehouse Grill."

He packs a wad of tobacco under his lip for the short drive through town. He's feeling good, grateful for the money order I've handed him.

"My bills are about $1,800 a month. With your $1,000, I just need to make another $200 and I'll have my mortgage." Although he made good money throughout his wrestling career—$75,000 alone in his first year, 1975—he never saved, something he now regrets.

"My body was my money. That was my ticket to make a living, and I had nothing else," he says.

Other than his bills, his only other major expense now is getting walked on, his form of therapy.

"You know I have a shoe fetish," he tells me, spitting tobacco juice into a paper cup.

See, people don't realize, you're born the way you are. Just like a gay person. He didn't become gay. When he came out the womb, he was gay. We born the way we are. We develop these things as time goes on. A lot of times these things control us and later on in life we learn how to control it. I like to get walked on, and my shoe fetish is nonsexual. I don't get no boner, it don't turn me on. But what it does do to me, it gives me a rush. And it humbles me. And my strength gets stronger. It's weird.

"Kind of like Popeye's spinach," I say.

"Yeah!" He likes the analogy.

"There's a girl, she wants to step on me today, but I'm with you," he says. He'll give her fifty dollars for a session. Sometimes he films it and has his friend Matthew at the laundromat put it on his social media (Matthew runs his Twitter account). It keeps him mellow, takes the edge off, keeps the rage down and the beast in its cage.

We drive past a sign for a local Juneteenth celebration.

"See, I don't like that," he says. "All this critical race theory. Let's say you're Caucasian and you see Juneteenth. You're not gonna feel good about that. We already have Martin Luther King Day, we have Black History Month, now we have Juneteenth. I don't like when I see something done for one group. A country is like a family. I like the Fourth of July."

Ever since he won the Mr. USA bodybuilding competition in 1979, Tony has made patriotism part of his character. He wears red-white-and-blue wrestling tights and leads the crowd in chants of "U-S-A! U-S-A!" during his matches, to this day. He and the Iron Sheik feuded in the late 1980s, wringing every last drop out of the hostage crisis.

He feels right at home in the Firehouse Grill, whose interior is painted fire-engine red, the walls decorated with an American flag and a bumper sticker that reads "Fire Fighters Can Handle Their Hoses."

"Hey, Tony!"

The greetings come from three people as we walk in and grab a booth.

"Do you have any of those chicken wings? With the garlic parmesan. And some baked beans," he asks the waitress.

Yesterday he alluded to the downside of his career, how he flamed out under the spotlight. Early in his career, old-timer Thunderbolt Patterson told him, "Kid, you have the world by the balls and you don't even know it."

"In your book [Atlas: Too Much . . . Too Soon, published in 2014], you talk a lot about how you became this guy you didn't like," I say.

"I felt I was better than others," he replies, picking the bones of his wings clean.

"I never lost at nothing. Every bodybuilding contest I went in, I won. Every powerlifting contest I went in, I won."

While this smacks of the "I sold out every building every night" exaggeration endemic to wrestling, I don't slow Tony's roll.

"Nobody could put me in my place. I was so tough. I wanted to fight André [the Giant] in the worst way."

Cooler heads prevailed, as Tony befriended the Giant rather than trying to slay him.

"André loved me because I never mentioned his size."

Every moment of every day in public, people stared and gawked at André, who at six feet ten and over four hundred pounds was every bit a real-life giant (his wrestling height of seven feet four was a work). He was never comfortable in a world built for mortals. He needed multiple seats on airplanes, and when hotel bathrooms proved too small, he would sometimes end up defecating on a sheet on the bed.

People don't want to feel different, Tony explains. "A midget don't want to be told that he's short. He knows he's short."

Tim White, a regular-sized referee, traveled with André to help him with logistics and accommodations.

"André told him that he would give him all the money he ever made, just to be him [Tim] for one day," Tony tells me.

While Tony's rise was meteoric, his fall was just as sudden.

"What messed me up was drugs. And that messed up a lot of wrestlers."

The rage inside was hard enough to contain without a pharmacy's worth of chemicals churning in his body. Steroids, marijuana, alcohol, and cocaine became regular road companions. Tony started missing shows, getting a reputation for being unreliable. In 1982, at his peak with the WWF, he no-showed an event at the Philadelphia Spectrum and flew home to the warm embrace of a plate full of coke and his favorite pair of women's shoes. He and S.D. Jones were being groomed for a run with the tag-team titles; Tony's negligence cost S.D. what might have been the big break he was waiting for. Tony acknowledges that and accepts it—he's never one to blame anyone but himself. S.D., who Tony chose to induct him into the Hall of Fame in 2006, still covers for his best friend, taking the blame.

"I was the one who killed the tag team. I was the one who had to step aside," S.D. said in his speech. But it wasn't S.D. who killed it.

After almost a year away, Tony called Vince McMahon Senior.

"Where in the hell have you been, Tony?" Vince Senior asked.

"Well, it's a long story," Tony replied. Vince Senior wired him $800 through Western Union to get him back to the East Coast and the friendly confines of the WWF. Toward the end of 1983, shortly before the Madison Square Garden card that inspired this book (at which Tony wrestled in a six-man match against the Wild Samoans), Vince Junior put the tag-team titles on him and Rocky Johnson, making them the WWF's first Black tag-team champions. Johnson's son would later follow in his dad's footsteps: you know him as The Rock.

But Tony didn't get along with Rocky and couldn't control the rage or the drugs. Vince Junior was now in charge and made a list of who he could trust to carry the ball. Tony had all the qualities—the body, the charisma, the moves, the fans' adulation—but he was not on the list. In May 1984, only six months after the Iron Sheik became champion, Tony got a letter from the office: "Your services arc no longer needed," it read.

Vince gave him another shot in September when Tony had started working for a rival promoter, Verne Gagne of the AWA. It was then that Tony got a glimpse of the ruthlessness that helped make Vince so successful.

As part of the WWF's international expansion, Vince had been planning a tour of Africa through Nigerian wrestler/promoter "Power Mike" Okpala and saw Tony as the perfect babyface attraction. According to Tony, Vince offered him $10,000 for the tour, but then sent him a one-way ticket to Toronto for a TV taping where Vince gave him a sheet of paper to sign. Tony's entire career had operated on handshake deals as he circulated among the various territories, and so he thought little of signing it. It turned out it was a contract prohibiting him from wrestling anywhere else. Tony says that when he asked Vince if he should call Verne Gagne to let him know, Vince reassured him that Gagne had already been notified. But according to Tony, that apparently wasn't true. Years later, Gagne told him Vince had never called.

The Africa tour never materialized, and for the next couple years, Tony's star faded. He kicked the drugs for a while, but he had lost his shine in Vince's eyes. He did more and more jobs until Vince let him go again in August 1986.

The downward spiral continued, bottoming out with a suicide attempt in a hotel room a few months later. His voice gets soft as he tells the story, the waitress taking away his plate and pouring me a cup of coffee.

"One of my regulars wants to have his picture taken with you before you go," she adds.

Tony smiles and agrees, always happy to accommodate fans, then turns his attention back to his story.

I was in New York, and I was married to Lisa [his third wife]. I was staying in a hotel in the Bronx. It had the dirty movies. Mirrors on the wall, mirrors on the ceiling, so you know the type of hotel it was. This Puerto Rican guy I know who worked there let me stay there. I was ready to kill myself. This guy, he said, "You really want to die?" He took a dirty rag, put it on the ground, opened a bottle of acid, and poured it on the rag. And I saw what it did to that rag. He poured some in a little cup and said, "Drink that."

As depressed as Tony was, when he saw the acid eat away the rag, he changed his mind. When S.D. Jones heard what had happened, he insisted Tony move in with him. Tony says that when Vince found out, he threatened to fire S.D.

"I kissed ass for two years and did everything that man [Vince] asked me to do. Then he just jobbed me out, jobbed me out, jobbed me out."

Wrestling may be staged, but winning and losing still matters. Nobody wants to become a "jobber," losing night after night, because it means you're not getting over with the fans, and if you're not over, neither is your paycheck.

Still, Vince had a soft spot for Tony, and brought him back in 1990 with a new look: Saba Simba, a babyface African warrior with a spear, headdress, and giant shield.

"Saba Simba, who went to Africa and found that his family totem was 'seven lions'—thus his new name—is roaring for action," wrote the WWF Magazine in introducing his gimmick.

"I came in as Tony Atlas, with my trunks on, and they said, 'You've got to go to costume,'" he says. By this time the WWF had grown so big and corporate that they had their own in-house costume designers.

"They said, 'Yeah, you're gonna be Saba Simba,' and I said, 'What the hell is a Simba?' I'm not a frickin' African. I'm not gonna pretend to be African. I'm a hillbilly."

The character fizzled, lasting only five months.

"Vince won't fire you in person. Vince would do this," Tony tells me, lowering his voice to begin a Vince imitation. He pauses.

"What's your name again?" he asks, suddenly aware that he's just called me "buddy" this whole time.

"Brad."

"Brad, I got to remember that."

[In his Vince voice]: "Brad, you're doing great. You're just as much a part of this company as anybody. You're one of my number one people. You're doing fantastic. Glad to have you on board.

"Then you go home for your three days' vacation. You open the mailbox; you got a letter from the office. It says, 'Your service is no longer needed.' You know who's just like Vince? They're like Siamese twins. Trump," he says.

A second suicide attempt went a little further, during the time he was homeless in Kennedy Park. He still has a four-inch scar on his left arm to remind him of how close he came. He cut the wrong way, inadvertently saving his own life.

Our waitress returns.

"Glen took care of your bill," she says.

"Who did?" Tony asks.

She motions to a short guy by the bar, sunglasses perched on his bald head, with a sleeve tattoo covering his right arm.

Tony walks over and extends his hand, smiling for a picture with Glen.

"How you doin', man?" Glen asks.

"Getting older and uglier, but OK," Tony replies.

"Naw, man, you're looking as good as ever," Glen says.

We walk back outside into the brilliant summer sunshine.

"The people here are all so good to me," he says. "I've noticed lately everyone is extra friendly to me because of *Young Rock* [the show about The Rock's childhood that ran for three seasons on NBC and featured a portrayal of Atlas along with many other wrestling notables]. After I'm off TV, not so much. And I realize these people like Tony Atlas, not Anthony White."

*   *   *

ON THAT BENCH IN KENNEDY PARK IN 1989, TONY SAYS HE MET AN ANGEL. The same angel we're on our way to visit.

Monika De Rance, a seamstress and artist born in Berlin during World War II, saw Tony sleeping under that bench in Kennedy Park and decided to not ignore him. She went a step further, asking about his situation. When she felt safe enough, she offered, "If you don't have a place to sleep, you can stay at my place." He ended up on a mattress on her floor.

"She didn't know who the hell I was. She never watched wrestling. She didn't even have a TV. She just knew I needed help," Tony says.

Three weeks after she took him in, Tony went into a coma, his body experiencing the shock of sudden withdrawal from crack cocaine.

"I dropped all the way down to 190 pounds."

Slowly but surely Monika built him back up. She became his fourth wife, and this one stuck. When his days as a wrestling regular were numbered, she encouraged him to seek out a second life as a trainer. She helped sign him up for classes so he could earn his personal training certification, work he's been doing in various gyms in the area ever since. Together they bought a duplex in Auburn for $78,000 in 2009 that Tony says is now worth $275,000, thanks to the influx of remote workers spurred by the pandemic. When Vince McMahon, who has always had a soft spot for Tony, brought him back in 2006 as a goodwill ambassador for the WWE, Monika provided the support and stability Tony had always been looking for, handling all of his finances as his paychecks came in.

On June 2, 2019, he got the chance to repay the favor. Tony was scheduled to wrestle at a show in Pittsburgh, but it got canceled. When he walked into the kitchen around four o'clock to discuss dinner plans, Monika, who is thirteen years older, suddenly couldn't talk. He called 911, and luckily an ambulance was only a couple blocks away.

"If that show wasn't canceled, I would have come home to a corpse," he says.

Now every day revolves around his visits to Monika at St. Mary's d'Youville Pavilion nursing home. This is why Tony has been so punctilious about his schedule and time since my arrival—Monika looks forward to his visit every day at one o'clock. He helps feed her from four thirty to five thirty, then puts her to bed at six o'clock. The stroke confined her to a wheelchair and limited use of her left side, but thankfully her mind is still sharp, and she is able to speak.

We walk into the lobby, wait to get our temperatures taken as part of COVID protocol, and put on masks. A woman brushes by quickly in the hallway as Tony reaches for a bag, narrowly missing a collision with his burly right arm. He laughs and turns to me.

"I'm a six-two, 285-pound Black man in Maine and no one can see me," he jokes, then calls after the woman, "You almost got clotheslined by Tony Atlas!"

We walk by Room 351, which reads "Monika White," and emerge into the rec room full of wheelchairs and natural light. The staff has set up karaoke, and an older woman leans over the microphone and mouths lyrics to no one in particular. Another group is huddled around a table working on a jigsaw puzzle, ignoring the singing. Tony jokes and laughs with the staff, who know him well. One of them says, "I've been watching you on *Young Rock!*"

"If we did *Young Tony* we'd have to film a horse and buggy!" Tony replies, cracking up the room.

Monika's face lights up when she sees her husband. She has straight silver hair recently brushed at the nursing home salon and is wearing a bright floral print blouse and purplish sweatpants with pink shoes.

"How did your morning go? Good?" he asks, taking her left arm and rubbing it, flexing her fingers.

"Don't break it," she says, laughing, rubbing her own arm.

"No, I ain't gonna break your arm," he replies.

"You can stop rubbing it, baby, I got it, relax, relax, honey. I got you now," he says in a soothing tone, almost purring.

We wheel her out to the courtyard and sit on a white bench under the shade of a maple tree.

After a few minutes Tony notices her looking a little uncomfortable.

"You want to get in that sun, don't you?" he asks.

She agrees and he wheels her out of the cover of the maple tree.

"We've been having this fight for thirty-two years. She would take me to the beach and lay out in the sun. I'm sitting there, you know, us Black people don't like getting the sun.

"This woman loved me so much. She was the first one," he says, referencing his past wives.

"She would say, 'I didn't marry Tony Atlas, I married Anthony White. You leave Tony Atlas in the ring.' Isn't that right, sugar?"

Monika laughs in agreement.

"That woman would walk through hell with kerosene drawers to help me. I could depend on Monika. And she could depend on me. She knows that I'm gonna be here every day. It's hard to find somebody in this world you can depend on. I've been let down too much. It started with my dad. He left my mother with nine kids. That's a big letdown for kids," he says.

I'm curious about Tony's first marriage, to a woman named Joyce, because she's the only one with whom he had kids. They met at the matches in Columbus, Georgia, when Tony was twenty-three. Joyce's sister dragged her to the show, and Tony noticed her hanging out afterward. They went on a date, and she got pregnant soon after. Tony was in way over his head. He asked his dad, "What should I do?"

"Do you love her?" his dad asked.

"I barely know her!" Tony replied. He had never planned on having kids.

They had a baby, a beautiful little girl named Nikki. But the wrestling industry was no place for Joyce. Tony considered his second and third wives to be "rats," the pejorative term wrestlers used to describe the women who hung out around the arenas looking to hook up. But Joyce wanted no part of the lifestyle. When Tony went off to work in Charlotte for the Mid-Atlantic promotion, she begged him to come back to Georgia, and then gave him an ultimatum: quit the business or I'm gone.

"I didn't know how to make a living. You want me to go back to washing dishes for sixty-five dollars a week now that I'm making $3,000? That woman asked a poor man that grew up in poverty to leave a $3,000-a-week job? Are you kidding me?" he says to me.

"I had what you call weekend visits. But Joyce wouldn't let me see Nikki. I worked on the weekends. I couldn't tell a promoter I wanted a day off. If I went on a Wednesday, Joyce wouldn't let me see her. I told Nikki that and she didn't want to hear it. She didn't want to hear what really happened."

Joyce took Nikki when she was four and moved back to her home state of Alabama, cutting ties with Tony.

He wouldn't talk to his daughter for another ten years, and even then, they were largely estranged until the late 2000s.

Throughout her childhood Nikki thought about her dad, wondered about him, even though she didn't know him. In the material Tony saved from his career that he shares with me, I find a photo of Nikki stuck in the pages of one of his old albums. She looks to be about fourteen, with a big smile like her dad's, wearing a green flannel button-up and resting her hands on a young boy's shoulders. I flip it over and find her handwriting on the back.

"To my father who I love very much and hope to come to visit me soon. Hope you like this picture of me and my brother. Love Always, Nikki White."

They're in closer touch now, but there's so much to make up for. He passes me his phone, showing me a recent text he received from her:

"I got married today!" it reads.

"Do you think you were a good father?" I ask him.

He looks away, then meets my eyes.

"No," he says quietly.

"No wrestler was a good father," he adds.

Monika's back is hurting, and so we take her back up to Room 351, where a pile of laundry sits on her twin hospital bed. Tony folds her laundry while they bring out her dinner. She coughs and he raises a tissue to her nose.

"Baby, blow your nose. When you cough, blow your nose," he says gently.

He spoon-feeds her pudding. They have a lot in common, he from the circus of wrestling, she from the literal circus, having been a performer who balanced on balls while holding a woman on her shoulders. When the toxic environment of sexual harassment got to be too much, she quit, refusing to trade sexual favors for career advancement. She finally found some peace in her work as a seamstress and in her artwork.

Later on at his house, Tony shows me his artwork, drawings all done with Sharpies of some of the biggest names in wrestling history—Hulk Hogan, André the Giant, Kane. One of the works in progress, outlined in black ink with the color partially filled in, is a drawing of the Iron Sheik putting Tony in the abdominal stretch.

"I liked Khosrow. He was funny. He was always nice to me," he says. I film a short video on my phone of Tony saying hi to Khos, just as I did with Alan Rice, which I tell him I will deliver in person in a few weeks when I get down to Georgia.

His drawings are another form of therapy, an outlet for the rage and a way to stay in touch with his past. He sees the Boys at the reunion shows and conventions, but so many have passed away prematurely, and the ones who are still alive he doesn't keep up with.

Despite all they endured together, day in and day out, thousands of miles on lonely dark roads and thousands more in the air, once they were away from the squared circle, they lost touch. Maybe it was wrestling's individualistic nature, a dog-eat-dog world where every man was at the promoter's whim, jockeying for position, trying to protect their spot. Maybe it hurts too much to be reminded of what you once were physically and in the public eye. Or maybe they don't want to acknowledge the people the Road and the business turned them into.

I bid Tony farewell, and after I'm back in my hotel room alone with my thoughts, Tony cracks a beer, grabs a Sharpie, and starts coloring in the lines.

*   *   *

I NEED TO SEE TONY'S HOMETOWN FOR MYSELF.

The Alleghany Highlands of western Virginia provide one of the most scenic stretches of my journey. Highways snake around verdant hills, the peaks of the Blue Ridge Mountains shimmering blue, a result of the chemical isoprene released by the trees. In the US's infancy, this was the border of the western frontier, the gateway to the "Great West" that the original Mr. USA, George Washington, envisioned opening up through the burgeoning rail industry. Rivers and railroads drove economic expansion, and when the 77.8-mile track from Clifton Forge to Hinton, West Virginia, was built in the 1800s, it opened up a path from the coast to Louisville, Toledo, and Cincinnati. Clifton Forge was strategically located on the James River near iron deposits, spurring an iron boom in the late 1800s that launched the Low Moor Iron Company in the nearby village of Low Moor.

The Iron Company originally owned and operated Low Moor's one store, what Tony called the commissary, where Tony's mother would buy provisions for the one meal per day she could afford.

When I exit for Low Moor on an overcast afternoon in July, I see a two-story brick building with black shutters in roughly the location that Tony had described for the commissary. It's not long before my California plates and photo-snapping outside the building stir some attention.

"Taking pictures, are ya?" a redhead who looks a few years my junior says from the front seat of her parked car. Her name is Amber, and she's wearing jean shorts and a red T-shirt that says "All American Mama."

"Did there used to be a general store or commissary around here?" I ask.

"You're looking at it. It used to be Averill's."

I explain the gist of my book and mention Tony Atlas growing up here.

"Oh yeah, I remember watching wrestling on Saturday mornings. And then I remember my brothers wanting to practice all the moves on me," she says.

The building is now a restaurant called Family Treets, and Amber works here. She walks me inside and gives me a tour, showing me several displays with artifacts, historical photos, and articles about Alpha Via Averill, who began working the store in 1941 and continued well into her hundreds. There's even a cabinet with yellowed index cards and people's names, a ledger of all the locals' running tabs. I scan the names for any evidence of the White family. But no luck.

By the time Tony was growing up here in the late 1950s, Low Moor's fortunes had started to turn. The Chesapeake and Ohio Railway had initially given life to the town, with Clifton Forge serving as a major hub for rail service and repair. Tony's grandfather worked for the railroad, but the replacement of steam engines with diesel at midcentury (along with the broader expansion of the aviation and automobile industries) crippled the local economy, a blow from which it has never fully recovered. While Clifton Forge has gamely tried to reinvent itself with a focus on tourism and the arts, Low Moor, home to only a few hundred people, continues to struggle. It's the same song that has played out in thousands of communities around the country, the wholesale displacement of manufacturing by services. The big employer in Low Moor now is LewisGale Hospital Alleghany, which sits just down the road.

I get back in the Fusion and snoop around Low Moor at ten miles per hour, trying to find some of the landmarks of Tony's childhood. Selma-Low Moor Road parallels the train tracks, bounding the lattice of back roads and homes whose yards blend into each other, unobstructed by fences. Rusted-out cars, furniture, children's toys, and machinery in various states of disuse spill across those yards; a faded Trump–Pence sign appears in one windowsill, an "I Heart Jesus" sign in another. When Tony was growing up here, the town was about 90 percent Black: now it's the opposite. A different shade of poverty, but poverty just the same.

In front of Mount Olivet Baptist Church, I pull to the side of the narrow road so I can jot down some notes. A yellow vein of lightning lights up the sky, threatening rain. I feel a car pull up to me and then stop. It doesn't advance. Then it honks.

I roll down my window and see an older man with a smattering of facial hair and a brown complexion.

"Who are you looking for?" he asks.

The road is so narrow that I can see clearly inside his car; his hands shake with a slight tremor as he leans forward.

"I'm looking for a wrestler who grew up here named Tony Atlas," I reply.

"Of course," he says with a big grin.

"Ahh-go [Argo]. We used to call him Ahh-go. I can't talk to you now because I have to go to the ER in Roanoke, but follow me and I'll take you to a guy named Reggie who knows him," he says, introducing himself as Frank Rowland.

"Ahh-go's house was right over there. There's nothing there now, but it was there. And some kid pushed him in a creek over there," he says. The Spike story!

We go all of one block before he turns left and we arrive at our destination, a ranch-style house with a red Chevy Silverado parked in the gravel driveway. As if he was expecting us, Reggie Dean bounds out of the house. He's white, with thin hair and a goatee, and looks to be about Frank's age.

"Talk to this guy," Frank says. "He's an author writing about Ahh-go."

Reggie doesn't invite me inside but is willing to talk for a few minutes.

"You sure as shit aren't a very good driver," he says. I realize I've parked in the middle of the road.

Frank takes off for the ER and I stand with my notebook out in Reggie's driveway.

"Were you in school with Tony?" I ask.

"No, he was younger than me. I did go over and saw him wrestle Ric Flair at the [Roanoke] Civic Center. I was telling everybody I hid in the back because I used to slap the snot out of his nose. I wouldn't get up too close because I was afraid he might recognize me," he drawls.

"He had an older brother, we called him Chayee, and come to find out, that's just the way they would try to pronounce Charley."

He recounts the match at the Civic Center, in which Flair, the heel, prevailed by hitting Atlas with a "foreign object." Tony crumpled to the mat, selling big, and the heat on Flair turned nuclear.

"There was this Black woman behind me, and she said, 'If I had a gun I'd shoot that yellow-haired motherfucker,'" Reggie recalls.

Reggie began working at the nearby Hercules manufacturing plant the day after he graduated from high school, and when it burned down in 1980, he moved on to construction and electric work.

I ask him if he remembers Redeye Hinton, the farmer who stabbed Tony in the back with a pitchfork after stiffing him on his pay.

"He was the kind of guy, he'd start a bunch of stuff with you, and then he'd call the law," he says of Redeye.

"Rodney [one of Redeye's sons] shot him in the back. Shot his daddy in the back. I don't even think he done time over it. He [Rodney] ended up killing himself."

"Tony told me there was a place called Scrappers Corner where he would fight," I say.

"That's just straight down the end of this road," he replies.

I follow Reggie's directions to the intersection of Sugar Maple and Selma-Low Moor, and at the base of a telephone pole, partially obscured by a bramble of purple flowers, is a white cross, marking the spot of Scrappers Corner.

Down the street, near the former White homestead (now bulldozed and completely overgrown), there's a creek bed with a slow trickle of water, the same creek where Spike killed Anthony White and begat Tony Atlas.

I creep down the bank, only about three feet high, and chuckle, remembering Tony's story of it being "ten feet up."

Only in wrestling.

MATCH 5

MR. MCMAHON VS. VINCE MCMAHON

sport *n*: an activity involving physical exertion and skill that is governed
   by a set of rules or customs and often undertaken competitively
entertainment *n*: something that amuses, pleases, or diverts, especially
   a performance or show
sports entertainment *n*: professional wrestling under Vince McMahon

I PULL INTO THE GREENWICH, CONNECTICUT, PUBLIC LIBRARY, AN ORNATE complex worthy of a university. The facility includes 105,000 square feet of bound volumes and digital assets complete with an art gallery, a theater, an "Innovation Lab," a "Business Wing," a café, and a floating staircase. Fresh from an $18 million renovation by the architect César Pelli, the main concourse gleams with natural light pouring through its floor-to-ceiling glass arches that look out onto garden courtyards.

Greenwich sits just over the New York border, thirty miles from the WWF's root chakra, Madison Square Garden, which is why Vince McMahon and his wife/CEO Linda moved the company here in the fall of 1983.

Vince always believed in looking the part—a town with Greenwich's pedigree helped establish the WWF as serious business. While other wrestling promoters dwelled in cigar-stained, dimly lit offices, Vince wanted suits and ties under fluorescent lights. Vince sought to invent an entirely new genre in which to categorize his "spectacle of excess": sports entertainment. He craved acceptance from Madison Avenue, wanting to trade armories and high school gyms for football stadiums.

He is P. T. Barnum on steroids, a six-foot-three, swaggering, cocksure capitalist with shoe-polish hair and eye-popping vascularity. Bombastic, brazen, and domineering, he personifies the larger-than-life ethos of the wrestling industry. After years of fantasizing about being one of his comic book–style creations, in the late nineties he finally said "fuck it" and created the character of "Mr. McMahon," a despicable corporate tyrant obsessed with money, even feuding in storyline with Donald Trump. In real life, Trump and McMahon are good friends—it's been reported that Vince is one of the only people Trump will clear a room for so they can speak in private on the phone.

Vince is obsessed with work (he only sleeps a few hours a night and never takes vacations), bodybuilding, and above all else, control. Writer Rob Miller recalls meeting him in his office to discuss a book project.

"He had the jawbone of a Tyrannosaurus rex above his desk," Miller recounts.

"What do you think of that?" Vince growled at Miller, a soft-spoken, polite lawyer from New Hampshire.

"It's there for intimidation!" Vince roared, in case there was any doubt.

While he most values strength and power, Vince is not without his quirks.

"He's not a normal guy," says Eric Bischoff, Vince's one-time archenemy as president of World Championship Wrestling (WCW) who later went on to work for him. On my way across the country, I stop in at Eric's sprawling ranch in Cody, Wyoming, to ask him about his former boss.

"The only time I've ever seen him really lose his temper is when he sneezes or if somebody else sneezes in a room that he's in. He loses his shit. He believes that sneezing is a weakness. If you can control your mind, you should be able to control your body," Bischoff explains.

But while Vince would eventually squeeze the entire wrestling world in his iron fist, it didn't happen overnight.

I ask the reference librarian if I can see copies of the *Greenwich Time* from 1983, and he refers me to the historian, who sets me up at a computer connected to a microfilm reader where I can view spools of back issues. There's only one machine for the entire library, so I wait patiently while a patron with plastic bags full of tchotchkes and worn spiral notebooks finishes what is likely a daily routine. Without an index, I'm looking for that needle in the haystack, hoping to stumble on some press coverage of Vince's arrival. While I plan on throwing a Hail Mary to see if I can meet with Vince face-to-face while I'm in town, for now I'll have to be content with whatever this antiquated technology can churn up.

Flipping on the microfilm light, I spin the dial back to the past.

*   *   *

ONE OF THE MANY IRONIES OF VINCE MCMAHON IS THAT THE MAN WHO became synonymous with wrestling in New York, who always made a point to differentiate his slickly produced TV show from the "rasslin'" down South, is, in fact, a Southerner.

He graduated from Fishburne Military School in Waynesboro, Virginia, in 1964 after growing up in three different North Carolina towns: Southern Pines, Weeksville, and Havelock. In Southern Pines, his family lacked indoor plumbing; in Havelock they lived in an eight-foot-wide trailer.

And for the first twelve years of his life, Vince McMahon was Vinny Lupton, son of Vicki Hanner and stepson of an abusive electrician, Leo Lupton.

Childhood matters. A lot. And although Vince has never spoken in detail about his life as Vinny Lupton, we know that the trauma he experienced early on formed the man who he later became.

In an interview with *Playboy* in 2001, Vince provided some rare insight into those early years, describing his stepfather Leo's physical abuse. Leo beat not only young Vince but also Vince's mother, Vicki.

Vince also alluded to potential sexual abuse from his mother.

"I lived with her and my real asshole of a stepfather, a man who enjoyed kicking people around. . . . It's unfortunate that he died before I could kill him. I would have enjoyed that," Vince said.

"Was the abuse all physical, or was there sexual abuse too?" writer Kevin Cook asked.

"That's not anything I would like to embellish. Just because it was weird," Vince replied.

"Did it come from the same man?"

"No. It wasn't . . . it wasn't from the male," Vince said.

Cook later went on: "It's well known that you're estranged from your mother. Have we found the reason?"

"Without saying that, I'd say that's pretty close," Vince responded.

Despite all that dysfunction, Vince loathes the victim mentality.

"I'm not big on excuses. When I hear people from the projects, or anywhere else, blame their actions on the way they grew up, I think it's a crock of shit. You can rise above it. This country gives you opportunity if you want to take it, so don't blame your environment," he said.

There's a narrative out there that in his teenage years, Vince was a hellion whose behavior could only be corrected through military school. That narrative, however, has come entirely from Vince himself. In the *Playboy* interview, Vince recalled a pugnacious adolescence of stealing cars, fighting Marines, and getting court-martialed at school, but his unofficial biographer, Abraham Josephine Riesman, found no evidence of such things in her reporting. She did break new ground, rounding up several of Vince's childhood acquaintances who say Vince was not a fighter at all; Riesman also could not find a record of a court-martial at Fishburne. Perhaps this youth-as-hellion story is all a work. If anything, even in high school Vince was the promoter we all know him to be, organizing homemade wrestling shows in the gym after school. Riesman even unearthed Vince's first gimmick: "Ape Man" McMahon.

What is undeniably true is that at age twelve, Vince met his real father, who up to then had done his best to pretend his son didn't exist.

"If I were to play amateur psychologist, which unfortunately every biographer has to do, whether they're qualified or not, I would say that Vince has spent his entire career trying to fill those ten to twelve years and that absence, which of course you can't do," Riesman tells me.

Vincent James McMahon ("Vince Senior") was the dad young Vince had been waiting for. Senior had met Vicki (Vince's mother) while in North Carolina serving in the Coast Guard, but their marriage would only last two and a half years. Less than a year after Vince Junior was born, Senior went back north to Washington, DC, where his father, Jess, had recently begun promoting concerts and other live events. Jess was part of the New York establishment, having started out at age seventeen managing a baseball team and working his way up the sports ladder. In 1925 he was named head booker for boxing matches at Madison Square Garden. His orbit eventually included wrestling, and when his son (Vince Senior) came calling for work in DC in 1946, Jess helped set him up as the general manager of Turner's Arena. By 1953, Vince Senior had founded the Capitol Wrestling Corporation, and soon after broadcasted live wrestling on TV from the renamed Capitol Arena on Thursday nights.

Foreshadowing the tactics his son would employ a generation later, Vince Senior used TV to build a bigger audience and drive box office receipts while partnering with Gold Dust Trio alum Toots Mondt to stage shows at Madison Square Garden.

While Vince Junior was dodging pipe wrenches swung by his stand-in dad, Vince Senior was being a father to his second wife, Juanita's, great-nieces and nephew, whose own father had bolted. If it hadn't been for Juanita—who reportedly took it upon herself to force a meeting between Senior and his two sons, Vince and Rod—you might not be holding this book right now.

Vince (who everyone in the wrestling business called Vinny in his younger days; best not to try that now) was immediately smitten with his dad, spending as much time as he could with him during the summers. He quickly jettisoned the last name Lupton and was rechristened "Vince McMahon Junior." In doing so he met his one true love—wrestling—an alternate reality where kicks and punches didn't *really* hurt, where every voice in the crowd mattered because those voices in fact controlled the action itself, where impressionable kids and frustrated dads could be as loud as they wanted without getting in trouble (in fact, the louder the better!) and then go home happy.

The illusion mattered. It helped hide a dark side that lurks within Junior, a side that may set him apart from the first two generations of McMahon wrestling promoters, men he clearly idolized.

"In a game of misinformation, my grandfather always told the truth. He was college educated and he kept office hours like a banker. He did business with some pretty tough customers, such as Frankie Carbo, but kept his integrity," Vince Junior said of grandfather Jess in 1991.

He added: "My dad was a fabulous human being, fair and warm."

Junior, by his own admission, is a bit more of a heel. When asked by a *Durham Sun* reporter in 1986 about his favorite grappler, he replied: "I would say that I idolized, when I was a youngster growing up, a wrestler by the name of Dr. Jerry Graham."

Graham was a cocky, platinum-blond heel.

"He was a persona non grata as far as the fans were concerned, and maybe that gives you some insight into my personality," Vince added.

*   *   *

A MAP OF NORTH AMERICA HUNG ON THE WALL IN TRAVEL COORDINATOR ED Cohen's office at WWF headquarters in the 1980s. As the person responsible for booking the hundreds of venues where the WWF held shows, Cohen needed to be able to see all of the US and Canada, especially with multiple tours operating at the same time.

But when Cohen looked at the map, he didn't see states—he saw wrestling territories, almost two dozen of them. Imagine each territory as a different color, the continent coming alive as a brilliant multicolored quilt. Some patches were enormous, like the one in the Midwest representing the American Wrestling Association (AWA), headquartered in Minneapolis; others were confined to a single city, such as the St. Louis Wrestling Club; the Texas patch was divided in three: World Class Championship Wrestling out of Dallas, Southwest Championship Wrestling out of San Antonio, and Houston Wrestling. Each territory consisted of a fiefdom run by a lord (promoter) or a handful of lords, and collectively they made up the professional wrestling industry from the early 1930s until the late 1980s. Wrestlers would circulate among them, brawny nomads legally classified as independent contractors, remaining in one territory for a year or so before the audience tired of their act, then moving on to the next. Many, but not all, of these territories formed a conglomerate called the National Wrestling Alliance (NWA), founded in Iowa in 1948 by a handful of lords who sought tighter control. But the alliance was always tenuous, strained by a 1956 antitrust lawsuit filed by the US Department of Justice (resulting in a slap on the wrist called a consent decree) and the even greater weight of the lords' egos.

Now imagine Vince Junior's favorite color is red. (I have no idea if this is true, but it seems plausible.) From Maine down to Washington, DC, the quilt shone red, representing the boundaries of the World Wrestling

Federation. But by 1983, little bits of crimson were starting to appear in other parts of the country: a blob in Southern California, a few dots in eastern Ohio, a smidge in St. Louis.

When Vince looked at the map, he saw the future, a canvas covered in the lords' spilled blood, a destiny that only he could manifest: complete and utter control of the wrestling industry.

By 1990, the quilt was mostly red; by 2001, it was monochromatic. In less than twenty years, Vince had created a virtual monopoly, and his WWF was a publicly traded company worth upward of $800 million, selling out the Astrodome with almost seventy thousand fans at WrestleMania X-Seven (17).

So how did he do it?

*   *   *

UNLIKE HIS DAD, VINCE NEVER SAW HIMSELF AS JUST A WRESTLING PROMOTER. He styled himself more in the tradition of Walt Disney, a cross-genre, mass-market entertainment mogul. In order to turn that map in Ed Cohen's office entirely red, he would need to double down on the DNA of professional wrestling, embrace its true nature in a way that most considered heretical.

Vince embraced the fact that professional wrestling, despite the lords' best efforts to convince the world otherwise, was *show*, and that its choreography was the key to his success. In the early 1980s, despite the occasional squabble, the lords presented a unified front in their enforcement of Kayfabe and their insistence that wrestling was a sport just like boxing or baseball. And in so doing, they emphasized realism to the extent possible in their matches, elevating former amateur wrestlers, football players, and "real" athletes who could handle themselves in and out of the ring. In their eyes, to end Kayfabe would be to kill the business.

But Vince happily held a knife to Kayfabe's throat. He wouldn't fully slit it until 1987, but shortly after buying out his dad and his partners for $1 million in 1982, he set the wheels in motion to revolutionize the industry.

His plan for a wrestling war operated on two fronts—the business side in the Office, setting up the infrastructure to be able to invade the other lords' fiefdoms, and the soldiers on the Road, the wrestlers who would

bump and sell their way onto lunch boxes, bedsheets, and prime-time network TV. His wrestlers needed to become *entertainers*, more Hollywood
actors than rough-and-tumble athletes. To do this, Vince needed absolute
control. This meant no more loaning his talent to other lords for big shows
or shuttling guys in and out of his territory. He introduced binding contracts, boilerplate deals giving him dominion over practically every aspect
of wrestlers' lives while offering few guarantees other than—Vince's favorite word—an opportunity. Vince locked up the merchandise rights and all
intellectual property associated with the wrestlers' characters, going so far
as to trademark their ring names. He owned you.

He and his wife, Linda (who with her paralegal background and
razor-sharp business acumen is tragically underrated in the story of the
WWF), put together licensing deal after licensing deal in the mid-1980s to
turn their wrestlers into literal toys. A deal with toymaker LJN in mid-1984
spawned several lines of action figures; the same year they capitalized on
the growing home video market by partnering with Coliseum Video (whose
parent company produced porn) for a series of VHS tapes. They created a
cartoon show, a magazine, and a music album, banned audience cameras
from their shows, and forbade professional photographers from outside
publications. The commercialization fit perfectly with the exploding popularity of MTV, and before long the "Rock 'N' Wrestling" connection was
born. Matches from Madison Square Garden were broadcast live on MTV
in 1984, drawing huge ratings. It helped that the expansion coincided with a
massive economic recovery in the US.

The gambit worked—by WrestleMania III in 1987 (headlined by Hulk
Hogan vs. André the Giant), which drew some seventy-eight thousand
fans to the Pontiac Silverdome (not the oft-publicized Kayfabe number of
ninety-three thousand), the following merchandise was on sale for Hulk
Hogan alone: foam hands, T-shirts, painter caps, pennants, posters, pens,
and headbands. According to internal company documents, the company
sold $498,270 worth of merchandise and $132,585 in programs that night,
more than half of what Vince had paid to buy *the entire company* from his
dad and his partners just five years prior.

Less than a year later, more than thirty million people would tune in to
NBC during prime time to watch a Hogan vs. André rematch, the biggest
TV audience in the history of American wrestling.

*   *   *

Vince's promotional baptism occurred when he began running the Cape Cod Coliseum in South Yarmouth, Massachusetts, in 1979. Contrary to popular belief, the McMahons never owned the building, but covered the lease and managed all aspects of the 7,200-seat arena. They moved into a nearby two-story Cape Cod hybrid-style home with a big party room downstairs, deep purple shag carpet, and a huge painting of Linda in the hallway near the entrance (when they bought their ten-acre property in Greenwich a few years later, they added a giant portrait of Vince on a Harley). Always mindful of looking the part, Vince had people from New York come down in a two-seater Jaguar to fit him for tailored three-piece suits in bright colors like lavender and canary yellow.

On February 21, 1980, the power couple created Titan Sports Inc., a literal mom-and-pop (they had two kids by this time, Shane and Stephanie) run out of the Coliseum as the corporate entity for what was now the WWF (they changed the name from the WWWF in 1979). While Vince Senior continued piloting the company to great success, regularly selling out Madison Square Garden, Vince and Linda booked concerts and other live attractions into the Cape Cod Coliseum, including such acts as the Grateful Dead, Van Halen, and Tom Petty. Linda oversaw all the mundane details of the box office and promotions, while Vince hunkered down in his cinderblock office working the phones and scribbling in yellow legal pads (even early on, Vince wrote everything down, acutely aware of the prospect of future litigation). The Coliseum was just his training wheels.

In 1981, needing a regular act to cover the lease, Vince turned to an unlikely source: ice hockey. He knew little about the sport, but a team called the Cape Codders had previously played in the Coliseum. New Englanders loved hockey, and the Eastern Hockey League was trying to reboot as the Atlantic Coast Hockey League, a low-level minor league. Vince had recently met a sandy-haired hockey ruffian with a shattered hand looking for a soft landing, Jim Troy, and saw Paul Newman from *Slapshot*. Troy was equally impressed.

"I met Vince at the Coliseum through a mutual friend, and he was a real-life character, like something out of a book, that bigger-than-life personality, and, you know, just full of energy," Troy tells me over black coffee and eggs over easy at the New Canaan Diner in Connecticut. A horrific fall off a ladder several years ago fractured the C3-C7 vertebrae in Troy's back, making it difficult for him to walk. Although his life is now spent on crutches, his blue eyes still maintain a sense of mischief. His life, now busy with scouting and coaching youth in ice hockey, has come full circle.

While Vince didn't have the coordination of a hockey player, he had the same indomitable spirit and fearlessness.

"He was absolutely jacked and trained like an animal," Troy says.

Troy would be his player-coach, assistant general manager of the nascent Cape Cod Buccaneers, and sidekick; since he was mostly retired (the shattered hand required career-ending surgery), the Bucs still needed an enforcer, or fighter, a time-honored if not bizarre tradition of the sport. Troy recommended Mike Breen ("Breener" to the locker room), a gregarious homebody from nearby Wareham who loved to scrap. In only thirty-nine games, Breener would rack up 118 penalty minutes for the Buccaneers.

Vince, Breener, and Troy, all young men overflowing with testosterone, partied together during that 1981–1982 season. Breener and Troy knew Vince was something special, the way he lit up a room by simply walking in.

Years later when Breener and referee Tim White were trying to open a bar but were short on cash, Vince asked how much they needed. Embarrassed, Breener said, "A lot."

"What's a lot of money?" Vince asked, his dimpled chin jutting forward.

"Well, like, $20,000," Breener replied.

Vince roared, unleashing his famous thunderous laugh.

"Twenty grand is not a lot of money!" he boomed. "A million dollars is a lot of money!" And with that, he had his secretary cut a check.

But before Vince could put his grand plan for the WWF's expansion into place, he needed to own the company, still the possession of his father. Vince Senior, now in his late sixties, was winding down, spending more time in Florida and enjoying steak dinners with his confidants at Jimmy Weston's after each monthly Madison Square Garden event. Vince Junior was the natural heir, even if the son's braggadocio gave the father some pause. Although his company was probably worth significantly more, Vince Senior and his three partners, old-timers Gorilla Monsoon (real name Bob Marella), Phil Zacko, and Arnold Skaaland, agreed to sell the WWF to Vince

Junior for $1 million in four installments, with the caveat that if Vince missed a single payment, the sale was off.

In the weeks leading up to the sale, Troy watched as Vince and Linda scrambled to come up with the cash. On June 5, 1982, the trio boarded a prop plane in Hyannis for the short flight to New York for a meeting with the old guard at the posh Warwick Hotel. Troy and Vince carried briefcases weighed down with $230,736, the down payment.

"We checked in to the Warwick, and I ended up going downstairs for a bite to eat while they got to the actual dotting of the i's and crossing of the t's. By the time I came back upstairs, everybody seemed pretty happy," Troy recalls.

Other than the handful of people in that room, nobody knew for a long time what had transpired.

"Even though he bought it, it was not something that was highly publicized. Even the other promoters didn't really know," Dave Meltzer of *The Wrestling Observer* tells me.

At the Madison Square Garden show later that night, Vince Senior was still calling the shots, jingling a set of quarters in his hand as he always did, pulling the Boys into the bathroom to discuss the finishes of matches. He would continue as the figurehead of the company well into 1984 before passing away from cancer that May.

Quietly, the torch had been passed.

*   *   *

IN ORDER TO MAKE HIS WRESTLERS HOUSEHOLD NAMES, VINCE NEEDED COAST-to-coast TV exposure backed up by a national tour. Wrestling was still a live event business, promotions made or broken based on their ability to use syndicated TV to drive people to the matches when the Boys came to town.

With Jim Troy's hockey career over, Vince gave him the title of senior vice president of Titan Sports and sent him out on a raiding mission. Although other lords had tried invasions before (for example, the AWA's incursion into Los Angeles in the late sixties and Georgia Championship Wrestling's expansion into Michigan, Ohio, and West Virginia in the early eighties), no one quite had the cojones that Vince McMahon did.

Troy, newly minted director of operations Jim Barnett (who had previously worked for the NWA), and Vince Senior's longtime associate Joe Perkins were tasked with working the phones and traveling the country to convince TV station managers to scrap their existing wrestling shows and replace them with the WWF's syndicated programs *Championship Wrestling* and *All-Star Wrestling*. Their offer was one few could refuse: they would pay the managers up to thousands of dollars per week to air their shows in exchange for a set number of minutes of commercial time. The WWF would fill this time with plugs for their own products and, more importantly, "per-inquiry" advertisements, companies hawking home products whose call to action was a phone number; for each phone call or inquiry the advertiser received, the WWF got a set fee.

Vince made a killing off of Clappers and Flowbees.

The plan worked. According to internal WWF documents, Troy, Barnett, and Perkins had added San Jose, Dayton, Tucson, Phoenix, Detroit, Akron, Los Angeles, Youngstown, and San Diego by October 15, 1983, to bring the number of TV markets to forty-four, up from just twenty-four in September 1982; by August 1986 they were in 201 markets.

Once the WWF's foot was in the door, Vince began running live events in these territories, creating a turf war. In 1983, he invaded Ohio to battle with promoter Ole Anderson and took on the NWA bastion of St. Louis, where old-timers Verne Gagne, Bob Geigel, and Harley Race were kings. In 1984, it was on to the South and Midwest, and although not all of his salvos were initially successful, he was creating the original new world order of the wrestling industry.

The other side of the TV coin was cable. With the US market growing from one million homes wired for cable in 1963 to 41.5 million by 1985, technology broke down the walls imposed by geography, allowing people in California to watch a show emanating from Connecticut. Wrestling was an instant hit: in 1982, Georgia Championship Wrestling on Ted Turner's Superstation, WTBS, was the most-watched cable show in the nation. The WWF itself had been on HBO and the MSG Network since 1973.

Jim Troy, it turned out, had some very valuable connections through his past in hockey. The former general manager of the Hartford Whalers, Ron Ryan, had taken over as president of New England Prime Cable Network/ PRISM New England (now NBC Sports Boston), a regional sports network in the burgeoning cable TV industry that carried the Boston Celtics. When Ryan expressed an interest in televising a series of fifteen wrestling and fifteen boxing events, Troy made the introduction to Vince, and shortly thereafter they had a deal to tape the shows at the Coliseum.

While that deal ended up as little more than a footnote in the WWF's meteoric rise, Troy provided the gateway to a bigger fish: the USA Network, which today still broadcasts the company's flagship show, *Monday Night Raw*. Troy had a connection at the MSG Network who was close to USA's CEO, Kay Koplovitz.

Troy got Vince a meeting with Koplovitz, and despite being no fan of wrestling, she relented after hearing Vince's pitch to replace USA's current wrestling program produced by Southwest Championship Wrestling with the WWF's new show, *All-American Wrestling*. Vince knew that the network had gotten heat from a recent angle in which one wrestler dumped pig feces on another, and he sold her on his promotion being geared toward kids (it helped that Southwest was also slow to pay its bills).

What connections Troy didn't already have, he quickly made, fashioning himself into a media expert. Vince dispatched him to National Association of Television Program Executives (NATPE) events, sometimes coming with Hulk Hogan in tow as the muscle and eye candy.

The combination of syndication and cable TV penetration along with expanded national tours paid off. While the other lords fought back valiantly, even pooling their resources at times, within a few years Vince put almost all of them out of business. His production values, merchandising, and risk tolerance were orders of magnitude above the competition, and one by one the regional territories went bust or were bought out.

*   *   *

MAJORING IN BUSINESS ADMINISTRATION AT EAST CAROLINA UNIVERSITY, Vince graduated with a 2.0 GPA, and then only after twisting his professors' arms. Even a man with his ego knew he needed help when it came to tightening up the fiscal side of the WWF.

Enter Bob McMullan, a twenty-nine-year-old internal auditor with Barnes Engineering from Greenwich, who got a call from a recruiter in the spring of 1983 about a job with a wrestling company out on the Cape.

Vince and Linda hired McMullan as their vice president of finance and made it clear that the company's ambitions were stratospheric.

"When I first met Vince, he laid out a plan," McMullan tells me over breakfast at the Morristown Diner in Morristown, New Jersey. He has the settled countenance of a finance veteran, well-dressed and perfectly groomed.

"He was very up front with these guys [the other promoters]. He had a vision and he was going to execute on it. They could be a part of it if they wanted."

Vince made offers to several of the lords to buy them out, but found few takers.

"These guys were close to Vince's dad, and here comes this kid who's going to tell them all how to run the business. It didn't go over well," McMullan says.

As the rejections piled up, Vince shrugged. You could join him or get steamrolled.

Despite his confidence, success was by no means a given. In fact, most doubted him.

"They [the WWF] were an interesting business," McMullan recalls of his introduction to the company. "They were all cash. And they never had any money. I saw all these agents who ran the shows and who ran the box office, and they would come in with all this cash. And I said, 'When's the last time you were here [in the office]?' 'Three weeks ago.' 'And so for three weeks you're walking around with all this cash?' I went to Vince and said, 'Look, these guys can't be walking around the country with this money. One, it's dangerous. Two, we're not insured. And number three, we need the money.'"

McMullan instituted a system in which road agents exchanged cash for bank checks right after a show, immediately providing the company with $250,000 in cash flow. This also avoided the situation of agents roaming the streets with tens if not hundreds of thousands of dollars in cash in briefcases for weeks at a time.

"They weren't sophisticated," McMullan says of the situation. When Vince bought out his dad in 1982, he had not consolidated the two companies (Capitol Wrestling Corporation and Titan Sports). With money moving between the two entities, valuations got confusing. McMullan put an end to that, discontinuing Capitol. He also introduced audited financial statements, opening the door to the McMahons getting a much-needed line of credit through the Bank of Boston. When one of Vince's buyout offers was accepted, such as his purchase of Georgia Championship Wrestling in 1984, it "was notes, not real money," McMullan says. In his two years with the company, McMullan ushered in a lot of positive change, witnessing the company grow from less than $10 million in gross revenue to $63.125 million in 1985 (in 1988, after McMullan was gone, the company passed the $100 million threshold).

"They were making money. They always made money," McMullan says. Even the original WrestleMania in 1985, for which conventional wisdom says the McMahons mortgaged every last scrap of their finances, may not have been as dire a situation as has been presented.

"I never saw Vince put a nickel in the business," he says. "It [Wrestle-Mania] was a gamble. If it didn't work, we would have been in trouble." But maybe not dead. The point is moot—the event grossed $9 million "before insurance proceeds" according to McMullan, with Hulk Hogan alone making $300,000 for the main event.

McMullan mythbusts left and right as we eat breakfast.

"So who do you think named WrestleMania?" he asks me, referencing the annual Super Bowl–like event that began in 1985.

"Well, from my research, Howard Finkel," I reply, mentioning the ring announcer who pulled double duty as one of Vince's office assistants.

"Bullshit," he says without hesitation.

"A crazy guy by the name of Rex Jones," he elaborates. "Rex Jones was brought in, he was a television guy, and Linda brought us into Vince's office, and we're all trying to think about how to do it. We were getting 'mania.' So Rex sits there and says, 'It's got to be WrestleMania, it rhymes with Hulka-mania,'" he recalls.

While costs ballooned with the expansion, McMullan implored Vince to get creative about his revenue sources. While the WWF regularly lent talent to the promotion New Japan for their shows under a gentleman's agreement between them and Vince Senior, to an outsider like McMullan, this was flushing money away.

"Why are they taking our people out of our markets and we get nothing?" McMullan says. "I convinced Vince to license [the talent], and we got a million dollars from New Japan," he says.

In those early Wild West days of cable, he even urged Vince to buy ESPN.

"Texaco owned ESPN, and when they said it was for sale, I said, 'Vince, why don't we go buy? I can raise money. Let's go buy ESPN,'" McMullan says, pausing to switch into a Vince imitation by lowering his voice: "'Wow, run our own sports network! That'd be fun. But I'd have to give up the wrestling.' And he couldn't do that."

One aspect of the company's financial model did worry McMullan: the wrestlers were classified as independent contractors, not employees, despite a full-time work schedule and boilerplate contracts that gave Titan complete control over their performers' time and likeness (for merchandising, public appearances, etc.). They were independent contractors, yet were forbidden from working for other promotions.

"The cost of workers' compensation would have been enormous. Millions of dollars a year. The economics would not have supported it," McMullan says.

He brought up his concerns about classifying wrestlers as independent contractors with Vince and Linda, who simply said they would rely on the advice of their lawyers. After all, the Boys could read what was in their contract and what they were agreeing to. McMullan knew that the only way this expansion could work financially was to maintain the status quo.

* * *

BREAKING KAYFABE, MERCHANDISING, SYNDICATION, INVADING THE LORDS' turf, expanding cable TV, improving production values, and getting the books in order paved the way for Vince, but he still needed more revenue to cover the massive increase in costs. Much of the world was still untapped when it came to the curious phenomenon of pro wrestling, especially Vince's cartoonish iteration. He flirted with running tours in New Zealand and Africa, but settled on a region flush with cash that could help fund his expansion: the Middle East.

Jim Troy and Mike Breen had spent plenty of time on the Road as hockey players, barnstorming in front of small but passionate crowds and getting in their fair share of trouble on and off the ice. But hockey was Sunday school compared to what they would encounter on the WWF's tours of the Middle East. The stories from these tours illustrate best just how insane the wrestling business could be.

Troy was head counselor on these missions, saddled with the impossible task of herding twenty-some young behemoths with an appetite for destruction through a land that was nothing like their own. The nations of the Middle East were hungry for content and had plenty of money to throw around; knowing this, Vince shipped tapes of his shows for airing on state TV, a welcome novelty and departure from the usual government propaganda. Between 1983 and 1985, the WWF would complete four tours of the region, hitting Kuwait, Egypt, Bahrain, United Arab Emirates, Qatar, Jordan, and Oman. In the process they would make a ton of money, witness all hell break loose, and in the case of Jim Troy, be lucky to make it out alive.

Right from the start, although lucrative, the trips were a disaster. The initial tour in 1983, which was supposed to include visits to Kuwait, Saudi Arabia, Bahrain, and Qatar, ended up as ten consecutive nights in the same venue in Kuwait when the deals with the other nations fell through. Wrestlers like Moondog Spot and Ivan Putski, accustomed to the familiar stage lights of Madison Square Garden, now found themselves desperately trying to remain fresh for ten straight events in a soccer stadium full of men wearing keffiyehs who bought a little too heavily into the action. One night, Mr. Fuji, a heel, had his opponent blade during the match, so that he gushed real blood. When the crowd saw crimson, they went wild, starting a full-scale riot to go after Fuji. Kayfabe was out the window.

Troy recounts:

I'm taking Fuji from the ring to the locker room and a guy throws a can of Pepsi at him. But it misses and hits me in the head. Being the hothead that I was back then, I leaped over the barrier into the crowd, and the people just spread like the sea. I ran for the guy [who had thrown the can], but just before I got there, the riot police intervened. They had these nightsticks that were probably three feet long and they just started cracking people. They jumped the guy, and had him down on the ground in zip ties.

And then when we left the stadium, we got all the heels on one bus, and I thought Fuji was going to be a dead man. I got on with them. We had the Kuwaiti riot police clearing a path for the bus. In the meantime the crowd behind them surged on and started rocking the bus, to the point where the wheels were coming off the ground. And this is, you know, a short bus. And then the riot police surged back and they were splitting people's heads open like they were watermelons. I mean just swinging those big clubs and taking their belts and just whaling the crap out of people.

The next night the Kuwaiti army showed up to make sure things didn't get out of hand again. But it only got worse for Troy. The Kuwaitis had only paid about a third of the $360,000 they owed Titan Sports for the tour as the trip headed into its final day. Back in Greenwich, Vince and Linda needed the cash to make payroll. Troy went to his contact, a Fijian promoter and liaison to a local prince, the night before the last show:

This negotiation ensues. And he says, "It didn't go as well as the prince wanted it to go. If we're going to do this, we're going to need to secure your passport." And I said, 'Nobody's taking my passport. This is the way it's going to be done or I'm not going to put the guys in the ring tomorrow night and sixty thousand people are going to tear your stadium down.' It was pretty tense . . . they still tried to take my passport. They had this bodyguard who was a big Egyptian boxer. He and I had an altercation. To make a long story short, that didn't last too long. And the way it was left when I left his office was that we were going to have to go to the bank the next morning, wire transfer the money for the balance to the Titan Sports bank account.

The Kuwaitis were not happy with Troy's strongarm tactics, so he wasn't surprised by what happened next.

"The next morning we're going to the airport. And we're going through customs and immigration, and my wife and son go through. I'm flagged. I can't leave the country," Troy tells me.

Troy would end up detained in Kuwait for two months, missing his sister's wedding. He made friends with people at the embassy and at the Marine guard and knew if he ever needed to make a break for it, he could get on a boat to Bahrain. Finally, a Kuwaiti court made a judgment that allowed him to return home. Even all these years later, Troy is still the ultimate warrior.

"It was good for the business. It was revenue that was important to the growth of the company at the time," he says.

A subsequent tour took them to Dubai, Qatar, Oman, and Bahrain, featuring one of the company's hottest feuds between "Superfly" Jimmy Snuka (real name: James Reiher), a Fijian babyface with a body of the gods, and Don "The Magnificent" Muraco, a churlish heel known for being an outstanding worker in the ring. Snuka would forever be a case of unrealized potential, a physical nonpareil destroyed by addiction to drugs and alcohol, and eventually a homicide defendant (in 2015 he was charged with the 1983 murder of his mistress, Nancy Argentino, ruled accidental at the time in a mess that Vince did his best to clean up).

While Jim Troy ran the tour, Mike Breen was along to referee.

Thirty-eight years later, Breener remembers it like yesterday. I track him down in the town of Scituate, Massachusetts, where he welcomes me into his spacious office as Scituate's highway and public grounds supervisor, and shares more Road stories.

One night after the matches at the Intercontinental Hotel in Dubai, Breener hit the bar with the rest of the Boys to blow off steam, and saw Snuka (who was married at the time) relentlessly hitting on a woman who clearly wasn't enjoying the attention. He walked up to try to help, enraging Snuka. But before chaperone Jim Troy could intervene to defuse the situation, he got an urgent call from the hotel's general manager: apparently one of the Boys was drinking a case of beer in the lobby and then throwing the empties up in the air to shatter on the floor. Troy says:

I managed to get him to stop smashing bottles. He's terrifying the entire patronage of the hotel. I got him going down the hall, and I'm on his right side, and he's got his arm around me, and I'm barely guiding him. He weighed well over 300 pounds. And we're going down the hall, two steps this way, two steps that way. His room is at the end of the corridor. And all of a sudden, he starts to go and I can't control him. We both go flying to the right, and the full weight of us hits the door of this hotel room. We bust through this random older couple's room. They're in bed, and I hit the floor in front of their bed. The woman starts to scream. The guy jumps up on the bed and doesn't know what to do. I thought he was gonna have a heart attack. I try to calm them down. The general manager comes in. We get a luggage cart and we load him onto it and manage with people holding his arms and legs to get him to his room, get him off the luggage cart and plop him on his bed.

The tour finished up in Bahrain. Breener and fellow referee Tim White were looking forward to sleeping in their own beds after more than a week of craziness on the Road, and settled in for the long flight home, a commercial flight. Snuka, already bombed when he boarded and continuing to drink on the plane, started throwing change at Breener from across the aisle, still fuming over Breener's interference with the woman at the hotel bar a few nights prior. When the seat belt sign went off, Snuka walked over to Breener's aisle seat.

"You guys are office rats," he said, his bloodshot eyes bugging out of his head, strands of stringy black hair sweeping his massive shoulders.

"You got any balls, boy?" he taunted, immediately followed by the clap of his hand against Breener's face.

But Breener was no typical referee, having fought his way through the minor leagues of hockey.

"I got up and I grabbed his hair and just twisted it like I would a shirt, and I think it shocked the shit out of him because I hit him with probably like fifteen friggin' shots," Breener recalls.

Most wrestlers of that era knew how to fight for real (promoters were known to fire them if they ever lost a bar fight), and so Snuka grabbed Breener around the waist, picked him up, and ran him all the way to the back of the plane, smashing both of them through the bathroom door.

"The next thing I remember is I hit the wall and then my head is right next to a silver toilet. And his fingers come down and he's trying to pull my eye out. So I take his finger and I bite it as hard as I can. Blood is everywhere, I don't know if it's mine or his," Breener says.

"The Magnificent" Muraco, Snuka's storyline rival, came over and pulled Snuka off and out of the bathroom. But no sooner was Breener free than The Tonga Kid (Sam Fatu) came up and slammed him. Breener fought back until he realized he was bashing the Kid's head into the plane's emergency exit door.

While Muraco and others tried to break it up, the poor flight attendants summoned Jim Troy, who reseated Breener and Tim White for the remainder of the flight. White, neither a hockey player nor a fighter, asked for six beers to settle his nerves while Snuka came up and apologized to Breener.

"I want to apologize, bruddha. My head was bad. You're OK," he offered.

"But him [pointing to White], he's the devil," he added with a sadistic look.

Snuka went back to his seat, the lights went down, a movie came on, and things seemed to settle down. But a bit later in the flight, Breener heard what he thought was White snoring, only to look over and see Snuka choking him out. The noise he had heard was White struggling for air.

Breener reared back and hit Snuka with the hardest punch he'd ever thrown in his life.

All shreds of sanity long gone, Snuka then started raining blows down on Breener all the way to the back of the plane until Breener introduced a pot of hot coffee, getting enough separation to sprint down the aisle screaming. By now the entire flight was awake and in an uproar, and Troy did everything he could to subdue Snuka once again and get him to the back of the plane.

The pilot emerged in short order and said, "I'm going to land this plane in Heathrow and you two are never going to see the light of day." When the copilot asked who was in charge, Breener pointed to Troy.

"Troy had a bag of Kuwaiti dinars, so him and the pilot went up the corkscrew, the little thing up top, and I don't know what happened, but he must have paid off the captain," Breener says.

When they landed in Heathrow, Breener and White booked themselves on a separate flight back to New York, and not long after, Breener gave Vince his notice. Getting bloodied by a 240-pound mind-altered, roided-up Fijian at thirty thousand feet was not on the agenda when Vince told him to come along for the ride that day in the Cape Cod Coliseum. Even when he told Vince what had happened, Vince said, "Breener, I'm telling you, things are going good. Do you like the business at all?"

"No, I don't like the business at all," Breener replied. While Tim White ended up staying on for decades, Breener never looked back.

The Road ate people alive.

*   *   *

BACK IN GREENWICH, VINCE WAS PLOTTING THE FINAL PIECE OF THE PUZZLE, the crown jewel to his national expansion: the acquisition of Hulk Hogan.

Hulk had left the WWF under less-than-ideal circumstances in 1981. He was finishing up his first tour with the company and wanted to film *Rocky III* instead of accepting Vince Senior's assignment to work for a fellow lord in the Carolinas.

"If you leave to do the *Rocky* movie, you'll never work for this company again," Vince Senior told him.

But the son was not the father. Ever since he had worked with Hulk during that run, Vince Junior kept it under his hat that this six-foot-five-and-a-half (Hulk's six-foot-eight billing was a work), 310-pound, tanned, blond bass player from Tampa, Florida, was going to be his golden goose when the time was right.

"It had to be Hogan. Hogan was the only one who could have made it work. There was nobody else, from day one," says Dave Meltzer of *The Wrestling Observer*.

In mid-1983, Vince recruited Ed Helinski and Steve Taylor, a writer-photographer duo from *The Citizen* newspaper in Auburn, New York, to help launch his new WWF-only magazine, *Victory*. The magazine would end up being Vince's tool to acquire Hulk.

With an initial print run of thirty thousand, *Victory* was a modest project, except for one small detail that figured big into Vince's grand scheme: just as his new *All-American Wrestling* show on the USA Network featured wrestlers from other territories, *Victory* covered other promoters' talent as well. (*Victory* would only last two issues before pressure from *Inside Wrestling: A Victory Sports Series* allegedly led Vince to rename it *WWF Magazine*.)

It seemed counterintuitive—why would Vince give ink to his competition, especially as he was bringing everything else in-house and making plans to invade their territories?

In order to drive his expansion, he needed more talent. Vince Senior, although in poor health, was still alive, and Junior wanted to at least maintain the pretense of civility with his dad's old friends. He couldn't come right out and try to poach talent, but he needed a way to get in touch with the top stars of all the other promotions. The magazine provided just such a cover.

"I would call down to Dallas, Texas, and talk to [promoter] Fritz Von Erich and say, 'Hey, we got this national magazine, do you mind if we send a photographer down there, maybe do a little story about you and your promotion for our magazine?'" Helinski explains. His photographer, Steve Taylor, would fly to Dallas with a stack of Vince's business cards in his hand, the perfect Trojan horse.

"These guys took the bait," Helinski says. "Steve was palming off business cards left and right, saying, 'Vince wants to talk to you.'"

In October, as the leaves in Greenwich turned color, Vince summoned Helinski, Taylor, and Jim Troy to his office. He had recently come back from a failed attempt to buy the AWA from Verne Gagne, and wanted to stick the rebuke right up Gagne's ass.

Gagne held the queen on Vince's chessboard in the form of Hogan, who possessed a quality rare in wrestlers that would set him apart: he wasn't afraid to stand up for himself. Since leaving the WWF, Hulk had become an international star in Japan and the hottest box office attraction in the AWA. But as charismatic as Hulk was, as larger-than-life, as solid gold at the ticket window, Gagne refused to make him his champion because, well, he wasn't built in the traditional mold. Gagne, an accomplished amateur wrestler, had held his own promotion's belt ten times (giving it to himself) and never liked the fact that under all the finger-wagging and ear-cupping that made Hulkamania a force of nature, he was a bass player from Tampa who would rather play Jimi Hendrix covers in high school than smash someone in the mouth on the football field.

"I think Verne [Gagne] was a little jealous," says Brad Rheingans, who wrestled for Gagne at the same time and befriended Hulk.

According to Rheingans, who spent a lot of time with Hulk on the Road at that time, Gagne helped Hulk develop his character and his in-ring skills, teaching him how to do interviews, to "Hulk up" when it was time for a comeback. But he also was hard on Hulk, mean even, demeaning him, calling him "dumbass" and "dipshit." Despite being a monster in size and stature, Hulk was a pretty sensitive guy and didn't appreciate the insults.

Vince, of sizable ego himself, wasn't about to let pride get in the way of the almighty dollar, and knew he needed Hulk to consummate his plan.

"Steve, I want you to go to the upcoming AWA show at the Rosemont Horizon and give this to Hogan," Vince said, passing him a card with his home phone number. Ed Helinski would call the AWA office to explain their plan to do a story on Gagne's wrestlers for the magazine, and Steve would have his opening.

"I'm gonna make Hulk Hogan the first million-dollar wrestler," Vince told them.

The plan worked. Taylor arrived at the arena before the show to shoot photos. Even with this apparent peace offering, the AWA agents were on guard, watching Taylor's every move. When he got up to Hulk, he got close enough to whisper, "I have Vince's card."

"Palm it to me when we shake hands," Hulk replied.

Hulk's enormous mitt dwarfed Taylor's as he felt the cardboard shift between their fingers.

A month later Hulk sent a telegram to Gagne from Japan, where he was on tour: "I'm not coming back."

Vince told him he would start with the World Wrestling Federation in St. Louis on December 27, the day after their big show in Madison Square Garden, where he would have Bob Backlund lose the championship to another recent acquisition, the Iron Sheik.

*   *   *

I EXIT THE GREENWICH LIBRARY, MY EYES STILL BURNING FROM STARING AT microfilm for hours.

I tap 81 Holly Hill Lane into my phone, an address that sounds like the name of a horror movie. A trickle of sweat escapes my tangle of thick black hair and runs down the side of my face. It's a bright, brilliant day, the zenith of New England summer, when the foliage is so dense and lime green that it seems to burst like fireworks, the streets awash in gobs of color.

Greenwich, already so tidy and idyllic, reaches near-perfection on days like this. Orthodontist offices look like bed-and-breakfasts, with little white signs swaying in the breeze hanging from street posts. Estates, not homes, are set far back from the street with pillared porches and lawns like football fields; I'm probably lowering property values just by driving the Ford Fusion along these pastoral roads.

Maserati, Porsche, Bentley, Ferrari—one after the next, the dealerships on Route 1 pass by until I turn left onto Holly Hill, a quieter road paralleling the main drag. There's a sign on the left for the Resource Recycling Facility, a euphemism for the town dump; just down that street is Christiano Field, where the WWF softball team, led by Jim Troy, played in the mid-1980s. Past the boarded-up Greenwich Pigeon Club, I reach my destination, an elevated two-story gray office building set on a hill, almost brand-new when Vince moved Titan Sports here from Cape Cod in the fall of 1983, and the site of that meeting to plan the acquisition of Hulk Hogan. The company was still small then, with maybe a dozen employees. Vince had a corner office. The front of the building consists of a glass rectangular facade with "81 Holly Hill Lane" written across the center.

I'm not exactly sure what I'm doing here. I walk up the driveway, completely empty on a Saturday, and walk across the ground-level carport. I'm surprised to find the glass door to the building open, and once inside, I spot a sign listing the occupants. The third floor, once occupied by Titan Sports, is now home to Greenwich Medical Associates.

I scamper up to the third floor, now fully aware that I am trespassing but eager to get a glimpse of the space where the WWF took root. The hallway to the suite is dimly lit, and a TV monitor has been knocked ninety degrees from its perch on the wall. I grab the metal handle to the suite entrance, certain it will be locked, but it turns, opening up the WWF's former headquarters. Now I'm really spooked, scanning the walls for cameras, my neck tensed and expecting to hear an alarm go off at any moment. The medical offices look like they had been evacuated mid-workday, with laptops out, paperwork strewn across desks; even a light is on in one of the examination rooms.

I creep around the doorway of the lit room holding my breath, wondering which office belonged to Vince McMahon. I brace myself while preparing an explanation if I am not, in fact, alone.

But nobody's home.

Before I leave, I take out my phone and open up Twitter. I have no special way of getting to Vince, and my emails to Linda have gone unanswered, so I tap out a couple lines asking him to meet while I'm in town. A needle in a haystack, but why not?

I head down the road to Stamford, where the company moved in 1986. Quickly outgrowing their quarters there, they moved again in 1991 to their present location at 1241 East Main Street, so close to I-95's Exit 9 you can almost reach out your car window and touch it.

The new location was classic Vince, staking out a spot on the east side of town where every motorist heading into New York City would have no choice but to see the gleaming beacon of the WWF's blue, white, and yellow logo atop the building. It's an odd spot for a commercial building, wedged between a main thoroughfare and a working-class neighborhood of modest dwellings.

Sprinkled with some Vince dust, the unremarkable four-story glass-and-steel building became Titan Towers, the capital of sports entertainment. The wrestling industry Vince entered as a young man, with its magazines advertising boner pills and women's apartment wrestling tapes, became a distant memory. Behind these walls now operates a publicly traded company worth an estimated $8.3 billion with fifteen million TikTok followers and programming broadcasted in thirty languages and 180 countries. The respect that Vince so desperately coveted from Madison Avenue can now be counted in his bank account.

I walk around the perimeter, snooping and peering into the parking garage, where a black stretch limo is parked. The front door is locked, and my attempt at the handle draws a big grin from the desk security guard, who probably sees this several times a day from curious fans. A statue of André the Giant looms over the entire lobby inside, but there's little else to see. Walking back toward my motel, I cross a freeway overpass and come upon a neatly dressed older man folding up a cardboard sign that reads "Please help" as he waits for the bus. His short gray hair is pushed back and appears wet with gel, and he's wearing tinted prescription glasses.

"Need some help?" I ask, unfolding a couple ones from the pocket of my mesh shorts.

"Financial? Sure!" he replies, lighting up and grinning, all gums.

His name is Norman, and he's in the trucking business. He tells me he was about to get back on his feet with a business partner, but that guy got caught embezzling.

"I cut my hair and I panhandle. The cops don't usually give me a hard time," he says. "It's better here than in Norwalk. It's those state troopers, they put a tag on you and if they keep seeing you they'll give you a ticket."

I nod. "Do you have a place to stay?" I ask.

He pauses like a man trying to figure out exactly how much he wants to share, then exhales and said, "Yeah. By the grace of God, yeah."

I point behind him to the twin flags of the United States and the WWE, America and its dream materialized, atop Titan Towers.

"Do you know what that is?"

He looks back at me, almost with pity.

"Shit, man, I was watching wrestling before you were even in diapers," he replies.

"There were multiple eras—when I was young, you had Bob Backlund and all those guys, then you had Hulk Hogan, that was the best era. . . . " He marches through the WWE's history, right up to last week's episode of *Monday Night Raw.*

Norman may be panhandling, but he's all up to date on his wrestling. Somewhere, Vince, the ultimate populist, is smiling. For now.

Later that evening I sit rigidly atop clammy sheets in the Red Carpet Inn, a flophouse in the shadow of Titan Towers that still sets me back ninety-five dollars in this inflated economy. I feel the smoke from past patrons seeping out of the blue (not red!) carpet and into my pores, my eyes fixated on a gaping hole in the wall next to the door.

A strong Wi-Fi connection is the Red Carpet Inn's saving grace, and I pull up a *Wall Street Journal* story from a few days ago: "WWE board probes secret $3 million hush pact by CEO Vince McMahon, sources say." The article reports that Vince, now seventy-six and still running the show, had allegedly signed a $3 million nondisclosure agreement with a forty-one-year-old WWE paralegal to buy her silence about their alleged affair. The WWE's board of directors had been investigating the situation for months, having been initially tipped off by the paralegal's friend via email, and in the process had stumbled upon other, older NDAs with past employees alleging sexual misconduct against McMahon.

Vince went on live TV two days later, probably the only CEO in America who would have the temerity to turn his sex scandal into a ratings opportunity. He opened the show by coming through the curtain to his "No Chance in Hell" theme music, getting a huge pop. He smirked, stretching both arms out wide to acknowledge the crowd, as if to say *these* are my people, fuck you, *Wall Street Journal*. He strutted to the ring with his exaggerated Mr. McMahon swagger, using his hands to conduct the crowd through his song's lyrics. Wearing a purple tie, he took the microphone and said a few lines about the WWE's motto, finishing with "Welcome to Smackdown!" before tossing the microphone to the canvas. No mention of the women, the allegations, the story. A complete no-sell.

The show earned its highest ratings in months, with 2.389 million people watching.

My phone slips out of my hand as I look up and consider all the WWF employees from the early years who I've interviewed these past few days. Nobody can argue against Vince McMahon the Wall Street mogul, the kid from a trailer park in North Carolina who became a billionaire. Vince took on the world and won.

But what about the man?

I want to know what his employees in the Office, the people he worked with day in and day out, think of him. Before leaving Connecticut, I seek out some of the lesser-known figures whose time with Vince is now a distant memory, some of whom have never commented publicly on their WWF past.

Outside of Troy and Breener, loyalists to the end, every former Office employee I interview expresses two things: immense respect for Vince's creative genius, work ethic, and success as a businessman, and serious misgivings about Vince the man and the workplace culture he created.

Bob McMullan, nearing the end of a storied career as a CFO with more than seventy deals to his name, looks back with some disappointment over how his tenure at the WWF ended. A week before he was told he was being replaced by a CBS exec named Doug Sages, Bob says Vince looked him in the eye and said, "We're not going to replace you." Doug was just coming in to help modernize their financial systems, not push anyone out, Vince assured him.

But in a refrain I hear over and over, Vince's actions didn't match his words.

When he learned of his dismissal, McMullan demanded a meeting with Vince.

"I was direct. I said, 'Vince, I've done a lot of things for you here. We should have had a conversation and talk like adults here. . . . But I don't appreciate you going behind my back and doing this as a surprise after I had a direct conversation with you,'" McMullan recalls. But like every other one of the Boys, Office or Road, McMullan was expendable, useful until he wasn't.

Vince was just doing what was "best for business."

Nelson Sweglar headed Vince's TV production for twelve years before moving on to produce boxing and other combat sports for ESPN. While he holds enormous respect for *what* Vince accomplished, he takes some issue with the *how*:

"We would have meetings from time to time on the fourth floor. Across from Vince's office there was a conference room with a long table. We'd be in there talking about ideas, and the way he spoke to some people. Howard Finkel in particular," Sweglar says.

"He [Finkel] might come up with an idea and Vince would say, 'That is the dumbest idea I've ever heard. Why would you say that?' Howard was his whipping boy. And there was no one who worked harder [than Howard]."

In all the years of working for Vince, after moving his family up from Baltimore in the early years and helping to build the WWF studios at 88 Hamilton Avenue in Stamford, Vince only publicly acknowledged Sweglar once.

"I thought I had more than paid my dues. After all those years . . . I would have liked to have an expression of confidence that I know what I'm doing," Sweglar says about his decision to leave.

"What was your first impression of Vince when you met him?" I ask Ed Helinski, the magazine editor.

"You don't realize how big he is. He's a tall guy. And he's soft-spoken as opposed to his gimmick on TV. You don't know how bad of a temper he had or how vindictive he is. You find out later when you work for the man," he replies.

Helinski lasted less than a year as editor before he was reassigned to merchandising, news that McMahon had one of his minions deliver. And when he was fired for good three years later, McMahon again did not do the dirty work.

"McMahon wouldn't do it. The McMahons would never do it. They got stooges to do it. And I was never given a reason why. They just said we gotta let you go."

Helinski's résumé was ruined by his stint in wrestling journalism.

"You do fiction," editors would say as he looked for his next job. He ended up in trucking management, recently finding his way back to covering local sports in upstate New York.

His replacements at *WWF Magazine* echo Helinski's experience. Ed Ricciuti joined the staff as executive editor in 1984 and lasted until 1993. A career journalist who has covered everything from crime to entomology, at age eighty-four, he now runs Green Hill Martial Arts in Killingworth, Connecticut.

"Kind of a little imperious," he says of his first impression of his new boss. Vince took one look at Ricciuti's attire and said, "We wear ties here."

Company culture in those early years was tough.

"It was not a good place to work," Ricciuti says. "Everything that human resources should have corrected existed at that place." But in 1983, human resources was not yet a thing. HR was simply Linda McMahon, the house mother of the fraternity.

When Vince tired of Ricciuti, he let him go.

Dropping the axe fell to Tom Emanuel, the magazine's publisher, who has great respect for Ricciuti. Under their leadership, a single issue once sold a million copies; the licensing rights to Germany alone netted them $1 million. Emanuel did everything he could to make his friend's exit smooth.

"They gave me a monster package. Vince didn't know. They said, 'Don't tell Vince, stay out of his way. Don't be around him. The other thing we'd like you to do is, can you set it all up and find us a replacement?'" Ricciuti recalls. That replacement, another Vince (Vince Russo), would go on to become infamous as one of the head writers during the WWF's "Attitude Era" years later.

Emanuel, a well-spoken Brit who the McMahons plucked from *Connecticut Magazine* in late 1984, still dreams about his time at the WWF. "That ten years is so deeply ingrained in my system. I don't ever remember being as happy or as miserable," he says.

The life was fast, hard, and cutthroat, in the mold of its emperor, whether you were one of the Boys on the Road or the suits in the Office.

And soon I will come face-to-face with the rest of the Six Packers who remember it all like it was just yesterday.

MATCH 6

TITO SANTANA VS. MERCED SOLIS

1984

THESE THINGS AREN'T SUPPOSED TO HAPPEN.

At three years old, Christal Lavary should be learning to talk, wobbling around the house, delighting her parents with each "first" as it happens.

Instead, Christal is clinging to life.

She has a rare and (if uncorrected) fatal condition, with eleven microscopic holes in her heart. Open-heart surgery is the only hope, and the surgery itself is highly risky. Her surgeon, Dr. Joseph D'Amato, the lead of the Pediatric Cardiovascular unit at the Children's Hospital in Newark, New Jersey, has some advice for Christal's mom, Pat: if Christal goes into the surgery with a strong attitude, it will greatly increase her chances of survival.

On January 4, the WWF's live event booker, Ed Cohen, gets an unexpected phone call in his office at 81 Holly Hill Lane in Greenwich. Things have been crazy lately, as Hulk Hogan has just come over from the AWA and will be challenging the Iron Sheik for the WWF title in Madison Square Garden in a few weeks. Most of the company is off in Hamburg, Pennsylvania, taping the next three weeks' worth of syndicated TV, but Cohen is in the office staring at that map of the US figuring out how the hell he is going to get everyone where they need to be as they expand to new markets all over the country, many requiring air travel.

The person on the other end of the call is Pat Lavary. She has a very simple request: nothing in the world brightens her daughter Christal's face more than seeing her favorite wrestler on TV, Tito Santana. Is there any chance, given that Santana is local to New Jersey, that he could take a moment out of his crazy schedule to meet Christal before her surgery?

A little under a month later, Pat writes a letter to Tito and Titan Sports in loopy cursive thanking Tito for his visit to see Christal in the hospital.

"I knew God would make me see him," the three-year-old told her mom afterward.

According to Pat's letter, the morning after Christal's surgery was a Saturday, meaning the WWF was on. But the TV in Christal's intensive care unit couldn't pick up the channel. Undaunted, Christal endured the incredible pain of each step as she walked down the hallway to be able to watch Tito wrestle on the TV in the waiting room.

Tito's heroism was as real as the repaired heart and toughness of that little girl who refused to tap out.

*   *   *

2022

THE 1970–1971 MISSION HIGH SCHOOL YEARBOOK, NAMED *THE EAGLE* AND representing the only high school at the time in Mission, Texas, is an astounding time capsule.

As I flip through the musty pages in the Mission Library, I can't suppress a smile at some of the honorifics and clubs that would never fly in today's world. Each class has a "Best All-Around" category (I suppose for the best person?) along with "Best Looking"; a page describing the "freshman initiation" displays four guys in women's clothes and refers to their "shapely legs"; and the Future Homemakers of America page includes the following description: "The primary aim of FHA is to promote a growing appreciation of the joys and satisfactions of homemaking. The club is open to all girls at Mission High School."

Among the seniors, I come across a photo of a handsome young man with thick black-frame glasses and swoopy black hair parted on the side.

He's wearing a sports coat and a patterned necktie perfectly knotted. His name is Merced Solis.

Merced appears all over the yearbook—homecoming king, #85 on the football team (along with All-District honors), #24 on the basketball team, and MVP of the Grapefruit Basketball Tournament; he even has a blurb in The Who's Who of Mission High, which lists him as a three-year letterman in football, basketball, and track, along with such accolades as "Best Looking" his sophomore year and the Sweetheart of the Future Homemakers of America.

In 1971, it's clear Merced Solis was the BMOC of Mission High.

Back outside the library, I push through the punishing ninety-seven-degree heat, made worse by gusts that feel like the exhaust pipe of a laundry dryer blasting full force in my face. The landscape is parched, a pastiche of dull browns and greens, the spindly trunks of the ubiquitous mesquite trees stretching across the horizon. Stubby palm trees provide urban decor, their leathery fronds bright green on top and girded with graying heaps of old growth that hang like tired beards.

The Coahuiltecan people hunted and gathered here along the lower Rio Grande Valley for thousands of years, leading a subsistence lifestyle necessitated by the limited natural resources of this coastal sand plain overlain with scrub vegetation. Prickly pear cactus pads and mesquite bean pods provided food, and when those sources turned scarce, the Coahuiltecan found nourishment in spider eggs and deer dung. Europeans began arriving in the early 1700s, hardy souls willing to eke out a meager living ranching, and in 1861, Catholic French missionaries from the Oblates of Mary Immaculate order obtained 20.1 square miles of land in modern-day Mission and built Chapel La Lomita, parts of which still stand.

The spread of the railroad and innovations in irrigation spurred the founding of the city of Mission in 1908, named after the La Lomita settlement. It's only a thirty-minute drive from the Mexican border. The town's first census in 1910 counted twenty-eight residents, one of whom was Merced Solis's grandfather, Matias Cavazos. Matias helped design and lay the pipes that carried water from the Rio Grande through a network of irrigation canals, solving the conundrum of water access and ushering in an agricultural boom. Entrepreneur John Shary, fresh from the redwood lumber industry in California, arrived in 1912 and saw gold in the shape of a grape-fruit. He acquired forty-nine thousand acres of land he named Sharyland, which he subdivided into forty-acre groves to experiment with growing cit-rus. His sweet grapefruit variety became legendary, branding Mission as the citrus capital of Texas, a title reinforced each January with the city's hosting of the Texas Citrus Fiesta.

I duck into the Mission Historical Museum, located in a building named after Shary, and encounter Aida, a museum employee wearing a denim face mask and shielded by a sheet of plexiglass hanging from the ceiling. She eyes me with some reserve, hesitant and unsure, until I explain why I have a notebook out. Her face brightens and she begins telling me about all the staff and their various roles before encouraging me to look around.

I do a quick march through the city's history until I come to a room ded-icated to contemporary events. There on the wall hangs a framed poster of a shirtless Tito Santana, Merced's alter ego, his arms crossed in defiance, a brilliant mullet cascading down his shoulders. It's from January 2008, when he was the grand marshal for the Parade of Oranges. The town is proud of its prodigal son—the city council named June 27, 2009, "Tito San-tana Day" for one of his return visits.

A few minutes later, Merced's cousin José Mario Cavazos picks me up to show me all the places where they hung out as kids.

"Everyone calls me Kito," he says, extending his hand with a firm grip.

"What does it mean?" I ask.

"There's no translation. I had a cousin Luis and he just put names to everyone."

Kito is the little brother everyone should have. Although he's in his midsixties, his pep is obvious in his frequent high-pitched chuckles, crack-ing himself up and rolling through the day like a prizefighter bobbing and weaving. He's short and stocky, with a white T-shirt hanging over camou-flage shorts, an American flag baseball hat, and a gold chain with Jude the Apostle hanging from its vertex.

We drive down St. Marie Street past Lions Park, where Kito and Merced would play baseball as kids and ride their bikes home in the dark, chased by a menacing dog named Red. They lived that romanticized 1950s child-hood full of independent play, Merced and his three siblings and a hundred first cousins (Merced's mother, Juanita Cavazos, was the oldest of sixteen) turned loose on the streets of Mission to invent games, using rolled-up socks as dodgeballs, shirts vs. skins.

"My grandfather [Matias] owned half a block. There were houses all around and in the middle was this playground. As soon as we woke up, we didn't even need breakfast, everyone went to the middle to play," he says.

Kito looked up to his cousin Merced, who the family called Nuné or Cookie, awed by his athleticism and kindness.

"I've known that guy all my life. He's like a brother," he says.

We stop in front of the old homestead on the southeast side of town. Back alleys running behind modest homes lined with chain-link fences are strewn with trash and other litter. Merced and Kito's childhood homes have long been torn down, replaced with rows of low-slung tan-brick apartments. Kito points out the plot where Merced's house once stood, now a coarse lawn with a prickly pear cactus standing guard behind the fence. An old couch and tires litter a yard nearby. Although Mission has experienced a building and population boom in the past twenty to thirty years, swelling from 45,408 in 2000 to 77,058 in 2010 (when Merced was born in 1953, there were about eleven thousand people), the cost of living has remained low; homes in the fanciest part of town go for just over $200,000.

Being three years younger, Kito idolized Merced, spending as much time as he could at the Solis house.

"He was awesome. He was athletic, he had a good build. You know, he has these big hands. But he was rough and tough too," Kito says.

Those hands set Merced apart as an athlete, but it took him a while to get going. Money was tight in the two-bedroom Solis house. All four kids slept in one room, sometimes five with Kito always hanging around—Merced and his brother Robert shared a bed, with Kito squished between them. There was one bathroom for the entire Cavazos family complex, located apart from the rest of the houses, and the hot water often gave out. When the football coach at Mission High asked Merced to try out in eighth grade, seeing the kid's long rangy arms and trim build, Merced was too embarrassed to ask his mom if they could afford the equipment. That sense of scarcity stayed with him throughout his life; he may make mistakes, he may hit rough patches, but he vowed that he would never be poor.

In his sophomore year, Merced discovered that the school covered the cost of football equipment, and he blossomed into a star halfback and strong safety, plowing his way through defenses and using those large hands to palm passes thrown his way. Football became his dream and his ticket out of Mission. Kito drives us past the high school, adorned with a giant *M* and the eagle mascot. The new football field, built long after Merced was gone, is named Tom Landry Stadium after another Mission native, the Super Bowl–winning coach of the Dallas Cowboys. The Friday Night Lights are alive and well in Mission.

Kito shakes his head.

"Oh, man. Everywhere you go, there's different buildings. The old buildings are torn down. And they make new buildings," he says.

We head a little farther south toward the home where Merced moved when he was in seventh grade, on Citriana Avenue.

While Merced was making waves at Mission High, he wasn't immune to the larger forces of the times. When he showed interest in the white girls at school, he quickly learned the cost of being Latino even in a majority-Latinx town. After meeting a girl's family he would suddenly get the cold shoulder, being told, "I don't think we should see each other anymore." Some of the white guys at school derisively called him "Mexican." But Merced got his most stark lesson in identity when he and his family packed up each spring to travel north for work as migrant farm workers.

Merced's father, also named Merced, was a crew leader, and every year starting when Merced was six, the family drove to Illinois for asparagus season, followed by Wisconsin and Michigan (cherries and strawberries), and then Indiana (tomatoes). They picked and bagged produce in the fields from six in the morning to six in the evening alongside 150 others, living in aluminum sheds with an outhouse. Being three years younger, Kito was always desperate to join the Solis family on the road, packing a suitcase each season with hopes that *this would be the year*. Although it was hard work, for kids it was an adventure, a chance to see a whole different part of the country.

"For us, it wasn't really work," Kito says.

"We had never really gotten out of Mission. It was like a vacation."

But while traveling those interstates from field to field, Merced saw the country's ugly side. He calls it "the look," a stare or expression that made him feel every cell of his brown skin. Kito recalls a time it got more overt, when they stopped at a restaurant and were simply told, "You shouldn't be here."

Merced was a soft-spoken, gentle young man who did his best to conceal the volcano roiling underneath. Football provided an outlet, a chance to bash heads without getting in trouble. He never looked for a fight, but if triggered, the volcano would erupt. Kito recalls:

> He had this girlfriend, and they were walking through a club. His girl said, "Somebody pinched my ass." When Merced turned around the guys were already in their car, ready to leave. Merced went up to the guys and said, "Hey, one of you motherfuckers pinched my girlfriend's ass." One of the passengers said, "I did, what the fuck are you gonna do about it?" The guy tried to open the door, and Merced got his leg and dragged him out. He punched the guy so hard he knocked him out. And then Merced was like, "Now I have to help the guy cuz I thought I killed him!" He was trying to revive him.

"He had such big hands, huge hands," he adds with a giggle.

West Texas State University in Canyon, a veritable factory of pro wrestlers (eight WWE Hall of Famers played football there) offered Merced a full ride, and he excelled as a tight end, earning first team All-Missouri Valley Conference in his senior year. His quarterback was a guy named Tully Blanchard, whose father, Joe, promoted Southwest Championship Wrestling out of San Antonio. Tully knew his dad was looking for a new Hispanic babyface to play to the local crowds, and suggested to Merced that he give wrestling some thought. Merced, not a wrestling fan and still set on a pro football career, declined.

He attracted the attention of pro football scouts, earning a tryout with the Kansas City Chiefs in 1975. He impressed enough to start every game of that preseason, but a severely sprained Achilles tendon hobbled him, and he was cut just before the season began. After a year in the CFL, the allure of the money in wrestling was too great to resist. Joe Blanchard told him he could make $90,000 a year, and with his football hopes dimmed, Merced made the switch to his new career. The training was rough.

"You can't fake gravity," he wrote in his 2019 autobiography, *Don't Call Me Chico*.

Although Blanchard had given Merced his initiation into wrestling, Merced cut his teeth in the Florida territory, based out of Tampa, in 1977. In his very first match, wrestling under his real name, Merced took on veteran Crusher Verdu in Miami. While Merced had learned the basics of how to take a bump, his training included a hedge—just in case he wasn't long for the business, his mentors didn't completely expose Kayfabe (if a guy quit after only a couple matches, he could at least attest to his friends that wrestling was "real"). Merced knew that the matches were staged, but like every other Six Packer, he had some doubts about how it all worked, what parts might have been more real than others.

Making sure to protect the business, Verdu was especially *stiff*, laying in his shots, hitting Merced for real. When he executed a powerslam, he landed so hard on Merced that he knocked the wind out of him. Realizing this was a test, Merced didn't overreact and followed the plan for the match, which ended in a time-limit draw.

To provide more seasoning for the rookie, promoter Mike Graham sent Merced to a fellow lord in Georgia, Jim Barnett, where the booker Ole Anderson welcomed him with greetings of "Hey, wetback" or "Hey, beaner." They also gave him a makeover, changing his wrestling name to Richard Blood, the real name of Ricky "The Dragon" Steamboat, who had recently left the territory. Merced had the same babyface good looks, youth, and athleticism as Steamboat, and Barnett figured he could replace him with a wink to Steamboat's real identity. But it was a couple years later, in the WWF, when Merced really came into his own.

The WWF, catering to the diversity of New York City, was known for its ethnic gimmicks, often featuring Hispanic, Black, and Native American wrestlers as babyfaces. Vince McMahon Senior was looking for a new Latino act, and given Merced's Mexican heritage, asked him to come up with a catchier ring name than "Merced Solis." Having always liked the story of Antonio Lopez de Santa Anna in the fall of the Alamo, Merced adopted the name Tito Santana. While Merced may have been from Mission, Texas, Tito was from Toluca, Mexico, which quickly became bastardized to the fictional "Tocula" when ring announcer Howard Finkel kept botching it. While Merced Solis and Richard Blood were mid-carders, Tito Santana would become one of the WWF's star performers of the 1980s.

Tito remained forever grateful to Vince Senior for giving him that break. "I really liked Vince's honesty with me," he wrote in his autobiography.

"In fact, he became a bit of a mentor for me when I really needed it back then. Whenever I would contemplate moving to a new territory or sometimes a change with how I was doing business, I would call Vince for advice."

*   *   *

I DRIVE TOWARD THE MEXICO BORDER, SOUTH OF THE 2-WEST EXPRESSWAY. This side of Mission reflects the past and perhaps the near future—open space, once planted over with fruit trees and other crops, now lies fallow until a developer gets approval to add another housing complex with names like "Tanglewood" and promises of "Living Together with Nature." Somewhere in the distance, hidden from view, is the Rio Grande, the source of life for the whole region.

After parting ways with Kito, I can't help but think about the other reason that Merced wanted to get out of here. He briefly discussed it in his autobiography, and Kito touched on it, but it's something I feel the need to bring up when I see Merced later in New Jersey.

One of the sources for that inner volcano, that volatility that could erupt with the right trigger, was Merced's relationship with his father, or lack thereof. While his dad was ostensibly the family head, leading them across the country for seasonal farm work, his leadership ended there. Once the family returned to Mission at the end of the season, his dad would disappear into the bars and pool halls, carousing around town. He made promises he immediately broke, telling the family to get dressed to go out to dinner and then never showing up, sometimes not returning until the next morning. Whatever money they had earned was quickly spent, forcing them to pick up work in the fields around Mission.

Merced's mom, Juanita, on the other hand, was his rock. Everything he learned about personal responsibility, about hard work, about doing the right thing, came from her. He knew better than to expect as much from his dad, and yet when he came home from college one break to find his father gone, he was still devastated. They lost touch in 1973 and had no communication for years.

When Merced met his wife, Leah, in 1979 and they started to get serious, Merced added one more vow to his list—I'll never be poor again, and when I have kids, I will be a much better father than my dad ever was.

*　　*　　*

MICHAEL SOLIS OBVIOUSLY DOESN'T REMEMBER HIS OWN BIRTH. BUT HE'S
been told how his dad almost missed it, having been wrestling in Baltimore
in the midst of a grueling-but-typical road trip for the WWF.

Tito Santana was the number two babyface in the company, behind
only world champion Hulk Hogan, whose fame occupied another zip code.
While Hulk was the larger-than-life superhero whose matches were short
and predictable, Tito as the Intercontinental champion (isn't that just
another name for World?) represented what it meant to be a good *worker*
in the wrestling business—that is, a technically sound wrestler with a large
arsenal of moves whose ring work looked believable. Tito's punch was one
of the best in the business. Watch old tapes and you'll swear his right hand
connects with his opponents' skulls. It was a technique he perfected early
in his career by hanging a Styrofoam cup from the ceiling on a string and
punching until it barely moved when he grazed it.

Hulk drew the houses, but workers like Tito Santana, "Macho Man"
Randy Savage, and Bret "The Hitman" Hart tore them down with their
breathless pace, agility, and ability to make the audience believe, even for
just a moment.

By November 17, 1984, Tito was well on his way to his most lucrative year
ever, making $176,000. That evening, he challenged his archnemesis, Greg
"The Hammer" Valentine, in the Baltimore Civic Center for the Intercontinental title, which Valentine had taken from him in London, Ontario, on
September 24. In the Kayfabe era, long before the internet, only the fans
in attendance that night in London were aware that Tito had lost the belt
(remember, newspapers rarely covered wrestling). If you weren't there
that night, you wouldn't know that after the match, Valentine had gone
on a rampage, inflicting such damage to Tito's right knee that he had to
be stretchered out (in storyline). The following night, September 25, when
Tito showed up in Troy, New York, at the RPI Field House, he was magically
the Intercontinental champion again, defending it against Valentine. The
match in London, Ontario, taped for TV, didn't air until October 13, and so
effectively Tito was champion for another three weeks.

While Tito was selling for Valentine in Baltimore, his face a mask of pretend agony as Valentine walloped him, back in New Jersey his wife, Leah,

was in real pain. Merced's mother, Juanita, was visiting from Texas, knowing Leah would give birth any day now, and when he called the house after his match as was his routine, Juanita told him that Leah was in labor and on the way to the hospital. When she arrived, the doctor wasn't even there yet, taken aback by the sudden delivery. Leah screamed for an epidural, while Merced made the drive from Baltimore to Morristown, New Jersey, a distance of almost two hundred miles, faster than anyone had done before.

"You can't go in there!" the staff shouted when the six-foot-two, 235-pound superstar came charging through the hospital dressed in a ski jacket and hat.

"My wife's having a baby!" he yelled back, forcing his way into the delivery room. Just moments after Leah's mom, June, cut Michael's umbilical cord, Merced burst inside. The nurse handed the swaddled newborn to the swaddled father, still bundled up from the late-fall cold.

Merced got a few hours of sleep only to have to head to the airport later that day for another match against Greg Valentine, in Toronto.

But in that moment holding his son, Merced couldn't have been happier.

*   *   *

THE FIRST THING THAT COMES TO MICHAEL'S MIND WHEN HE'S ASKED ABOUT his father is the sense of constant motion, the coming and going. And yet despite being gone on the road all the time, Merced always felt close by.

Above all else, Merced was a family man. He rang up exorbitant long-distance telephone bills checking in from hotel rooms and pay phones on the road, even parenting his three boys through the phone when they were too much for stay-at-home mom Leah to handle.

"He made a concerted effort to come home when he could. If he was in a nearby area, in Boston or somewhere in New England, he would try to get back home, spend the night, even if he was going to be traveling out the next day," Michael tells me on Zoom from Nairobi, Kenya, where he is global director of partnerships and localization for the nonprofit Trocaire. He has a mane of wild curly hair, a handsome, angular face, and his dad's long build without the bulk.

He recalls his dad being caring and attentive, but strict.

"He was always this presence. He created a lot of discipline in us. I think we always had this admiration of him, but also a bit of fear," Michael says.

That fear loomed a bit larger for Michael, the middle child, than for his two brothers because he had a lot less in common with his dad than they did. Matt, the oldest, and Mark, the youngest, were jocks who loved wrestling. When Merced took all three of them to watch him wrestle, Matt and Mark were quickly absorbed in the matches, while Michael found himself checking the clock and wanting to hang out with Mom.

"My favorite wrestler was Miss Elizabeth," he says, referencing "Macho Man" Randy Savage's valet.

"My dad and I never really connected on sports, as much as I tried. I was a terrible athlete. One time [playing basketball] after halftime, when the ends switched, I shot the ball in the wrong basket and missed," he says with a grimace and laugh.

"My dad was just like, 'Who is this kid?'"

When Michael learned how to write, he began dotting all his i's with hearts, much to his dad's horror.

"I was always trying, like, 'What can I do to connect with him?'"

He was a talented artist who loved to sketch (princesses were his specialty), so he figured he'd try some portraits of his dad.

"I always found him really difficult to draw, because he's obviously very macho. But he had this long flowing hair. So I would try to capture the hair, but every time it would just look like a woman or something," he says.

Occasionally at school there were fairs where students could buy trinkets to bring home to their parents. Matt and Mark had brought home things that their dad immediately liked.

"When are you going to bring me something?" Merced asked Michael.

Determined, Michael went to the next fair and was immediately smitten with a giant eraser that said "big mistake." He knew his dad, the gentle giant, would love it, a big eraser for a big guy. He rushed home from school to give it to him.

Merced was expressionless. He didn't get it. Another swing and a miss.

When Michael announced at the dinner table that he was going out for marching band, his mom was delighted and supportive.

"That's social suicide," Merced said.

They fought and tangled, both prone to let their tempers get the best of them. And yet every time Michael had a concert or a jazz band performance, Merced was there.

"As painful as it probably was for him to sit through all that stuff, he always did. And he always said lovely things about it afterward," Michael says.

Michael knew he was different. Although his parents preferred to ignore the obvious, Michael struggled realizing he was gay in a world and in a family that wasn't the most progressive. Merced was a devout Catholic; Michael's two brothers were clearly straight.

Following his graduation from college, Michael joined his parents one evening for dinner with their neighbors Barbara and Sal across the street. The conversation turned to a lesbian couple in the neighborhood with whom Merced was very close. He and Sal began speculating on which woman in the couple "wore the pants" or was "the man."

Michael was furious.

"How can you talk like this? You can't just assume that for every same-sex relationship one person is going to be the man and the other person is going to be the woman! It's not like that! And there's no point in talking about them behind their backs. Just ask them if they have gender roles," he said.

The dinner party came to a screeching halt.

Back at the house, Michael marched upstairs to see his parents. He braced himself for the worst (would they kick me out of the house?) but couldn't wait any longer.

"I'm gay," he told them.

He recalls: "My dad just looked stone-faced, like, 'Oh my God, what is this thing I've created?' My mom was like, 'That's fine, that's fine, that's fine, it's fine.'

"The next day, my dad was like, 'I think everyone explores their sexuality. I saw it a lot with the wrestlers. Some of them were sleeping with each other, and you know, they went on to get married, to have kids, and they had normal lives. So, you know, you can still think about that as an option.'

"And I was like, 'I don't think it really works that way.'"

Merced went on to say that he would never tell his family back in Mission, who were too devout, too conservative, to handle such news.

It took some time, but gradually Merced processed reality and came to accept it. He loved his son dearly, always had, always would. During a visit back to Texas, when one of his nephews started insulting gay people, Merced snapped, his temper flaring.

"My son is gay, and you will not talk that way!" he yelled.

Michael says, "He started asking me, 'Are you seeing anyone?' I saw growth in him. He came really full circle, a very long way from challenging those beliefs that I think he inherited. He's been open and there for me. And a loving presence."

When they were kids, before Merced retired from wrestling full-time in 1993, he would take the three boys on the Road every time he was performing anywhere close to New Jersey. Out on the Road, in between the kids fighting over who got to ride shotgun and devouring Chicken McNuggets, Merced led spelling and Spanish lessons, mixing in life advice.

"My dad would be driving, and there were all these dynamics happening. That's where we learned about the birds and the bees. He would give us relationship advice. He told us about the girl who broke his heart growing up, because she was white and he was Mexican and the father didn't want her being with him," Michael says.

Even now, the few times Michael makes it back to the US to visit, they have their best conversations on the Road.

"That's kind of where we touch base, when we're often going to and from the airport."

Coming and going. The Road is where the Boys are most at home.

*   *   *

SOON I'LL HEAD TO SUBURBAN NEW JERSEY TO VISIT MERCED AT HIS HOME, but I've got some time to kill in Midtown Manhattan, home to Madison Square Garden.

I pass by all the iconic sites—Rockefeller Plaza, St. Patrick's Cathedral, Radio City Music Hall; an Applebee's wedged into the indomitable series of high-rises seems completely out of place. I walk along sidewalks four-deep with bodies, past blue-and-yellow umbrellas marking Sabrett hot dog stands, walking fast because slowing down feels like it would result in instant trampling. Billboards soar around me, their electronic screens switching from one outrageous distraction to another.

I duck into a coffee shop, pulling notepads and books out of my backpack. Merced was initially reluctant to talk to me when I reached him several weeks ago via text. Much like Tony Atlas, his first question was, "Is there any compensation for this?" And just like Tony, my explanation of why you don't pay your sources didn't seem to matter much.

"I put too much time in our business for me not to get compensation. Nothing against you, but that is how I feel. If it is worth my time, I will consider it," he explained.

We agreed to $750 for two hours of his time, with my usual provision that I will disclose the arrangement.

Given my limited time, I know there's only so much we can cover. Much of Tito Santana's career has already been documented in the public domain. The same way the captain of a professional sports team is not necessarily the best player, Santana was effectively the captain of the WWF roster during its 1980s boom period, even more so than Hulk Hogan. While Hogan was far and away the top star, becoming the industry's first $1 million man just as Vince McMahon had promised, Santana developed into a beacon of reliability, looked up to by the Boys and respected by the Office. When Vince rolled the dice with the original WrestleMania in 1985, he featured Tito in the opening match, knowing that he would set the pace for the rest of the event and draw in the audience. Other than Hulk, he is the only wrestler to compete in all nine of the first WrestleManias, and in his eleven years as a full-time competitor for the WWF, he missed all of two shows, one for the birth of one of his sons and the other because a hurricane canceled a flight in Buffalo.

He was a staple of my Saturday-morning wrestling diet, a perennial babyface who made everything look so fluid and natural in the ring. Although his biggest success came in the mid-1980s as Intercontinental champion, I remember him better as tag-team champion with Rick Martel. Named "Strike Force," Martel and Santana were high-flying, mullet-wearing pretty boys felled only by the dastardly tactics of a heel tag team named Demolition, Ax and Smash. Santana was the perfect target for heel color commentator and future Minnesota governor Jesse "The Body" Ventura, who insisted on calling him "Chico" and drew on every racist stereotype in the book to demean him, par for the course at the time. His catchphrase, well before guys like The Rock made careers out of catchphrases, was a simple "Arriba!" with a pump of his fist.

But above all else, Santana was a role model. In a business and an era when no one seemed to escape the jaws of the Road, from womanizing to drugs, Santana appeared to rise above, so much so that the Boys called it the "Tito thing"—having a long career and then going home to a loving, stable family when the lights finally dimmed.

"One of the most impressive things about the guy is that he took care of the home. Even while he was doing all this and enjoying the success, he kept a level head and he and his wife have raised three amazing young men," fellow wrestler Shawn Michaels said when inducting him into the WWE Hall of Fame in 2004.

Tony Atlas, one of the few people from wrestling Tito would consider a good friend, always admired his pal's ability to keep a level head. In his autobiography, Tony spent a chapter detailing all the sordid debauchery of the Boys' behavior, but wrote, "Tito was the only wrestler I knew who wouldn't hang out with the Boys. That's why Tito is still married today. He honored his wedding vows and didn't mess around with other women."

"No wrestler was a good father," Tony had told me. Perhaps Tito is the exception.

In his own autobiography, Tito also discussed the hookup culture on the Road, describing the "rats," the women who frequented the shows.

"I was happily married and did not partake in such carnal temptations. But there were many of the Boys who did! (Shame shame!)," he wrote.

Once again, however, the truth is inconvenient. Undoubtedly Tito was a good family man, often traveling alone on the Road and staying out of trouble. But in my research, I discover a recent news story that reveals his sainthood to be a bit of Kayfabe.

"Wrestler Jenni Santana on finding out Tito Santana is her father," reads the headline on 411mania.com.

Jennifer Haas, who lives in Las Vegas, discovered through DNA testing a couple years back that Tito is her biological father. She was born in December 1980, which puts her conception right around the time that Tito had met his wife Leah but well before they were married. When Haas took up wrestling in recent years, she started using the ring name Jenni Santana.

"We had a conversation and we had talked about getting to know each other and meeting up. And then, I don't really know what happened. It just kind of went silent. So, I'm not really sure. Eventually, hopefully, we'll get to know each other more," she was quoted as saying in the article.

*   *   *

THE SANTANA HOME IS TUCKED BEHIND TOWERING OAK AND MAPLE TREES IN A quiet, forested neighborhood of Ledgewood, New Jersey. From the street, you can catch glimpses of its dark brown wood paneling set on a hilly 2.8 acres. It was brand-new when Tito and Leah bought it in 1986, their dream house only thirty-six miles northwest of New York City, the perfect nest for raising their three boys.

Tito's still a little groggy from a quick trip to California, a flight on Friday and then back the next night, his first flight since the pandemic started. It was a personal appearance, signing autographs and taking selfies with fans dying to talk about Strike Force and his feud with Greg "The Hammer" Valentine.

He goes downstairs to the den, his place to think. When the kids were young, this was their playroom, where they could wrestle their friends and have sleepovers. Now it's the grandkids' turn. But on a quiet Monday morning in summer, it's Tito's gym and retreat.

He lies under the bench-press bar, tape wrapped around it where he places his hands, a white towel under his head. He stares at the white mineral fiber tiles on the ceiling. There's a twinge in his left knee where he tore his meniscus a few months back in a match, maybe his last match with the way it's feeling. He went to execute a simple move, planting his leg to deliver a hip toss, and the knee gave way. The doctors advised against surgery and gave him a cortisone shot to numb the pain.

He knocks out a couple of sets, then reaches up to massage his neck where two herniated discs remind him of the thousands of bumps he took into the turnbuckle, his head snapping back as his upper back hit the padding.

Compared to many of the Boys, he's in great shape. He's alive for one, which is no small thing. Sitting atop the plush gray couch on the other side of the den are seven "Wrestling Buddies," stuffed dolls of Hulk Hogan, Big Boss Man, Jake "The Snake" Roberts, Road Warrior Hawk, The Ultimate Warrior, "Million Dollar Man" Ted DiBiase, and "Macho Man" Randy Savage. Four of the seven stars of the late 1980s—Boss Man, Hawk, the Warrior, and Savage—are now dead.

Tito attributes his good health to his avoidance of steroids and the party drugs that ruined so many careers and lives. "The Tito thing" was real, taking care of his body, checking on the family, always aware that one day the ride would stop and he would have to get off.

The den holds the few mementos he's saved from his career; most of his old ring gear and memorabilia he's sold to collectors over the years. On the wall hang his plaques from both the WWE and the Professional Wrestling Halls of Fame, along with several portraits of him in wrestling attire. One of his favorites is a pencil sketch of him in his prime, titled "A Friend" and signed "Tony Atlas White '96." The rest of the decor is generic jock—a Guinness sign, several football jerseys (Steve Young, Joe Montana, Emmitt Smith). A stack of wrestling magazines from a fan sit on one table, while a recent Hungry Hungry Hippos kids' game has been left out on the coffee table in front of the couch.

He walks over to a rack of dumbbells to work other muscles, thinking about his appointment later today with this writer from California who's working on some book project. People never tire of hearing stories from the glory days when wrestling was on Saturday mornings and the world all seemed a little simpler. He grabs a bottle of water and walks back upstairs.

*   *   *

AS I PULL INTO THE DRIVEWAY I REALIZE I DON'T EVEN KNOW WHAT TO CALL him. Over text, I've been using Merced, but does he prefer Tito?

I park the Fusion next to a Ford Escape and a Mercedes hatchback and admire the stone walls and paths of the courtyard, a beautifully landscaped entrance.

The Intercontinental champion is waiting for me.

He walks out of the garage and extends his hand. It's massive, just like Kito said.

"Tito, nice to meet you," he says.

He's wearing a gray hoodie that reads "Philadelphia, PA," black sweatpants, and gray sneakers. He's tall, with broad shoulders, and his thick black-framed glasses are a callback to his senior yearbook photo. His hair is brown but white at the roots, cut short and a bit spiky, and thin enough that I can see the top of his head through the forest of follicles. He exudes calm and stability.

He walks me inside and we immediately bump into his wife, Leah, who I am shocked to discover also calls him Tito.

They met at a nearby bar called The Quarry in 1980, when Tito was in his first run in the WWF and was living in a one-bedroom apartment where he'd let fellow wrestlers Dominic DeNucci and Mikel Scicluna crash for fifteen dollars each per week. Leah was in town visiting her family, on vacation from her job at a travel agency in Hawaii. Tito was immediately smitten. They rang up huge phone bills over the next several months until he convinced her to move to Minneapolis with him, where he was wrestling for Verne Gagne's AWA. They've been together ever since.

In his WWE Hall of Fame induction speech, Tito put over Leah like a million dollars, his voice trembling with emotion: "When you get into wrestling, there's a lot of sacrifice that comes with it that a lot of fans don't know. And, God it's hard to be on the Road. To miss your kids' birthdays. Your wife's birthdays. You miss so much because you love this business. And what this business has done for me, what it's given to me and my family. I'd like to say that I could take credit for my kids," he began.

"And I owe it all to my wife."

Now it's Tito's turn. Lately, he's been on babysitting duty for his two-year-old and three-month-old grandkids.

"Now that I'm around my son's kids, I see them growing. I watch them taking their first steps and talking. I come home at three o'clock and take over with the little girl, and by five thirty I'm exhausted," he says, sitting across from me on the gray couch in the den.

"I realize my wife raised all three of my kids by herself, and you know she never complained. I appreciate her now more than I did even back then."

He speaks with the slightest of accents, evident in the way he emphasizes terminal syllables; in "babyface," the stress is on "face."

Most people when given a chance to interview Tito Santana will go to his prime, perhaps his experience wrestling in the opening match at the first WrestleMania or his legendary feud with Greg "The Hammer" Valentine. But I want to start at the end.

"When your career was winding down with the WWF and you were doing the Matador gimmick, and they didn't really have any merchandise going along with it, did that make you feel they weren't that invested?" I ask.

To give Tito a fresh start in 1991, Vince McMahon had reached into his box of gimmicks and grabbed El Matador. Tito was suddenly a bull-fighting champion from Tijuana who pulled his hair back into a ponytail and wore bright ankle-length green tights and pink boots. The commentators at least acknowledged that El Matador and Tito Santana were one and the same, but they asked him to reinvent himself.

"Yeah. I went to Tijuana to learn how to fight bulls, to get trained so I could have an understanding of the gimmick. And the guy who was there told me, 'Vince invested close to half a million dollars on this; they must have big plans for you,'" he replies. But when he called the merchandising department to see what line of El Matador products were in development, he was crushed.

"The lady said, 'We have a new El Matador figure.' And I said, 'Anything else?' And she said, 'No, not at the moment.' When I hung up, I told my wife, 'They don't have any plans for me.' It was pretty depressing. If you weren't involved in the main bouts, all you were doing is working like a dog and just barely making a living."

Just because Tito was on TV all the time and wrestling in front of thousands of people each night didn't mean he was rich. Wrestlers received no health or retirement benefits and weren't guaranteed anything beyond that night's match. Payoffs were notoriously unpredictable—Tito received $1,200 for a mid-card match in Philadelphia in 1984 against the Iron Sheik, but only $750 for a match against the Sheik a month earlier in the same building when it was the main event. Unless you were at the top of the card, WWF pay was modest. For example, according to documents I obtained as part of a lawsuit discovery file, Randy Colley, a typical mid-card wrestler who performed as "Moondog Rex," made just $61,758 in 1986.

One day in 1993, Tito looked around the locker room and realized there was no one left from when his run had begun a decade earlier. Even the great Hulk Hogan was gone, put out to pasture by steroid revelations and Vince's insistence on featuring a "New Generation" of superstars.

"Linda McMahon called us dinosaurs," Tito says.

"The next day I flew into Newark, and then drove to Connecticut [for the next show]. I walked into the building and asked Vince if I could speak with him. We went into his little office, and I said, 'I see you're not doing anything with El Matador. I think it's time for me to go.' And he said, 'I think you're right.' I gave my two-week notice."

Tito is one of the few people to leave the wrestling business on his terms, something that a control freak like Vince doesn't like.

"I used to always hear it from Hulk—Vince likes closure. He wants to be the one that closes the story. And with me he was never able to get that. I gave him my notice, and I never called him back needing work. He liked guys to go back. He liked to be needed. But I never even called him back to complain about my shitty residual checks that I got," he says with a laugh.

Tito was only forty, still in excellent shape. He could have gone to another promotion, maybe to WCW (World Championship Wrestling), but that wasn't the Tito thing. His family was waiting.

Still, he was terrified by the uncertainty, having no idea what lay ahead.

After giving his notice and taping his interviews, he got out his booking sheet and saw he was scheduled for a town in New York a hundred miles away.

"I broke down. I was scared. I didn't know what I was going to do. I'm pretty religious, and so I prayed to God, saying, 'All I ask is that you allow me to keep my family living the life that I got them used to.'"

He went home and told Leah, who, as always, didn't miss a beat, ever the loyal partner.

"We'll do whatever we have to do. I'll go back to work. We'll sell the house and move to Texas. Whatever it is, I'm with you," she told him.

"It was like the world came off my shoulders," Tito recalls.

He got to work, cycling through a series of false starts before finding his footing. There was a job selling Quorum alarms (potentially a pyramid scheme), an attempt to open a gym, and a brief stint helping to run a wrestling promotion with wrestler Sgt. Slaughter. Then he and Leah bought a hair salon, which she took to running.

But it was teaching that called him home. Unlike most wrestlers, he had a college degree to fall back on, having graduated with a bachelor's in physical education and a minor in Spanish. He picked up some shifts as a substitute gym teacher and plunged into the challenge of getting his teaching credential. For his entire career he had relied on his body; now it was time to scrape the rust from his brain.

His son Michael told me in our Zoom call: "I remember doing my homework on the family computer in the family room, and just looking over at him on the couch studying, and I just had a soft moment. He was really trying to do something that doesn't come naturally to him."

He eventually passed the exam. As soon as he saw Michael, who has a bachelor's from Princeton and two master's degrees, he was ecstatic: "Michael, I passed the test, I passed the test!" he said giddily.

He was hired full-time to teach elementary school physical education, then moved over to Eisenhower Middle School to teach Spanish, where he has worked for the past twenty-one years. Tito Santana doesn't exist within the walls of his classroom; it's Señor Solis.

He has now spent more time as an educator than he did as a full-time wrestler. These days his students need to check Wikipedia to realize who he is. And that's just fine with Merced. One more year and he'll hang up the chalk, right next to the boots and tights.

*   *   *

"TELL ME ABOUT YOUR RELATIONSHIP WITH YOUR DAD," I SAY, TAKING A SIP OF water and bracing myself for a glimpse of Tito's legendary temper.

He remains calm, his hands in his lap, lifting his heels off the ground over and over with some nervous energy.

"My dad was . . . " he begins, stopping to think carefully about what to say next.

"He ended up leaving my mom. My dad never did anything as a family with any of us. I didn't consider him a good dad. But he was still my hero," he says.

"What do you mean by that?" I ask.

"Well, I loved him. And I was looking for his love that I never really got."

Despite his dad's womanizing and poor handling of money, Merced's mom, Juanita, remained by his dad's side until he made the choice to leave for her.

Merced came back from college during his sophomore year to find that Juanita had moved in with one of his sisters while his dad was living with his mistress. Livid, Merced and his brother, Robert, put Juanita in the car and decided to stage an intervention.

They drove to their dad's favorite place for breakfast.

We told my mom to stay in the car. My brother was a big guy, like 265 pounds. And my dad was a 220-pound guy, big himself. So they're [dad and his mistress] in the booth. The woman says, "What did I do to you?"

My brother says, "What did you do to me? Your broke our family up and you ask what you did to me." So what I did, she was from Mexico, so I went to call the border patrol. They came and took her. We told my dad, "You have to choose. Are you going to pick her, or are you going to try to make a life with our mom?" And he said, "I'll go with you." So we drop my mom off at my grandmother's and she took a nap. While my mom was sleeping, she [the mistress] somehow came back and my father left with her again. When he left again, my mom decided, "That's it. I'm done fighting for him."

It would be another ten years before Merced would see his father. By that time he was Tito Santana, making good money and a star on TV. His dad would call him when he needed money, which became more and more frequent, and Merced reluctantly obliged. When he retired from full-time wrestling in 1993, he told his dad it would be the last time he could give him money because the tap was no longer flowing. A few years after that, he got a surprise call.

"My brother called me about one or two in the morning. He says, 'Dad just died in a car accident.' My dad was a player; he had another girlfriend in the car. And she died too. My brother said the funeral is going to be at whatever time. I said, 'Robert, I'm not going to the funeral. To be honest, I don't feel like I lost my dad. Tell me how much it's gonna cost on my end to bury him. But I'm not going to the funeral.' I didn't drop a tear."

Leah woke up while he was talking to Robert. Merced turned to her and said, "I don't feel like I lost my dad."

She looked at her husband tenderly.

"You lost your dad a long time ago," she replied.

*　　*　　*

FOR ALL THESE YEARS, MERCED HAS BEEN A GOOD DAD TO HIS THREE KIDS. And now, out of nowhere, there's a fourth. A daughter, Jenni.

Our two hours together are almost up, and so I pivot to the hardest question of all.

"I've done all this research on your life and career, and this thing came up recently with you, I guess, having a daughter," I stumble.

He reacts as if he had been expecting this question.

"Well, luckily it happened before I was married. When I was single, you know, living the life. When she [Jenni] was thirty-eight years old, I got a letter at school that I have a daughter," he says, his voice still flat.

Shortly before Thanksgiving, Jenni's mother had written Merced a letter. Jenni had recently found out that Merced was her father, and after giving it some hard thought, decided she wanted to meet him. Merced had no recollection of Jenni's mom—it had been a one-night stand.

"I said, what the fuck am I gonna do? I can't fucking do this to my family right before Thanksgiving and Christmas. I didn't know how to handle it. I was hoping it would go away. I didn't answer it."

His voice is gaining steam now, more animated and forceful, like all those babyface comebacks he made in the ring over the years. Not anger, but a mix of frustration and disappointment with himself.

"I don't know how many months later, I think it was during COVID, my wife gets a certified letter at the hair salon, which she has to sign. I'm here in the living room, sitting watching television, when my wife throws the letter. 'Oh, so you have a daughter.'"

Leah was crushed. Broken. Wrestling's family man, the one who was supposed to be above it all, *the Tito thing for Christ's sake*. Was it all a work?

Merced was completely lost. I can see the pain on his face right now. Nothing in the world means more to him than his family, and he could see how close he was to losing that. But he also understands his daughter's perspective. Jenni just wants to get to know her real father.

After speaking with him on the phone a few times, Jenni showed up at a wrestling convention a month ago and introduced herself to Merced. She introduced him to her daughter, Merced's granddaughter. He let her talk. But as much as he feels for her, it's too hard on the family for him to build a relationship with her right now. Maybe down the road.

Leah took it the hardest, doing the math, wondering when exactly this happened and if Merced had in fact cheated on her.

"She asked me, when I got COVID, and I don't think I was thinking straight. She said I told her that I screwed around a little bit. And she wants to know when the last time was that I screwed around. I can't remember the last time," he says.

His oldest and youngest sons, Matt and Mark, both married with kids, also took it hard. But Michael, the middle child, the one who drew princesses and failed at sports, who could never quite connect with his dad growing up, Michael was the one who understood the situation best, who was the most sympathetic.

"I had a few one-to-ones with him when I was home, and I think he really appreciated it. He was very open, he was very genuine, he was very honest," Michael told me.

"This big image of the wrestler who made it all work, he really embraced that. And this unearthed some mistakes that he made back on the Road. He wasn't always faithful. Maybe he was more like his dad than he thought.

"But I think, and I've never told him this, but he has so many qualities that he doesn't share with his dad. He's never used us. He's always just proven to be there for us."

Tito Santana is flawless, a perfect babyface who spreads virtue around the world, fighting evil.

Merced Solis is human. Like the rest of us.

*   *   *

MICHAEL WAS STRUGGLING DURING THE FIRST FEW WEEKS OF LAW SCHOOL. As great as the opportunity was, it wasn't what he wanted. He didn't actually want to be a lawyer. He wanted to work abroad, see the world, have experiences.

One night he had a dream.

He was driving through grassy fields, through big open country, when he came to an intersection. He felt paralyzed, unsure of where he was going, which way to turn.

All of a sudden, this Jeep came rolling up. It was his dad. The window rolled down and he said, "Michael, just come on in."

He woke up from the dream and said, "I've got to call my dad."

He dialed.

"I'm gonna drop out of law school. Can you pick me up?"

Merced dropped everything. Michael got in the car.

Back on the Road.

MATCH 7

SGT. SLAUGHTER VS. BOB REMUS

I N THE EARLY 1960S, THE TOY COMPANY HASBRO WAS LOOKING FOR AN answer to Mattel's Barbie doll.

Director of marketing and development Don Levine found it in G.I. Joe, an 11.5-inch plastic figure with a generic military look marketed to boys, inspired by the 1945 film *The Story of G.I. Joe.* After the doll first appeared in 1964, Hasbro quickly rebranded it as an "action figure" (*boys don't play with dolls!*), and within two years, its sales provided two-thirds of Hasbro's profits. Separate figures for the Army, Navy, Air Force, and Marines soon emerged (sadly, Coast Guard G.I. Joe was left out).

The Vietnam War cooled interest in the brand in the 1970s, but the Reagan Revolution of the early 1980s restored enthusiasm for the military.

Hasbro carpe'd the diem.

A new line of smaller, 3.75-inch figures debuted, complete with back stories and personas, à la comic book characters. A nemesis for the Joes was defined, the evil terrorist organization COBRA (what was up with cobras in the 1980s? There was the cobra scene in *Raiders of the Lost Ark*, Cobra Kai, the Stallone movie *Cobra* . . .), and the cartoon *G.I. Joe: A Real American Hero* became a smash hit (I challenge any child of the eighties to *not* remember the theme song). Rejuvenated, Hasbro officials began looking for a real-life sports hero to serve as an ambassador for the brand.

The timing was serendipitous for Bob Remus. The Minnesota native had hit it big in the World Wrestling Federation, helping to lead Vince McMahon's national expansion. After seven years of dues-paying in which he had cycled through four different identities ("Beautiful Bobby," "Bruiser Bob," "Super Destroyer Mark 2," and "The Executioner"), he finally hit his stride with "Sgt. Slaughter," a swagger stick–wielding drill instructor with a hat, pencil-thin mustache, and aviator sunglasses who called fans and opponents alike "pukes," "slime," and "maggots." He embodied the character perfectly: six foot five, almost three hundred pounds, with a chin that jutted so far out under his lip that it almost touched his nose. He splashed onto the WWF scene in 1980 and generated incredible heat in his battles with Pat Patterson and champion Bob Backlund. After Remus moved on to more success in the Mid-Atlantic promotion, Vince McMahon Senior brought him back in 1983 to reprise the heel role just as Vince Junior was beginning his quest for world domination.

Following the TV tapings held in Allentown, Pennsylvania, every three weeks, Vince Senior and Junior would sometimes hit a local bar. Some of the Boys would join them.

Bob got to talking with Vince Senior about his character.

"Mr. McMahon, if you think I'm a great villain, you ought to see me as a hero," he said.

Vince Senior looked confused.

"Sgt. Slaughter a hero? What are you talking about? You could never be a hero; you're a Marine drill instructor," he replied.

Bob laid out his idea. Although it had been a few years since the Iranian hostage crisis, the whole ordeal still stung in the American psyche. And the Iron Sheik had recently returned to the WWF and become champion.

"You know what, Mr. McMahon, we never got to punch the Ayatollah Khomeini right in the nose," Bob said, taking a sip of his drink.

"He got away with all that," he added.

"Why don't you let Sgt. Slaughter go after the Iron Sheik for America?" he concluded.

Vince Senior rolled it around in his mind like the quarters he always jingled in his hand.

"Yeah!" he exclaimed.

Just as suddenly he sank back down.

"Wait, no, no, no. You almost had me," he said.

"Sergeant," he began (he always called Bob "Sergeant"), "you could never be a hero."

Behind him, Vince Junior's ears perked up. He loved the idea, loved subverting expectations, loved the idea of turning the ultimate heel into the ultimate babyface. It was the kind of risky proposition that got his blood pumping.

And now *he* was in charge. None of the Boys knew that Junior had bought the company from his dad in 1982, nor that Senior was sick with cancer and likely wouldn't be around much longer. This was Vince Junior's show now.

Junior set up the angle at the next TV taping: after winning his match and performing his usual anti-American antics, the Iron Sheik crossed paths with Slaughter in the aisle while leaving the ring. The two exchanged words, with Slaughter having had enough of the Sheik's desecration of America. A few weeks later, Slaughter confronted the Sheik again, said he was tired of reading about Americans dying overseas while the Sheik ran his mouth, and then led the entire audience in reciting the Pledge of Allegiance. The small but delirious crowd in the Allentown Agricultural Hall erupted in chants of "U-S-A! U-S-A!"

Bob Remus was right. Almost overnight, Sgt. Slaughter was a hero.

Later in 1984, Bob's attorney was chatting with a friend who worked for Hasbro, and he mentioned the company's desire to have a celebrity athlete as a spokesman for G.I. Joe. The Sgt. Slaughter character came up, and soon afterward Bob had a chance to make his pitch at Hasbro's Pawtucket, Rhode Island, headquarters. He pulled up to the building in his camouflaged limo, a 1973 Cadillac with a past life as a hearse that he had painted in military camouflage to fit his character. Most people would park the car and head into the building for the meeting, but most people are not professional wrestlers.

Bob had his driver circle the block as slowly as possible, the Stars and Stripes lashed to both front fenders, drawing as much attention as possible from workers in the surrounding buildings. By the time they actually parked the limo, fans clogged the street cheering on Sgt. Slaughter.

It didn't take long for Bob to land the job, a five-year ambassador deal.

Sgt. Slaughter was the only real person to ever become a G.I. Joe character, with his own action figure and role on the cartoon. Except Sgt. Slaughter wasn't actually a real person—he too was a fictional character sprung from the imagination of Bob Remus.

*   *   *

I ACTUALLY DON'T REMEMBER SGT. SLAUGHTER DURING THAT 1984 RUN IN THE WWF. He left the company in December of that year, when I was only four years old. I do remember his return in 1990, because when he came back, both his character and the world were very different.

Iraq, not Iran, loomed front and center as America's nemesis. Saddam Hussein's invasion of Kuwait on August 2 spurred the US's military buildup called Operation Desert Shield, and tensions were sky-high. Never one to avoid controversy, Vince McMahon saw an opportunity—just as heel Sgt. Slaughter had subverted expectations to turn babyface in 1984, now he could turn heel again to capitalize on the conflict in the Middle East.

Sgt. Slaughter returned wearing his campaign cover and fatigues and carrying his swagger stick, except this time he railed against America turning soft and weak. He took it one step further, announcing himself as an ally and agent of Saddam Hussein and wearing an Iraqi military uniform to the ring. He enlisted "General Adnan" as his sidekick, a real-life Iraqi pro wrestler and childhood friend of Hussein named Adnan Alkaissy (they played chess and dominoes together as kids). It turned out Hussein was a huge wrestling fan, and with Adnan as Iraq's native son, in 1969 Hussein ordered him to organize a wrestling show at Al-Shaab stadium in downtown Baghdad. In his 2005 autobiography, *The Sheikh of Baghdad*, Adnan claims two hundred thousand people watched him wrestle at that event (undoubtedly Kayfabe, given that the stadium was built for sixty thousand). For several years, Adnan staged shows at Hussein's bidding; while he was rewarded handsomely, he didn't feel like he had much choice to refuse the dictator's wishes.

Adnan had since settled in the US, and given his uncanny resemblance to Hussein, it's no surprise that Vince saw him as the perfect accomplice for Slaughter. In the ultimate twist, after several months of defaming America and pledging allegiance to Saddam Hussein, Adnan and Slaughter added a third to their army: Colonel Mustafa, instantly recognizable to fans as a repackaged Iron Sheik. He wore the same mustache and curly-toed boots, but now he donned an Iraqi military uniform and a beret instead of a keffiyeh and an agal. There was no attempt to explain the transformation, no nod to his past identity or blood feud with Slaughter. It bothered Khos greatly to portray someone from Iraq, the country with which his native Iran had just concluded a long and especially brutal war (if you'll recall, it was my remark about Adnan being the other Middle Easterner to make it in pro wrestling that triggered Khos's death threat against me). But it was a steady paycheck, and if you wanted work, you bowed down to Vince, the emperor.

Nicknamed the "Triangle of Terror," Adnan, Mustafa, and Slaughter terrorized the WWF, building to the main event at WrestleMania VII, where Slaughter defended the WWF championship against Hulk Hogan. If you watch that match carefully, you can see a bit of the Kayfabe magic being exposed. About fifteen minutes in, Slaughter climbs to the top rope and jumps off, ramming his knee into a prostrate Hogan's lower back. Face down, Hogan sells the move while tucking his left hand under him so he can pull out a tiny razor blade taped to his right wrist without the audience seeing.

A moment later, Slaughter exits the ring to get a steel chair while Hogan moves over to the ropes. Rearing back, Slaughter hits Hogan on the head with the chair, and as the Hulkster crumples to the mat, he swipes the razor blade over his forehead with his right hand. He drops the blade on the canvas as Slaughter goes to cover him for the pin, which the referee alertly picks up and puts in his pocket, concealing the evidence just before beginning his count. Hogan kicks out, and in a classic example of Vince McMahon's TV magic, the next camera shot shows blood pouring down the right side of his face. To the fans in attendance, Slaughter has bloodied their hero's head with a chair.

"Hogan is split wide open!" exclaims commentator Bobby "The Brain" Heenan.

A couple minutes later, a crimson-masked Hogan escapes the camel clutch (now Slaughter's adopted finishing move), drops his leg across Slaughter's neck, pins him, and saves America (sound familiar?). As Hogan celebrates in the ring waving the American flag, the camera catches a smiling Donald Trump standing at ringside, clapping.

But it wasn't 1984 anymore. It was the 1990s, and American pop culture was becoming more sensitive to the blatant exploitation of geopolitics, especially as American lives were at stake. The heat on Slaughter was enormous, so intense that he sometimes wore a bulletproof vest under his wrestling gear. But it was "white heat," dangerous heat, in which the audience's disdain was not in good fun but legitimately dangerous. People felt disgusted with Slaughter's character and equally disgusted with Vince McMahon for creating that character during a time of war.

At the same time, the WWF's popularity, stratospheric since Hulk Hogan beat the Iron Sheik to become champion in 1984, had finally waned. In a 1991 survey of 114 sports conducted by the firm SMG, pro wrestling ranked dead last in popularity; in 1983 it had come in eighth. Fans had tired of the cartoonish presentation and of Hogan himself, who soon found himself in the crosshairs of a steroid scandal. The media wrote of Vince's poor taste in the Desert Storm angle, and with sluggish advance ticket sales and security concerns, Vince moved WrestleMania VII from the almost ten-thousand-seat Los Angeles Coliseum to the sixteen-thousand-seat Sports Arena. It would take another six years, and the emergence of "Stone Cold" Steve Austin and The Rock, before the WWF would experience its next surge.

Although the WWF brand was tarnished, Slaughter's heel turn drew a lot of attention. Part of what made his betrayal so effective, other than being a G.I. Joe action figure, was that he had also been a real-life Marine, serving in Vietnam for six years.

Or that's what he said, what he still says to this day.

But Bob Remus was no more of a veteran than Donald Trump or Joe Biden.

It was all a work.

*   *   *

SGT. SLAUGHTER DOESN'T WANT TO TALK TO ME, AND I'M NOT SURE WHY.

I write him a letter explaining the project just as I do with every other Six Packer, but hear nothing back. I get his agent, Paul, a realtor from Norwalk, Connecticut, on the phone, and I immediately dislike him based on his supercilious tone. His first question: "Is there a payday?" is followed by a laundry list of reasons for why Slaughter won't talk to me and a reminder that even the WWE had to pay him to participate in interviews for their documentaries.

"I'll run it by him, but I don't think he'll do it," he says.

I check out Slaughter's Twitter account and try to reach him there. Sarge is a prolific retweeter and abuser of emojis, but he is so active on the platform that I imagine there is no way he is actually running it, just as Tony Atlas and the Iron Sheik have other people tweet for them. I can't picture a seventy-three-year-old Sarge hunkered over an iPhone debating the finger-point versus bicep emoji.

I use every research technique in my arsenal to investigate his story and learn some basics—he is divorced, has two daughters, lives in Burlington, North Carolina, and grew up outside Minneapolis in a town called Eden Prairie. Through an Eden Prairie History Facebook group, I track down a couple of his high school classmates who initially engage with me but then go mute when I ask for a phone call. I find his daughter Kelly's YouTube show *Slaughter Daughter*, in which she and her dad recount stories from his wrestling days. I leave a comment saying that I'd love to get in touch with Sarge, but when I check back a few hours later, my comment has been mysteriously deleted. I enlist the help of wrestler Kevin Sullivan, one of the Boys from Slaughter's era who I met years ago at a WrestleMania.

"I talked to Sarge, and he said he's going to call you this weekend," Sullivan texts me.

I'm still waiting.

And most curiously, I reach one of his childhood best friends, Danny Raustadt, on the phone, who receives me warmly and says he recently returned from a high school reunion with Sarge. We make plans to speak in depth a few days later, and in the interim, I receive the following text:

"I spoke with Sarge. He prefers I not contribute."

The Sarge appears to have muzzled his troops.

Time to hit the road: Eden Prairie or bust.

*   *   *

IT LOOKS LIKE IT'S SNOWING IN EDEN PRAIRIE IN JUNE. BUT IT'S EIGHTY-FIVE degrees outside, and on closer inspection, those fluffy white flakes drifting down from bright blue skies are the seeds of cottonwood trees, broadcasting their progeny all over the prairie.

The Eden Prairie where Bob Remus grew up bears little resemblance to this carefully planned suburb of diffuse affluence. At his heart, Bob's a kid from the sticks. In 1960, when he was in junior high, the town had only two thousand residents despite having been in existence for more than a century. These were the boonies of Minneapolis, farm after farm along the Mississippi and Minneapolis River watersheds, an expanse so idyllic that East Coast writer Elizabeth Fries Ellet bestowed the name Eden Prairie during a mid-nineteenth-century visit.

Bob's dad, Rudy, was a roofer, and in their little house on the prairie, Bob and his family would congregate around the TV on Saturday nights to watch local wrestling.

In 1962, Eden Prairie graduated to township status, and a few years later families began selling off their land to be subdivided for massive office parks and housing developments. By the year 2000, the population had swelled to more than sixty thousand, and today 2,800 businesses call it home. In 2010 *Money* magazine named Eden Prairie the number one place to live in America.

This premeditated perfection means, however, that it lacks any historic charm. There is no old downtown, and city hall is a modern, low red-brick building that looks like an office park. I walk inside and downstairs to the History Center run by the Eden Prairie Historical Society to meet with their president, Kathie Case, who's agreed to play partner detective in my search for Remus's past.

Historical societies are a boon to researchers because they care deeply about the kinds of things that most others do not. They tend to have thorough knowledge about what happened to people from many decades back, and have accumulated records (old newspapers, high school yearbooks, old photos) that otherwise would have ended up in a landfill. The people who run them are typically saints willing to drop everything to help in some quixotic chase.

Kathie Case fits the bill perfectly. She and her husband, Ron, who is Eden Prairie's mayor, bought an old farmhouse (dating to 1874) that was slated for destruction back in 1988, then renovated and expanded it three years later. Kathie fills her weekends with Historical Society activities, from movie screenings to house tours.

"I pulled out some old high school newspapers," she says, handing me some manila folders with remarkably well-preserved copies of *The Eyrie*. She has a helpful spirit, and is wearing a frilly white top and jeans.

"I've been asking around to see who might have known Bob Remus," she adds. Kathie had never heard of Bob, but she also grew up in nearby Bloomington and would not have overlapped with him in her youth. It seems Bob has kept a low profile when it comes to linking his two identities: there is no public acknowledgment of Bob/Sgt. Slaughter in any of Eden Prairie's records or publications honoring its people.

I take a seat in a room full of historical artifacts, including articles of vintage clothing, an old piano, and a classroom from one of the early twentieth-century one-room schoolhouses with its rows of austere wooden desks.

Given that Bob was born in August 1948, I flip through the school newspapers from the 1960s until I get to the June 3, 1966, issue, which announces that eighty-seven students are slated to graduate in Bob's class. His chin is unmistakable in his senior yearbook photo, his head lowered and tilted a bit to the side, wearing a playful grin.

"Look at this," Kathie tells me, handing me an article with the headline "Wrestlers make up for past starvation."

"During the wrestling season the wrestlers starve, but afterward, watch out," the article begins. It goes on to recount a post-season banquet in which twenty wrestlers devoured eighty-five pounds of food and five gallons of liquid.

"'Big Bob' Remus was the last to finish, along with eating the most," it reads.

In addition to being on the wrestling team, Bob excelled at football.

According to the yearbook, the Eden Prairie football team had its best season to date in 1965, and Bob was named to the Minnesota Valley All-Conference team at the position of tackle. It makes sense with his imposing physique that he would have played on the offensive *and* defensive lines.

"You know what?" Kathie says. "You should talk to his football coach, Curt Connaughty."

"He's still alive?" I say in disbelief.

Kathie makes a few calls, and later that day I get Curt on the phone. He spends much of his time visiting his wife in the Friendship Village senior living facility in Bloomington. We make plans to meet there.

"It's just off the 494 going west," his ninety-one-year-old voice crackles through the phone.

"You go off of 169 . . . " he continues, insisting on giving me detailed directions even though I've stated multiple times that I can just put it in my phone.

"You got that? You sure?" he asks.

*   *   *

EVERY FRIDAY NIGHT DURING THE FALL, CURT CONNAUGHTY STILL GOES OUT to the Eden Prairie High School football field to run the game clock. He retired as assistant principal thirty-six years ago. He founded the football program sixty-five years ago, when Eden Prairie had all of thirteen kids in its graduating class. Those early years were rough on the gridiron.

"We were not very good," he says on a terrace at Friendship Village. We've staked out some outdoor space while the facility's staff organize a movie night inside.

"None of them knew anything about football. I don't think the parents ever played football. They were all farms here. Basketball and baseball were the two sports they thought about."

He's a spry ninety-one, with gray hair, wearing a teal sweater and green corduroy pants.

"When did you first meet Bob?" I ask.

"Well, I forget the year, but I had him in phys ed," he says. "He was a big kid, just such a nice guy, a polite young man. And a good football player."

Bob played football all three years of high school (it was three years back then), and by his senior year, the team was actually pretty good, finishing fourth in the Valley Conference. What Coach Connaughty remembers most about Bob is that he was too gentle, too nice.

The image of a snarling Sgt. Slaughter spitting into the camera and beating his opponent with a riding crop pops in my head, the perfect juxtaposition to the shy kid Curt remembers.

"He was always afraid he was going to hurt somebody. I'd say, 'Bob, all these people have pads on, they've got shoulder pads, they've got kneepads, they've got everything,'" he says.

"We'd do all kinds of things to get him irritated, get him mad."

It took some prodding to unleash the aggression that Bob had locked up inside. But when it came out, he dominated.

"He was up there with the better players we had," he says.

Curt always said if they could just get to a hundred kids in a graduating class, they could field a good football team. Eden Prairie is now one of the largest high schools in the state, and the school has won twelve state championships since 1996.

The wail of a dump truck in reverse drowns out our conversation for several seconds.

"They're doing a bunch of work. There was a whole wing there and they just tore it down last week," he says. More change, more growth, more expansion, and yet for Curt, a lot still stays the same in his community.

Bob has never forgotten where he came from, even if he seems to prefer to keep those roots hidden. When he comes into town, he makes a point to get in touch with his old classmates and mentors.

"Bob came back just a week or so ago, and I didn't get the message on my phone. They wanted me to come down to meet him at the Lions Tap, a hamburger place. The teachers weren't allowed to go there when I first started because they serve beer," he says.

While Curt never saw Sgt. Slaughter perform live, he caught glimpses on TV and has enormous respect for what his pupil accomplished.

"They do have some great moves. One guy jumping off the post and landing on the other guy. That's some acrobatic stuff," he says.

I wish Curt luck with the next football season and head back into the cottonwood seed storm toward my hotel. I have some sense for what a young Bob Remus was like, but still have no clue why he remains so elusive.

Back in my room I pull up some articles and interviews online and start to piece things together. Although most of Remus's life has been clearly documented, there is inconsistency in his account of what he did between graduating from Eden Prairie High in 1966 and his entry into pro wrestling in 1973. In newspaper articles from the 1980s, he refers to serving in the Marine Corps before wrestling. Even more recently, long after Vince McMahon vanquished Kayfabe and wrestlers began speaking out of character outside the ring, Remus continued to insist that he was a military veteran.

In a 2009 "shoot interview" (where wrestlers are supposed to speak out of character; these types of paid interviews became common in the 1990s after the WWF ended Kayfabe), Remus said he was in the Marine Corps for six years as a drill instructor before getting into wrestling, but later in the interview unwittingly contradicted himself, saying that when he moved to Vancouver at the start of his wrestling career, it was his first time leaving Minnesota. There are no Marine bases in the state.

More egregiously, on the *Jim and Sam Show* on Sirius radio in 2019, he went into detail about his alleged time in Vietnam.

"Two tours of Vietnam," he said when asked of his service.

"What did you do over there?" the host asked.

"I would say basically just infantry. Making sure all the grunts didn't go AWOL on us and keep them all in line."

"Were you messed up when you came back?"

"We didn't really talk about it much. We weren't acknowledged as being heroes or anything like that. So we never talked about it. There's some bad experiences and I did a lot of things I normally wouldn't have done unless I was ordered to do it," Remus replied.

The interview went on in even more detail, Remus making claims that simply were not true for Bob Remus. Perhaps he would say that that was Sgt. Slaughter talking. Even though the rest of the interview was conducted "out of character," Remus wore the Slaughter outfit the whole time, including the campaign cover, aviator sunglasses, and a camouflage sports jacket. He still looks the part, dyeing the pencil mustache and shaving what remains of his hair.

The interview sparked some outrage among veterans. The *Marine Corps Times* ran an article with the headline "The man behind pro wrestling legend Sgt. Slaughter tells stories of combat tours in Vietnam. But he never served." The article states that the WWE told their reporter that such appearances by Slaughter are meant to be in character. Remus himself declined to comment, all the more reason for me to seek him out for a response.

In a longer piece in *MEL Magazine*, investigative reporter David Bixenspan dug up a 1985 article from the *Baltimore Sun Magazine* in which Marine Captain Jay Farrar reported receiving fifty complaints in one year alone from veterans offended by Remus's alleged stolen valor. The authors of that piece asserted back then that Slaughter had never served. Seeking to put the issue to rest once and for all, reporter Steve Bryant filed a Freedom of

Information Act request and received confirmation on Department of Navy letterhead in early 2020: Remus was no veteran.

Even when these articles came out and were posted all over social media and the internet, Remus never admitted his military service was a work.

Why, after all these revelations and decades after Kayfabe died, does Remus not clear the air? Does one inhabit a character for so long that it becomes easier to continue living the illusion? Is he afraid of some public backlash? My instinct is that it looks worse to continue the charade in light of the facts, but the only way to find out is to ask those who know him.

And to ask the man himself.

*   *   *

PRO FOOTBALL PLAYERS ARE NOT KNOWN FOR THEIR INTELLECTUAL CURIOS-ity. Yet George Adzick, drafted by the Seattle Seahawks in 1977 out of the University of Minnesota, a 1973 graduate of Eden Prairie High School, and a friend of Bob Remus, is displaying just that in his backyard on Lake Riley.

"It's a very nutritious lake," he tells me as we grab seats overlooking a picturesque section of shore, the sun sinking on the horizon. He hands me a summer ale, the perfect complement to the evening.

"It's four hundred acres, about sixty feet deep. The Sioux Indians occupied this. There's a watershed that runs very aggressively to the Minnesota River just three hundred yards down the bluff," he says, motioning toward the lake.

"There's a mound down there, next to the creek. Sacred. And there's a mound up on the bluff," he says, referencing the middens the Sioux left behind, heaps of animal parts and other artifacts that can be used to reconstruct the customs of past societies.

"I tried to work through the Eden Prairie Historical Society to find an interpreter from the University of Minnesota, Native American studies. Shit, they won't even return my calls."

His build is also not what you expect from a football player. He's tall, about six feet three, and wiry, with gray-green eyes and short gray hair. He crosses one leg over the other, almost daintily, and drags on a cigarette. He has a thoughtful, pensive expression on his face.

George is a child of the late sixties, the cohort after Bob's that started growing their hair long and questioning authority. His brother, Mark, was more a contemporary of Bob's; Mark played quarterback at Eden Prairie and Bob blocked for him on the offensive line.

"Verne Gagne bought a farm on the west end of the lake," he says, motioning in that direction.

"He put the ring up in the barn, and that was where his [Bob's] training camp was."

The same camp where Khos got his start is where Remus's wrestling origin story began. A sportswriter friend of his named Bill Tweet was covering Gagne's camp in 1972, and one day invited Bob to tag along.

Bob watched the wrestlers go through their paces, hitting the ropes and exchanging holds. Little did he know that a dozen years later he would headline Madison Square Garden with the swarthy Iranian standing in Gagne's ring.

Gagne invited the audience to get in the ring to try it out. Bob, having wrestled in high school, volunteered. Gagne expected any of his students to have their way with a random person from the crowd, so he picked Ric Flair and asked him to lock up with Bob.

Bob held his own against Flair and another student, Ken Patera, prompting a frustrated Gagne to sic trainer Billy Robinson on him. Robinson, a stout, rugged Brit blind in one eye, was known for being sadistic with the trainees; he had intentionally injured Khos when he thought he was getting too cocky.

Now Robinson set to teaching Bob a lesson. When Bob was in a vulnerable position on all fours, Robinson dropped his shin on the back of his leg, a cheap shot. Bob fought back and impressed everyone while defending himself.

Afterward Gagne pulled him aside.

"Where'd you learn to fight like that?" he asked.

"I just felt like he was taking advantage of me, and I have to work for a living. I work for my dad," Bob replied.

"What's your name?"

"Bob Remus."

"Are you related to Rudy Remus?"

"Yeah, that's my dad."

"Hell, I know your dad. He put the roof on my house!"

Gagne invited him to join the next training camp, the following year.

The training camp, the house, and Verne Gagne are now all long gone.

"He had 125 acres and 2,500 feet of lake shore," George tells me as the sun dips a little lower.

"It got subdivided. It's all houses now, five-acre lots."

After training with Gagne, Bob bounced around the lords' territories looking for the right character. Landing on a gimmick in which fans want to invest emotionally is the hardest part for a young wrestler. Tito Santana and Tony Atlas had the advantage of being attractive, strong Latino and Black wrestlers, respectively, in an era when that sufficed for a star baby-face role. Bob was just a big white guy.

His first gimmick was in the Vancouver territory, where he wrestled as a pretty boy with colorful tights and frosted hair named "Beautiful Bobby."

Bob Remus may be many things, but sex symbol he is not.

It flopped spectacularly (fans interpreted him as a gay character rather than a ladies' man, the exact opposite of the impression he wanted to make). "Bruiser Bob," a generic tough guy, was next.

Around 1976, the same year Khos morphed into the Iron Sheik, Bob caught a movie on TV called *The D.I.* in which Jack Webb played a callous drill instructor. He was the perfect heel. Bob ran it by Verne Gagne, who dispatched him to the Central States territory in Kansas City, where he learned from one of the masters, veteran grappler Harley Race. For the next year, he refined the role of the evil drill instructor, evolving from "D.I." Bob Slaughter to Sgt. Slaughter.

He never looked back.

"He went through phases until he finally landed on Sgt. Slaughter. That was his calling. And he's still Sgt. Slaughter," George says.

"What was his personality like?" I ask George.

He smiles, eager to sing his friend's praises.

"A lovely man, a successful person and a person of heart. You'll never hear anything but a kind word about that man. I never saw him angry, and there's a lot to be said for that, particularly in his occupation," he says.

While Bob traveled the world on the wrestling circuit, George went off to college and the NFL, eventually settling in the New York City area. They fell out of touch until getting reacquainted when Bob hit it big in the WWF in the mid-1980s.

In 1984, Sgt. Slaughter was at his peak. He had signed the G.I. Joe deal with Hasbro, which incensed his boss, Vince McMahon, who was launching his own line of wrestler action figures with LJN as part of his merchandising blitz.

"I can't let you do that, Bob," Vince said.

Always a strong self-advocate, Bob pushed Vince for more transparency around merchandise royalties and pay. He could see the ambition in Vince's eyes and knew that Vince needed the wrestlers as much as they needed him.

He asked for a meeting with Vince at 81 Holly Hill Lane and brought his lawyer, immediately pissing off Vince, who hated lawyers.

"Vince, all I want is to be paid the same as the other guys. André [the Giant] and [Hulk] Hogan," he said.

"You are getting as much as they are," Vince replied.

"No, I'm not."

Vince paged his CFO, Bob McMullan.

"Bob, tell me what André made last weekend." He paused as McMullan responded.

"And Hogan?"

The numbers were very close.

"And how about the Sarge?" he asked.

He got his answer and slammed the phone down, embarrassed. It was nothing close to André and Hulk's pay.

In that moment Vince agreed to Bob's demands, but as seemed to happen so many times with Vince, what *he said* and what *he did* were two very different things.

In a follow-up meeting, Bob again brought his attorney to 81 Holly Hill Lane. Vince was flanked by his Office lieutenants.

"I discussed it with my people here, and here's what you're going to get," Vince said, puffing his chest out.

"Well, that's not what we agreed on," Bob's attorney replied.

Vince moved right up to Bob's attorney, pointing his finger inches away from his face.

"You attorneys don't belong here. You don't belong in our business," he growled.

But Bob's attorney was no lightweight. He grabbed Vince's finger and pushed him back on his tiptoes.

"Keep your fucking finger out of my face," he warned.

No one spoke to Vince like that.

"You don't own Sgt. Slaughter. Robert Remus owns Sgt. Slaughter!" the attorney said.

"I'll be damned, I own Sgt. Slaughter, I made Sgt. Slaughter!" Vince shouted back. He had begun trademarking all of his wrestlers' character names so that he could control their merchandising rights in perpetuity.

With that, the attorney reached for a paper in his briefcase and handed it to Vince.

It was from the United States Patent and Trademark Office. Way back in the Central States territory, Bob had had the forethought to trademark his character, anticipating just this situation.

The feud between Bob and Vince culminated when Bob didn't show up for an event and Vince fired him, leading to a million-dollar lawsuit for breach of contract. Bob countersued with a million-dollar suit of his own. Bob was finally angry. Coach Connaughty would have been proud.

Having finished our summer ales, there's one thing left for me to ask George. What did he make of Bob's military claims?

"Did Bob do any military time?" I ask.

"I don't think he was in the Marines. Yeah, I'm sure he wasn't," he says.

"His first occupation was as a barber," he adds.

A barber? I almost fall out of my seat.

Following his graduation from Eden Prairie High, Bob enrolled in vocational school in Minneapolis and learned to cut hair.

"He gave me one of my worst haircuts ever. It wasn't straight. I had a little cowlick and he kind of snipped it down and made it worse. We've had a good laugh over that," George says.

While Sgt. Slaughter was ducking grenades in Vietnam, Bob Remus was giving bad haircuts in the Glen Lake neighborhood of Minnetonka.

Bob has been telling the Vietnam story for so many years that even the Boys believe it. In his 2007 autobiography, *Hitman: My Real Life in the Cartoon World of Wrestling*, Bret Hart recounted a conversation with Bob back in 1984 when he detailed his experience in the military.

The dissembling goes so deep that one has to wonder if Bob, or the other Boys for that matter, can even separate myth from reality in their memory.

For example, following my meeting with George, I watch a shoot interview with Bob in which he said he won the tag-team championship with a wrestler named Pak Song in the Mid-South territory in 1976. But in fact he won that championship with Buck Robley and teamed with Song the following year in an entirely different territory (Georgia).

He had no reason to lie—he simply didn't remember the facts correctly.

In some cases, like many of the Boys, he never knew them to begin with.

On his daughter Kelly's *Slaughter Daughter* YouTube show, he recounted his real-life friendship with Khos, how they crossed paths in Kansas City and shared many pre-match meals together as they fine-tuned their new characters of Sgt. Slaughter and the Iron Sheik, respectively. Yet despite their closeness, even Bob didn't know what was a work and what was a shoot.

"His real name is Khosrow Vasari," he said, messing up Khos's last name.

"He was an Olympian, a silver or bronze medalist," he says. Again, Khos never competed in the Olympics. He won medals wrestling for the US in the AAU national championships.

But to Bob and Khos, does the truth even matter? At seventy-three years old, Bob is still living the life of Sgt. Slaughter. This April, Hasbro announced that they were coming out with a new Sgt. Slaughter action figure.

Yo, Joe!

Although Bob may not care, some of those who served our country apparently do, based on the recent news articles and past complaints to the Navy.

The question remains: Why continue to Kayfabe?

I'm heading to Bob's home base in Burlington, North Carolina, to find out.

*   *   *

LET'S BE CLEAR: I DON'T LIKE DOING THIS.

Those who recall my ambush of Carlton Fisk in *The Wax Pack* know that I am willing to go to some extreme lengths to meet my subjects. Showing up unannounced is generally not the most tactful or considerate way to approach things in life, but sometimes the circumstances call for extreme measures, provided you accept the consequences.

It's in pursuit of an answer that I approach Bob Remus's house on a scalding-hot day on the third of July, appropriate given that we're on the eve of Sgt. Slaughter's favorite day of the year.

A few turns before his street, I pass a small shopping plaza with three storefronts—a general store, a nail salon, and Special Touch Hair Salon. I wonder if Bob gets his hair cut there and offers some pointers.

Not wanting him to see my approach, I park the Fusion in the shade of a nearby cul-de-sac and walk toward his porch. The neighborhood feels new, with large lawns and yards and patches of forest interspersed with houses.

This is Bob's sanctuary. Golf is one of his favorite pastimes, and it doesn't get any better than having your house directly on a golf course (the fourteenth hole). In the basement he keeps plastic storage bin after bin of memorabilia from his wrestling days, a trove of material that other wrestlers would have long since tossed or sold. But Bob has never needed the money, having been deliberate and careful in planning his career. While most of the Boys rode in the fast lane, Bob kept a level head, knowing the carousel would stop spinning sooner than later and he would have to get off. He never got caught up in drug abuse and never did steroids, substances that contributed to so many wrestlers' premature deaths.

When the Iraqi sympathizer angle ran its course (eventually Sgt. Slaughter turned into a babyface again, of course, asking for his country back), Bob phased himself out of active wrestling. He was in his midforties with a bad back, and knew it was time to transition to something less punishing on his body.

Ironically, given the legal battles he had had with Vince McMahon, Bob became one of Vince's behind-the-scenes lieutenants in the late 1990s as a road agent, responsible for organizing the matches and finishes at live events. He may have respected what Vince had accomplished, but he always kept a skeptical eye toward his boss's methods of doing business. When asked on the *Stories with Brisco and Bradshaw* podcast what the difference was between Vince Senior and Vince Junior, he replied, "Well, one of them had a heart."

I realize that my surprise visit could go very badly. Notebook in hand, backpack strapped on, I walk toward his driveway. The house is long and ranch-style, painted yellow with black shutters. Stone pillars mark the entrance to the driveway, stamped with a plaque reading "The Roost." Two flags, Old Glory and the University of North Carolina, hover above a short brick stairway leading to the front porch.

In the backyard, out of view, is Bob's prize attraction, a fountain and koi pond on the patio. When the WWE came to interview him recently for a documentary on the Iron Sheik, he spent all day cleaning that area only to see rain force the taping indoors.

There are no cars parked in the driveway, and I can't see inside the garage.

I mount the front steps slowly, trying to see every windowpane at once to detect any movement. There's a sign tacked to the wall with a drawing of the fourteenth green in back that reads "The Remus Roost."

My heart pounds just like it did back in 2005 in Khos's living room when he threatened to kill me. Now his stage nemesis might finish the job.

I ring the doorbell and wait. Seconds feel like whole minutes. I stare down at my feet, half wanting someone to answer and half not.

I knock this time. How long do I wait? No sound, no signs of life.

With a mixture of relief and disappointment, I turn and walk back to the street. As I pass into the neighbor's section of road, a large dog bounds toward me, barking loudly. Its owner, a short, compact guy in his early fifties with a thin strip of facial hair and a visor, calls off the furry muscle and approaches me with some suspicion and a bottle of water.

"We don't get people just walking around here much," he says. "Can I ask what you're doing here?"

The word "wrestling" is barely out of my mouth when he breaks into a grin and hands me the water.

"There's your guy!" he says, pointing to Bob's house.

"Yeah, I was just there. Looks like nobody's home," I say.

"He's in and out; he keeps to himself. He's been there since the nineties maybe?"

He introduces himself as Andy. He's quickly gone from neighborhood watchman to excited wrestling fan.

I slake my thirst with a gulp of the cold water, sweat running down my sideburns.

"I used to watch all that. We got tickets one Thanksgiving or Christmas to Starrcade, when Greg Valentine wrestled Roddy Piper in the dog collar." I can tell he could go on for hours.

I thank him for the water and head back to my car.

I always knew when I started the journey that it was unlikely that all of the Six Packers would meet with me. Some people don't want to be found, and despite my best effort to force an encounter, I have to accept that I did everything I could and still came up short.

Maybe one day Bob will lower his guard and realize there's no shame in admitting that Sgt. Slaughter is a work even while the inspiration he generates is a shoot.

Although Bob is AWOL, I have to get back on the road to make my appointment with the next Six Packer, who lives in Atlanta but who I am scheduled to meet in Charlotte.

He's a man who spent much of his career under a mask. And he's one of the few people to ever take on Vince McMahon—and win.

MATCH 8

THE MASKED SUPERSTAR/ DEMOLITION AX VS. BILL EADIE

March 1990

Bill Eadie is really looking forward to seeing *The Hunt for Red October*.

It's date night with his wife, Sue, near their home in suburban Atlanta, a rare night off from the grueling road schedule of the WWF. Things are going gangbusters for Bill, now in his fourth year of playing "Ax," who along with "Smash" (portrayed by Barry Darsow) comprise one of the WWF's most popular tag teams, Demolition.

To the uninitiated, Demolition may look like extras from an S&M video—they stride to the ring wearing black masks, dressed in strappy black leather covered with silver studs. When they take their masks off, they reveal full KISS-style face paint in silvers and blacks and reds. Once the bell rings, they live up to their moniker, wrestling in a heavy, clubbing style full of punches and stomps.

While Smash is the more voluble and charismatic of the duo, leading promos with his threat to "kick your stinking teeth in," Ax is the quiet muscle. His black hair is slicked straight back, his eyes glacial blue, and when he speaks, it's in a deep, gravelly tone that is all business.

Demolition started out as heels managed by Mr. Fuji (real name: Harry Fujiwara), who plays the Japanese heel stereotype to the hilt. From time to time, as was the case with Jake "The Snake" Roberts and "Rowdy" Roddy Piper, a heel character was so irresistible, so damn cool, that despite the Office's intentions, the fans began cheering them. Case in point: Demolition. With their thumping metal entrance music (*here comes the Ax, and here comes the Smasher*), intimidating interviews, and shit-kicking costumes, the fans turned them into babyfaces.

Bill will make $221,149 from the WWF this year, and Demolition are readying themselves for a title shot at WrestleMania VI in a couple of weeks, where Bill will earn $13,249 for a match that lasts nine minutes and fifteen seconds. That's $23.87 *per second.*

Best of all, Bill can sit here at one of his favorite restaurants as one of the most popular wrestlers in the world and go completely unrecognized, a luxury few of his colleagues share. Ax's face paint does wonders to obscure his true identity. In fact, for most of his career, Bill has enjoyed anonymity. In his previous gimmick, the Masked Superstar (the character he portrayed the night the Iron Sheik won the WWF championship), he never took off his mask. Once on a trip to Disney World with the Boys, Bill grinned as he watched fans accost Ric Flair and Blackjack Mulligan while he blended right in. More people were following the wrestlers than were following Mickey Mouse.

Sue, like so many wrestlers' wives, has been the family glue, raising their two daughters, Julie and Heather, as Bill traveled the world. The couple met in Cambridge, Ohio, where Bill was coaching high school football and teaching history and psychology. One of the students at the school suggested he meet Sue, the student's aunt, who was fresh from managing a gym in Tacoma, Washington, and looking at nursing school. Bill and Sue were an instant match, and after a year of dating, Sue gave him the ultimatum: we're getting married or I'm leaving. When he got into wrestling a few years later, she patiently stood by while he transformed into Bolo Mongol (a crazed, mute Mongolian), then the Masked Superstar, the Super Machine, and now Demolition Ax. When he toiled making twenty-five or thirty dollars a night trying to break into the business, she held down the fort with her job as a nurse.

Having been on dozens of wrestling tours to Japan, Bill developed a love for shellfish. For tonight's pre-movie meal, he polishes off a plate of shrimp with lobster sauce. On the walk across the street to the movie theater, he starts wheezing a bit, but doesn't think much of it. They get to the theater early, grab their tickets, and settle in for the previews.

But something is off. The wheezing doesn't go away, and Bill's throat suddenly feels like it's engulfed in flames. His whole body tingles, burning up, and he stands and wobbles to the aisle of the mostly empty theater.

"Honey, I'm going to the bathroom," he says.

He gets to the exit, presses his hands against the cold steel door, and is overcome with a chill just as he feels himself falling through the exit, collapsing on top of a man coming in with a tub of popcorn.

Sue bolts up from her seat and rushes to Bill's side. He sees a swirl of colors like he's looking through a child's kaleidoscope, then in his mind begins going up a tunnel toward a light. He sees three file cabinets filling up with mud and oozing over all the papers inside while he frantically shuffles through them, trying to get organized. He's taking inventory of where things stand—the house is paid off, he has life insurance, the cars are paid for. And then it hits him: *I'd better call Vince and tell him I'm not going to make it to WrestleMania.*

In an out-of-body moment, he finds himself looking down at the room, seeing his wife and paramedics next to his body.

"I can't find a pulse," he hears one of the paramedics say.

He sees himself hooked up to a machine showing a flat line for his heartbeat. Then the machine beeps. A sign of life.

"I got blood pressure," one of them says.

"Twenty-five over fifteen."

Bill is back in his body, and feels himself being lifted on a gurney into the back of an ambulance. He pulls Sue in with him. Doctors later inform him that he had eaten so much shellfish in Japan over the years that a toxic amount of iodine had built up in his system, and the seafood dinner triggered an allergic reaction that had stopped his heart.

A couple weeks later, Bill is in the ring at WrestleMania VI, winning the tag-team championship of the world with his partner Smash.

Demolition is on top once again.

* * *

2022

OVER THE (MONONGAHELA) RIVER AND THROUGH THE WOODS IN SOUTH-
western Pennsylvania, I arrive in Brownsville, Bill Eadie's hometown.

I cross a high-rise bridge to enter a place that time forgot, tucked into
the cliffside, a fairyland of teal-steepled churches and gabled houses in
Gothic Revival, Queen Anne, and Federal styles. There's even a castle!

On Front Street, the main thoroughfare at the turn of the nineteenth
century, historic brick houses with stone foundations and slate roofs creep
all the way to the edge of the street, reflecting a time before sidewalks.
Incorporated in 1815, Brownsville hit its first peak when President Jeffer-
son commissioned the building of the first interstate, called the National
Road, which passed right through here. The road offered reasonable passage across the Appalachian Mountains for stagecoaches heading to the
western frontier. Brownsville already served as a major hub for boat traffic
given its location on the mighty Monongahela, a tributary connecting to
the Ohio River in Pittsburgh forty miles to the north.

I have my doubts, given that he spent most of his career under face paint
or a mask, that the people of Brownsville will even know who Bill Eadie is.
From what I've read, he isn't one to call attention to himself. But I want to
know what traces of Bill Eadie can still be found here.

I park by the river behind the restored Flatiron Building and look
across the street to a row of absolutely-not-restored buildings. The story
of Brownsville is the story of countless small towns across interior America, of boom and bust and the ruins left behind. A magnificent three-story
brownstone building with arched windows and pillars sits abandoned and
decaying, with the words "Second National Bank" on its facade.

Inside the Flatiron Building, now a historical museum and art gallery, a
time-defying woman named Norma Ryan greets me.

"Welcome to Brownsville!" says the ninety-year-old. Her gray, wavy hair
is still damp from her morning shower, and she's wearing black pants, a
green-and-blue-striped shirt, and sandals.

We stand in front of a large 3-D topographic map showing Brownsville and its surrounding areas. Orange and yellow dots mark the rugged

landscape like a smattering of Reese's Pieces, representing the locations of all the past coal mines, the former lifeblood of the entire region.

"In the late 1800s, they discovered coal in this area," Norma says, sweat beading up on her forehead. It's midmorning and the summer heat is already oppressive (when they restored this building, originally constructed in 1831, they did such an authentic job that they didn't include air conditioning).

"And that is when we hit our biggest boom. We had the richest coal here. It's what made Pittsburgh the steel capital of the world. Brownsville was the shopping mecca for all these coal mines in the surrounding area. So on Saturday nights in the era when I grew up, when you came downtown these sidewalks were so full of people that if you wanted to get from one building to another, you literally had to walk out into the street to get back to the sidewalk."

Brownsville peaked with about eight thousand people in 1940. If coal was its lifeblood, the Monongahela was its chief artery, used to ship coke (coal after having its impurities burned off) up to the steel mills in Pittsburgh. When steel production began declining, Brownsville's fortunes turned as well.

"In the midfifties, most young people went to college and left the area. There were no jobs here, so you weren't gonna stay," she says.

But Norma never gave up on her hometown. After she cut hair for forty-four years, the locals urged her to run for mayor, and she won the seat in 1989 to become the first (and still only) female mayor in the town's history.

"When I got to the city council, they weren't used to women on there," she tells me with a twinkle in her green eyes.

"Especially ones who talk a lot."

Since then Norma has been front and center of the Brownsville Area Revitalization Corporation, a nonprofit charged with the heavy lift of pumping life back into downtown.

"Do you know Bill Eadie?" I finally ask.

She does not, but the name sounds familiar enough to ring a few bells.

"One of the projects I'm working on is a reunion this weekend. There's like ninety people coming in, and I'm telling the history of the Jewish families in town," she says. She can't stay and chat, but invites me along for a driving tour she is giving to the reunion's coordinator, a fiftyish woman named MG who it turns out lives near me in California.

"It's a small town; maybe we'll bump into someone who knows Bill," she says, leading me to her cream-colored Kia Amanti with a scraped bumper, the backseat strewn with brochures.

We drive by the river on Water Street, Norma pointing out the locations of the old "patch houses" where mining families lived amid groves of box elders and birch.

We stop at a cemetery to scout locations for tomorrow's festivities. MG explains that the event is a family reunion for Ray Klein, an eighty-five-year-old restaurateur who runs several restaurants at Stanford University. Ray, who grew up here as part of one of the only Jewish families, met MG several years ago and hired her to coordinate his personal projects like this.

"We have one Jewish person still living here in town. He's special needs," Norma says.

A young maintenance worker fusses over a headstone in the Jewish section of the cemetery, with all of nine people buried there (none since 1932). Klein provided some of the funding to restore and maintain the gravesites, which will be a stop on the reunion tour tomorrow.

"Brad, you should come!" MG says, Norma nodding in agreement.

As random and fun as this adventure is, I let them know I have to be on my way tomorrow to meet with Bill himself.

On the way back down the hill, Norma points out several more landmarks, then points to someone walking along the street.

"See that kid over there? That's our last Jewish person," she says. He looks to be in his fifties or sixties, wearing jeans and a black tank top.

"He's a kid?" I ask incredulously.

"Well, when you're ninety, everyone's a kid," Norma says, cracking us all up.

Norma was right about bumping into someone around town. A few minutes later, we're in Fiddles, the fifties-style diner downtown (which opened in 1910, making me wonder what the theme was for the first forty years), no more than two minutes when she says, "Woody, come over here. I want you to meet somebody."

"Woody," otherwise known as Ed Nicholson, was a fire chief in town for forty-five years and a 1958 graduate of Brownsville High. He's wearing a black baseball hat that says "Army Veteran," and the many folds over his eyelids and creases under his eyes suggest a lifetime of hard work.

"Did you know Bill Eadie?" Norma asks after introducing me.

"Oh, sure," he says, the wattle of his neck moving up and down as he speaks.

"His parents were Albert and Babe, and his uncle Jim was the police chief," Woody says.

"We sure had some really good athletes back in those days," he adds.

Bill played high school football and excelled at track, he tells us.

We grab a seat on the wooden benches lining the window, the same benches that were here when Bill and his friends noshed on hot dogs and slurped milkshakes after school. Fiddles is a Brownsville institution full of quirks, such as the ATM that only dispenses ten-dollar bills and the menu's numbering system, ostensibly easier for the waitstaff (though the logic behind the system baffles me, with the breakfast specials ordered #1, 8, 29, 37, and 337, reminding me of my favorite TV show of all time, *Lost*).

Woody mentions the location of the Eadie home, but given that he was several years ahead of Bill in school, he doesn't know much about him personally. For that, I benefit from Norma's detective work—following our tour of the town, she provides me with the names and phone numbers of several of Bill's high school classmates, a few of whom I'm able to reach on the phone to fill in details.

"There was no better place to grow up than Brownsville," says Dottie Patton Melchiorre, Bill's classmate who now lives in eastern Pennsylvania.

In the early sixties, life for teenagers revolved around sock hop dances at the Sons of Italy on Friday nights and playing the jukebox at places like Browns Drugstore.

Dottie met Bill when they entered junior high together.

"He was shy, kind of quiet," Dottie recalls.

"I was in a few classes with him. And . . . " Her voice trails off, ending with a chuckle. "He wrote in my yearbook that 'it was a shame that we didn't get to know each other a lot better.'"

"So maybe he had a little crush?" I offer.

"I'm thinking maybe he did," she replies.

Dottie went on to become an elementary school teacher and principal, and decades later she found out Bill was wrestling as Demolition Ax and would be performing at an arena nearby. She went to the matches with a student who loved wrestling and his father, and made a sign that read, "Hi Bill, Dottie says hi."

"Did he see it?" I ask.

"I think he did, because we were pretty close to the ring, and I thought I saw a glimmer in his eye," she replies.

That was the last time she saw Bill.

I reach another classmate of Bill's, Mike Smith, who was his football teammate. "We played ball together, and he was sort of a quiet individual. He wasn't rowdy like some of us," Mike says.

Every person I speak with about a young Bill echoes this sentiment, that Bill was a quiet kid.

"He was laid-back and nice, real nice," Mike says.

Ironically, Mike and his buddies would get together on the beach and put on pro wrestling exhibitions, mimicking their local favorites like Bruno Sammartino, but Bill didn't participate. He wasn't into wrestling.

"Track was his best sport. He was only about 175 [pounds] but was about six two, six three. He always had a little crew cut like we all did back in them days. He was a good hurdler, high and low hurdles," Mike says.

The physicality and conditioning of sports appealed to Bill; Dottie remembers him and the other jocks going over to coach Jack Henck's house day after day to train in his garage. The hard work paid off—Bill earned a full ride to West Virginia University for track, where he was team captain his junior and senior years. He was also no slouch academically, making the dean's list. He led by example, talking only when he needed to. But when he opened his mouth, people listened, a quality that served him well years later in wrestling.

Only a few months after graduating from college in 1968, he had already accomplished his dream of becoming a physical education teacher, securing a position at East Liverpool High School in Ohio, where he also coached track. A year later he moved over to Cambridge High School, where he taught history and psychology, and where he met Sue.

During a visit home to Brownsville in 1972, Bill was hanging with his neighbor and buddy Gary Klingensmith when Gary's dad, Marion, a former pro boxer, invited them to the wrestling matches at the Pittsburgh Civic

Arena. Marion was serving as one of three Pennsylvania Athletic Commissioners regulating pro wrestling.

Marion got Gary and Bill backstage, and in the locker room, wrestler/promoter Geto Mongol (real name: Newton Tattrie) took one look at the strapping young men and asked if they had any interest in becoming pro wrestlers. Bill hadn't thought much of wrestling—he watched it on TV on Saturday afternoons with his grandma growing up, but had never really been a fan—but seeing the guys toss each other around the ring that night, he knew it was something he could learn to do. He knew he could always go back to teaching, but the window to be a wrestler only remained open for so long. Never wanting to have regrets in life, Bill decided to go for it.

For the next several months, Bill made the ninety-minute drive every weekend from Cambridge, Ohio, to Mars, Pennsylvania, north of Pittsburgh, to train with Geto. His first day was a lot like mine in New Jersey at the East Coast Professional Wrestling School—except not at all. While I took a couple of bumps, on Bill's first day he stood in the center of the ring, crossed his arms, and flipped over to take a hundred back bumps in a row. A wrestler named Lawrence Whistler (who would soon wrestle as Larry Zbyszko, and eventually end up in the WWE Hall of Fame) had started training recently under Geto, and joined Bill for these sessions. Although the training was grueling, Geto's facilities were nice, with insulation and paneling, a far cry from the dilapidated Minnesota barn where Khosrow Vaziri and Bob Remus trained.

Right from the start, Bill's true identity was concealed as he tried different masked gimmicks, such as "The Paramedic." His break came when Geto offered him the chance to replace his Mongol tag-team partner Bepo (the future Nikolai Volkoff). Much like Caryl Vaziri losing her handsome husband Khos to the shaved head and handlebar mustache of the Iron Sheik, Sue Eadie lost Bill to the costume of "Bolo Mongol," who sported a bald head with a sixteen-inch ponytail in back, a tuft of hair sticking straight out in front, and a Fu Manchu so thick it looked like a horse's tail on Bill's face.

Because his face was always hidden or obscured, Bill's friends back in Brownsville had no idea that he had become a wrestler. To a person, each of them tell me they were shocked to learn that their quiet, studious classmate had become a snarling villain.

"He was always one of the nicer guys," Pat Kostelnik Ward tells me over the phone.

"I just didn't picture him being a wrestler."

To learn the rest of the story, I need to get to Bill himself. Leaving Brownsville in my rearview mirror, I head to North Carolina to hear how Bill Eadie got the best of Vince McMahon.

Because wrestling always needed Bill more than Bill needed wrestling.

*   *   *

No matter what may be obscuring his face, Bill's eyes always give him away. Ice blue and piercing, shot through with feeling, they paradoxically suggest more warmth than cool. Look at old footage of Bill as Demolition Ax or as the Masked Superstar, and those eyes betray the face paint and mask.

The years have added some bulk to his face, and on this warm summer afternoon, he squints a bit, his cheeks reddening with the sun. His dark hair is sparser but still slicked straight back, gray at the temples. He's wearing a red-and-white-checkered button-down shirt and blue shorts with a silver wristwatch. He still has a barrel chest, a remnant of the thick, burly physique he flexed in the ring.

Although he has spent much of his career as a teacher, he has never stopped being a student. He studies me as I unpack my backpack on the back patio of his daughter's house, which is furnished with a large couch and a rattan chair with a red cushion. An overhang provides relief from the sun, and cicadas whir among the backyard trees like a loud sprinkler system. Bill, seated in the chair, is quiet and polite, his blue eyes tracking me as I take out my tape recorder, notebook, and folder of research material.

Even at seventy-five years old, he still works a couple days a week, tutoring at a juvenile detention center. All Bill wanted growing up in Brownsville was to be a teacher, and after his wrestling career wound down in 1991, it wasn't long before he was back in a classroom. Wrestling is just something that happened while he was making other plans.

"When you were done with the WWF, you worked for a company called Global Protection," I say, starting at the end and sitting across from him on the couch. We're at his daughter Heather's house in Mooresville, North Carolina, near Lake Norman, just north of Charlotte. He and Sue have come up from their home outside Atlanta to watch their grandson while

Heather's away in Florida on vacation; his other daughter, Julie, is housesitting for them. He's fresh from a dip in the backyard pool, which shimmers in view in front of us.

"Yeah, that was our security company, Nick Busick and myself," he replies.

Nick was a former police-officer-turned-wrestler with the gimmick "Big Bully" Busick in the WWF. Recognizing their obvious muscle and wrestling notoriety, a local strip club owner approached Bill and Nick about working security at his establishments, and before long the pair had a management company providing security for thirteen clubs, two hotels, and three restaurants.

Then tragedy struck. A patron at one of the clubs who got a little too handsy with the dancers came storming back in after having been kicked out and shot the club manager in the heart. He died five days later.

"After that happened, I was up most nights all night. I had twenty-six or thirty-six guys stationed all over the city. And I'm thinking, 'What if someone goes in there and shoots them?'" Bill tells me.

Having gone from one seedy underworld (wrestling) to another (strip clubs), Bill heeded the call to return to teaching.

"Heather had just graduated from high school and was going to college. I said, 'Honey, I think I'm gonna go back to teaching.' She says, 'Dad, high school is not like it was years ago,'" he says.

The days of the sock hop were long gone.

"So I went over to the local school, and I sat in the lobby, in the cafeteria," he continues. "And I mean, there were kids running around. They were going nuts. And this was in a good school!"

Regular high school was no longer the place for him. A juvenile detention center, however, proved to be the perfect fit. Although the kids were tough, the environment was tightly controlled.

"I had to go through five doors to get to my office. Classes were limited. They had officers there that never left," he says. For the past twenty-five years, he's worked with these at-risk kids, far longer than the lifespan of Demolition Ax, the Masked Superstar, or Bolo Mongol.

When I ask Bill what he likes about his work, he crosses his right ankle over his left knee and addresses me with the same thoughtfulness with which he imbued his methodical promos as the Masked Superstar.

"I like the fact that I can take kids that society's thrown away and teach them. They want to learn. Most of them act out because they've been told they're failures. And they're really not. They're not bad kids. Just, society never gave them a chance," he says.

That deliberation, that calm but forceful way of speaking, added realism to his interviews as a wrestler. How did he learn that?

"I got it from listening to my manager, Boris Malenko," he says.

Following his run as Bolo Mongol, Bill was repackaged overnight in the Mid-Atlantic territory by promoter George Scott (the same promoter who gave Tony Atlas his first push) as the Masked Superstar, a cerebral master of psychology who brutalized his opponents. Malenko, a master of promos, taught Bill how to stand apart. Bill, as usual, was a quick study.

"He said, 'Listen to the people around you. Listen to the other heels especially. If they're yelling and screaming, you talk. If they're talking, you raise your voice and make it emphatic. And don't say anything outlandish that people can see through.'"

In other words, be a man of your word. Don't promise to break every bone in your opponent's body, because that's unrealistic. Show some vulnerability, but then come in for the kill with a sadistic level of determination.

Sitting in this poolside cabana in 2022, Bill Eadie lapses right into a promo straight out of 1977 to prove his point.

"You and I are going to have a battle tonight," he says, locking his blue eyes on me.

I freeze, lowering my pencil.

"I'm willing to get hurt. Matter of fact, I know I'm gonna get hurt. But I know you're gonna get hurt too. And you're not gonna be the same man at the end of the night as you are sitting here bragging," he says in a clear tone, never raising his voice.

I'm ready to tap out before the match has even begun.

Following through on your word means everything to Bill.

His parents back in Brownsville instilled that lesson, part of a childhood every bit as loving and supportive as Tony Atlas and Tito Santana's childhoods were dysfunctional.

"I read somewhere that your dad always said your word is the most important thing you have," I say.

"They were both hard workers," Bill says of his parents.

"My grandfather was a hard worker. My uncle was a hard worker. So I saw it as natural."

He pauses, his words catching in his throat, and presses his fingers to his eyes.

"I get teared up when I think of them."

He holds the thought a beat longer, then regains his footing.

"It's true. The kids I'm teaching, I tell them, 'The last thing you have is your word. Don't lie to somebody on purpose. And so many people lie to you and mislead you,'" he says.

Which brings us to Vince McMahon.

In the late seventies and early eighties, Bill spent ten to fourteen weeks each year wrestling in Japan, where he made $90,000 to $110,000 per year. Vince McMahon Senior, frequently there due to his working relationship with the New Japan territory, admired Bill's work as the Masked Superstar and asked him to come to New York to work for the WWF. Bill balked, preferring the southern territories where he and his family had settled. But his close friend André the Giant, who would soon be full-time in the WWF, kept pestering him to give it a shot and join him. Bill finally relented in August 1983, just as Vince Junior was ramping up his national expansion.

Behind the scenes, Junior battled his father for authority, as he had been since buying him out more than a year prior. But no one knew. The Office did its best to keep the Boys in the dark.

"He was just basically an announcer," Eadie said of Vince Junior in a 1992 deposition for his civil lawsuit against Vince and the WWF (more on that soon), unaware of the Office politics.

While Junior was recruiting Hulk Hogan and priming Jim Troy for his raid of syndicated TV stations across the country, Senior continued to book the monthly cards at Madison Square Garden.

"He told me when I would be starting and basically how much I would be making and when I would be leaving. That's how he ran his territory," Bill testified in the lawsuit.

A handshake deal, just as it always had been. Bill knew Senior was a man of his word.

"I always called Vince McMahon's father Mr. McMahon. I call Vince [Junior], Vince," Eadie said.

Almost twenty years before Vince Junior would adopt the persona of Mr. McMahon in his battles with "Stone Cold" Steve Austin, his father had been the real Mr. McMahon.

Vince Senior immediately booked the Masked Superstar into a main event program with champion Bob Backlund, which meant Bill was quickly making good money. On the two Madison Square Garden cards before the one that inspired this book (October 17 and November 21, 1983), the Superstar wrestled Backlund. There were whispers that Hulk Hogan was coming into the territory, which means Bill knew he might be in line to be a transitional champion between Backlund and Hogan.

"Vince Senior told me they were bringing in Hogan, and he's going to be world champion. So he mentioned to me, 'I don't want to have you win the championship and one month later, lose it, because it's gonna hurt your reputation,'" Bill tells me, taking a swig of water.

That honor would go to the Iron Sheik a month later.

Bill knew he wouldn't be in the WWF long, per his agreement with Vince Senior. But it was obvious from the start that something was amiss. For one, the company kept making him sign contracts, or "booking agreements." Up to now, almost all promotions operated on handshakes and verbal promises, but now Vince Junior wanted everything in writing. A glimpse at one such agreement signed by Eadie and McMahon on January 6, 1984, is staggering for how unconscionable it appears to be. It's simple and unsophisticated, less than three pages long with sixteen enumerated clauses. What it amounted to was giving the WWF complete and exclusive control over the work of its wrestlers.

The wrestlers were to provide their own transportation, food, lodging, and wardrobe. The WWF had the exclusive right to book the talent when and where they saw fit. Clause 11 read, "Although Talent works for Promoter as a private contractor and can leave at will to work for another promoter, Talent agrees to grant Promoter first right of refusal for Talent's services."

Perhaps most egregious of all, the agreement gave the WWF complete control over the talent's "name, likeness, abilities, and personality," and "Talent grants to Promoter the unqualified right to use the Promotional Products indefinitely at Promoter's discretion and to waive any right Talent may have to any income received by Promoter at any time in connection to the sale or use of such Promotional Products."

In other words, Vince owned all potential merchandise rights with zero obligation to pay the talent a single cent.

The only guaranteed compensation consisted of fifty dollars per television taping. For regular bouts, the WWF simply committed to a fee that will "consist of a percentage of the gross gate receipts as determined in accordance with the status of the Talent's match and the prevailing practices of the wrestling community."

Bill, college-educated and a former teacher, felt he was being swindled. He pushed back—what were the actual percentages? He received a paycheck every two weeks, but there was no transparency around the formula and process used to determine payment. He would complain sometimes to Vince and sometimes would get extra pay as a result.

He resisted signing the boilerplate contracts, but was told he would be out of a job if he didn't.

Creatively, Vince Junior was never fond of the Masked Superstar gimmick. He didn't like masked characters in general, and perhaps more importantly, it wasn't something *he* had created. At a Madison Square Garden card, he found Bill in the hallway. This would be the first of many times Bill Eadie told Vince Junior "no," a word he wasn't used to hearing.

"I don't like the mask. We're going to take the mask off and go another route," Vince Junior told him.

"I don't think I work for you. I work for your dad," Bill replied.

"No, you work for me," Junior insisted.

"OK," Bill said, walking toward Vince Senior at the end of the hallway.

"Mr. McMahon, can I talk to you?" he asked.

"Sure, Bill."

"Your son wants me to take the mask off. Do I work for you, or for your son?"

"Hell, you work for me," Senior replied.

Bill marched back to Junior.

"Well, what did he say?" he asked.

"He said I worked for him," Bill replied.

Vince was livid.

"It was downhill from there," Bill tells me.

Mask or no mask, Bill quickly tired of the WWF and left in early 1984. André the Giant convinced him to return in mid-1986 as part of a short-term tag-team gimmick called The Machines, and while back in New York, Bill began brainstorming the Demolition character with fellow wrestler Randy Colley, who had previously performed as Moondog Rex. Their idea went through several iterations (including monkey and hockey masks) before settling on the black studded leather and face paint look that would soon become so iconic.

There was only one problem: as soon as Colley took off his mask to reveal his painted face as Demolition Smash, the fans instantly recognized him as the former Moondog. Since Bill had always performed under a mask, his true identity was safely unknown.

Colley was quickly switched out with Barry Darsow, who became the new Smash. Vince Junior, now firmly and obviously in command backstage (his father passed in 1984), was enamored with the look and feel of Demolition.

"Goddamn, we're going all the way with it. You're going to be able to retire on the money you make with this," he told Bill and Barry.

For a few years, Vince kept his word. Demolition was featured as a top tag team, winning the tag-team championship three times.

And then, Bill had the allergic reaction to shellfish that temporarily stopped his heart.

Despite that near-death experience, Bill was released from the hospital that night after the doctors diagnosed it as an allergy and stabilized him, and he went right back on the road. The ring doctors who performed routine checkups on the wrestlers prior to the matches began noticing an irregular heartbeat on Bill. He reported feeling fine, but the doctors said the irregularity was a cause for concern.

One such doctor, Dr. Jeffrey Unger, a consultant at the time for the WWF, recommended that Bill come to his clinic for a battery of tests.

Here's where things get very strange.

According to Bill's deposition, Dr. Unger admitted to Bill that he was not a specialist and therefore could not properly interpret the tests he performed. He suggested Bill see a heart specialist at Emory University, Dr. Paul Walter. But in the meantime, Dr. Unger allegedly called Vince to recommend that Bill no longer wrestle. Why he did this before Bill had been fully evaluated is unknown; Bill thinks that in some way it was to curry favor with Vince. All Bill knows for sure is from that point forward, Vince lost faith in Bill as a wrestler. He recruited a third member of Demolition, Crush (played by Brian Adams), to replace Bill while he underwent further testing with Dr. Walter.

"The doctor developed this test where they go up through your groin with an electrode to test your heart. It goes up in your groin, then into each chamber, and he gives you a charge. He said, 'You're gonna feel a little flutter.' Next chamber, a little flutter. He said, 'Hell, you're OK,'" Bill tells me.

Dr. Walter said Bill's heart was fine and that the irregular heartbeat had been triggered by the allergic reaction. He gave him a medication, "and within twenty minutes the heartbeat was regular.

"Vince called me at the hospital," Bill goes on. "He said, 'Bill, I don't want you to worry. You've got a job for life. I'm gonna take care of you.'"

A man's word is his bond, just as his father had taught him. When Bill got out, he and Vince had several discussions over the ensuing months about Bill transitioning into a role as a road agent with the Office. He was forty-three, starting to slow down physically, and looked forward to a job that was less punishing on his body.

On November 19, 1990, at a TV taping in Rochester, New York, Vince once again discussed the plan for Bill to become an agent after the upcoming pay-per-view event, the Survivor Series. What Bill didn't know was that Vince was likely making promises he knew he couldn't keep. The company's popularity had diminished and cuts were coming. The WWF couldn't afford to keep running the same number of live events.

Three days later in Hartford, Connecticut, Bill stepped into the ring to wrestle as Demolition Ax, having no idea it would be for the last time. He wasn't booked for any more matches, assuming he would soon begin his agent duties. But Vince came to him and said he was sorry, but he couldn't work it out. He might have more work come the spring or summer, but for now, he couldn't offer him more than two or three days a month.

So much for a job for life.

It was the apparent lying that bothered Bill the most. He would have understood if Vince couldn't afford to pay him—business was down, times were tough. But don't make promises you can't keep; don't promise someone a job for life and then snatch it away.

Following his departure from the WWF, Bill had feelers from their biggest rival, World Championship Wrestling (WCW), but they were afraid of Vince suing them if they brought him in as Demolition Ax (Vince owned the character of Demolition, despite Bill, Randy Colley, and Barry Darsow having invented, refined, and lived it for years). Bill picked up some work with a smaller independent group called the Global Wrestling Federation, but they quickly ran out of money. He was effectively forced into retirement.

Here's where the lawsuit comes in.

On August 6, 1991, he filed suit against Vince and the WWF in the US District Court for the District of Connecticut, claiming breach of an oral contract, unjust enrichment, fraudulent misrepresentation, fraudulent inducement to contract, and quantum meruit (a reasonable sum of money awarded for work performed when the amount due was not stated in a contract). Bill sought $2.5 million, money that he felt should have been paid to him based on his performance.

The file for this case takes up four large boxes held in the archives at the federal courthouse in Bridgeport, Connecticut. They have never been digitized, and so the only way to get them is to physically go to the courthouse and request them. Which I did.

As I sit here in Bill's daughter's backyard more than two hours into our conversation, he has no idea that I've seen those files (the discovery process unearthed a gold mine of internal WWF documents). In past interviews, Bill has been very clear that he is legally prohibited from discussing the case, but since I've already read all the files, I know what happened. Except for the very end.

Bill's calculation that the WWF owed him $2.5 million for unpaid fees during his stint as Demolition Ax wasn't actually focused on his direct payoffs for matches, but on all the ancillary revenue streams Vince created that enabled him to take over the wrestling business. Royalties on merchandise, for example. As earlier stated, Vince's boilerplate contracts actually didn't obligate him to pay the talent anything for the T-shirts, action figures, posters, and so on sold with their likenesses. According to those internal documents, a single Demolition Ax action figure sold 225,912 units in the first quarter of 1991 alone for a gross of $810,985.84. Of that, Bill received only $11,353.80, or 1.4 percent. Perhaps to Vince he was being generous, given he was under no contractual obligation to give Bill anything. But this could be seen as robbery.

This is where things get difficult, and where my status as definitely not-a-lawyer is relevant—the court of common sense is not the court of law. Vince's defense in the suit was that Bill signed a contract and Vince fulfilled the obligations of that contract, which, strictly speaking, is true. But it's not that simple, as my crash course in contract law teaches me. For one, Bill never signed a contract upon returning to the WWF in August 1986 and wrestled without one until the WWF corrected the apparent oversight and had him sign one in June 1990. The WWF excused this by citing the contract he had signed in January 1984 as the Masked Superstar, which said, "This agreement shall terminate on December 31, 1984, unless extended for an additional period of time at the sole discretion of Promoter."

In a letter/agreement from Vince to Bill dated June 20, 1990, on WWF letterhead, he asserted, "This letter will serve as an amendment to your contract. It acknowledges that effective September 1, 1987, you began wrestling for Titan Sports, Inc., d/b/a The World Wrestling Federation under the ring name and characterization of 'Ax'/'Demolition,' which name was created and developed by Titan, and that all rights granted to Titan under your contract dated January 6, 1984 as extended, including all terms and conditions therein, are and will remain in full force and effect."

In my mind there are a couple of things wrong with this letter—one, Bill began wrestling as Demolition Ax on January 5, 1987, not September 1; and two, Bill and Randy Colley created the name and characterization of Demolition, not Vince and the WWF. Of course, the fact that Bill signed this letter didn't make his case any easier.

In addition to the pittance Bill received on his merchandise, he pointed out that talent did not share in pay-per-view revenue. Here, Vince had made a killing. In the late eighties, he and his lieutenant Jim Troy stood on the vanguard of the pay-per-view business, a more lucrative revenue stream than closed-circuit because fans could watch big events like WrestleMania from the comfort of their home. Bill wrestled on several of these events, but here's the thing—he only received a cut from the live attendance, not from the money the WWF made from pay-per-view. According to the lawsuit, the WWF should have paid Bill $2,273,670 as a percentage of their gross pay-per-view revenue.

As you might expect, the WWF fought back hard as they always do. Vince, who once despised lawyers and was furious with Bob Remus for introducing one to his contract discussions, now had his ass saved by them (as he would time and again, to the present day). The WWF disputed the percentages Bill used to come up with the amount he was owed and did a yoga class's worth of backbends with various procedural challenges.

Many people have sued the WWF over the years, and many have been crushed by the McMahon legal machine. But not Bill. The suit dragged on for years, well past the point when most would have given up. The docket alone for the case is thirty-five pages long with 332 entries. At some point, it wasn't even about money anymore for Bill. It was about principle.

Toward the end of the docket, it says the case was settled on May 7, 2001, for an unspecified amount. As is customary, Bill was forbidden from discussing any details.

But I need to know. Not an exact amount, just whether or not it was an amount that made Bill happy, because that means he would have bested the almighty emperor.

I pack up my backpack and thank Bill for his time, extending my hand.

"I know you can't say how much. But were you happy with the settlement amount?" I ask.

He grins like he's about to head to Fiddles in Brownsville for a hot dog and milkshake.

"Oh, yes," he replies, those blue eyes twinkling.

*   *   *

THE BILL EADIE STORY DOESN'T END THERE, EVEN IF MY TIME WITH HIM DOES.

Following his eleven-year lawsuit with the WWF, Bill never appeared on their live programming again, which is a remarkable feat considering Vince's pattern of eventually bringing everyone back. It is likely no coincidence that Demolition is not in the WWE Hall of Fame despite that body having inducted much lesser talents, and despite Demolition being one of the top tag teams in the company's history.

The lawsuit just discussed also would not be the last time Bill met Vince in court. This time, the stakes were much, much higher, challenging the core model of the now-WWE itself.

On July 18, 2016, Bill and fifty-nine other former WWE superstars filed a lawsuit against Vince and the WWE in the US District Court for the District of Connecticut, charging sixteen counts ranging from misclassification of talent to fraud without specifying a dollar amount of damages.

The upshot of the charges was that the WWE allegedly illegally misclassified wrestlers as independent contractors, rather than considering them employees, depriving them of a bevy of legal protections, and that the company allegedly knowingly exposed the talent to brain injury without taking the proper safeguards for them to heal to avoid long-term damage. These were heavy, explosive charges that, if upheld, would completely change the wrestling industry.

The action followed on the heels of football players' suit of the NFL, which was settled in 2013 with eighteen thousand former players receiving $765 million. That case emerged from the public uproar that stemmed from Dr. Bennett Omalu's 2005 publication of a study of former Pittsburgh Steeler Mike Webster's brain (made famous in the 2015 Will Smith movie *Concussion*). The research suggested that Webster had suffered from chronic traumatic encephalopathy (CTE). Although Omalu initially claimed to have discovered and named the disease, CTE was simply a new name for an old condition: dementia pugilistica, or "punch-drunk syndrome," first described in boxers in 1928. The long-term risk of concussions and head injuries was amplified by former Harvard football player and pro wrestler Chris Nowinski, who retired from wrestling in 2003 after suffering a series of concussions.

The death of several high-profile ex-players and their subsequent CTE diagnoses led the general public to put pressure on the NFL, and as a result, the league knew they had to make the game safer for their players. Nowinski helped lead the charge, founding the Concussion Legacy Foundation and shining a spotlight on the NFL's practices. But young pro wrestlers were dropping dead at a much more alarming rate than football players. A *USA Today* study of wrestler deaths between 1997 and 2003 revealed a death rate seven times higher than the general population. Wrestlers were twenty times more likely to die before the age of forty-five than football players. This was an epidemic, but did anyone care?

Sadly, the answer was not enough. The spate of wrestler deaths was largely and perhaps correctly attributed to the abuse of anabolic steroids, which contributed to heart issues. But the brain injuries represented a less obvious and just as sinister threat to wrestler health. It was easy to dismiss the danger of head trauma in wrestling—*it's fake, how could it be that dangerous?* But as we've well established in these pages, even if staged, the physical pounding wrestlers take is very real. Many of the punches, kicks, and chair shots really do connect, and unless one lands just right, bumps on the mat can jar the brain as well. Concussions were common and undiagnosed in the Six Packers' era; "You just got your bell rung, you'll be OK," was a common refrain. But the repeated blows to the head for decades on end add up.

The lawsuit contained a litany of head-injury-related pathologies reported by the plaintiffs, signs of CTE (the disease can't be definitively diagnosed until after death). In his portion of the 219-page revised complaint, Bill said the following:

"After an injury the referee or trainer might throw you a cold towel. You were expected to carry on with injuries, perform every day. You had to be ready to move on to the next city. The office did not give a damn if you were hurt unless it was going to impact the actual show." Among his current symptoms he listed recurring headaches, dizziness, and loss of memory.

The complaint was about more than money—it was a call for reform of the entire industry. In addition to health insurance and disability payments to cover their current ailments, the plaintiffs asked that moving forward, all wrestlers be classified as employees by WWE rather than as independent contractors.

It is stunning that the WWE continues to consider wrestlers independent contractors when they have exclusive control over their appearances and run them on a schedule that is essentially full-time (of course this was even worse in Bill's era). I'm reminded of my interview with former CFO Bob McMullan, who told me Vince and Linda McMahon could never have afforded to expand the WWF the way they did if the wrestlers were classified as employees. The company would have had to pay into Social Security, Medicare, disability, and unemployment insurance, and the Boys would have had all kinds of protections under OSHA, the Family Medical and Leave Act, and the National Labor Relations Act, including the right to unionize.

According to the IRS's website, "You are not an independent contractor if you perform services that can be controlled by an employer (what will be done and how it will be done)." The WWE's claim *not* to control the services of its wrestlers requires truly acrobatic logic.

So if this seems so obvious, why is the WWE still getting away with it, and why was the lawsuit that Bill participated in thrown out by a judge before it even got to the discovery phase?

On the former, it appears once again that wrestling's reputation as silliness keeps it from being taken seriously by those who could effect change. There is a world in which fans could delight in the spectacle's camp *and* know that its practitioners are kept (relatively) safe, but that would require the same level of outrage the public levied at the NFL.

On the latter, there's only one way to find out: ask their lawyer.

*   *   *

KONSTANTINE KYROS ISN'T EXPECTING A VISITOR TODAY, AND I'M NOT expecting a two-hour crash course on tort law while standing in his doorway.

I'm back in New England for a quick stop at my childhood home in Rhode Island, and after realizing that Konstantine's office is in Massachusetts, decide to make the short drive. My phone calls to Konstantine have gone unreturned, but I have an address for his business in the town of Hingham, a coastal hamlet south of Boston with an estimated median income over $200,000. Given the nature, scope, and size of the lawsuit, when I put the address into my phone's GPS, I expect to be led to a sleek, downtown law firm with a fancy lobby.

This can't be right, I say to myself as the GPS brings me to a side street well away from the town center.

You are arriving at your destination.

I'm at a house.

Konstantine's house.

It's a large, two-story home painted yellow with a pillared entryway, a gravel driveway, and a stand-alone three-door barn or garage.

I ring the doorbell, and a moment later a lanky man with gray floppy hair and a trimmed beard answers.

"Hi, Konstantine? I'm Brad Balukjian, I'm a writer working on a book about former wrestlers. I tried calling you but didn't hear back, and was in the area so thought I would just try to drop by," I explain.

He seems mildly shocked and maybe even a bit impressed by my intrusion, but not enough to invite me inside. He agrees to answer some questions, although he prefers I not tape-record him (no one is more skittish about being recorded than a lawyer).

For the next couple hours, I get a lot of practice learning how best to shift weight from one foot to the other while standing in place. Konstantine has a lot to say, almost as if he was waiting for someone to show up on his doorstep so he could unload his frustration about the case against the WWE.

He began his career hanging out his shingle as a solo practitioner, often working personal injury cases. He got involved with the NFL lawsuit, specializing in hunting down players from the league's early years and ended up representing 185 former players.

"How did you get involved with the wrestlers?" I ask.

"I thought, 'Why not go after the WWE? Those people seem like they're in bad shape,'" he replies with traces of a Boston accent.

He put together a simple website asking any wrestlers suffering from a ring-related head injury to get in touch, and got a call from a former WWE talent named Billy Jack Haynes out in Oregon. Billy Jack got the ball rolling, and before he knew it Konstantine was neck-deep in the network of hobbled ex-wrestlers. His client roster swelled (all on contingency, meaning Konstantine only got paid should they prevail in court), as did his list of potential claims. He ended up with seven lawsuits filed in a variety of jurisdictions, including the suit that Bill Eadie participated in. The court wasn't pleased with this divide-and-conquer strategy, and the cases ended up consolidated in federal court in Connecticut.

Eadie et al.'s case was dismissed by Judge Vanessa Bryant on September 17, 2018, before the discovery process even began. According to Konstantine, she was so disgusted with his behavior during the suit that she awarded sanctions, demanding that he pay the WWE's legal fees.

"There was no merit evaluation in this case. And the judge's account of me was completely inaccurate," Konstantine tells me.

I had read Judge Bryant's justification for dismissal and sanctions and now listen to Konstantine rebut her points. I'm no legal scholar; I don't know which side to believe. What is unambiguously true, however, and which Konstantine admits to, is that the initial complaint included egregious typos due to a sloppy cut-and-paste job from the NFL lawsuit (text referring to the "NFL" instead of the "WWE," for example). It was not a good look. It's also clear that this lawsuit was David vs. Goliath. Although he had initial co-counsel, the case generally pitted a plucky solo practitioner against the veteran legal army of K&L Gates and their bulldog Jerry McDevitt (the same attorney who kept Vince from going to prison for alleged conspiracy to distribute steroids in the 1994 case *United States v. McMahon*). From the jump, McDevitt hammered Konstantine, putting the focus on his alleged missteps rather than the merits of the case.

Bryant's decision to dismiss seemed to rest on two primary points: that Konstantine had not done an effective job of factually linking the specific charges with the WWE's behavior and that the statute of limitations had expired on the charges. Konstantine asserts that those statutes could be tolled. Another argument for the defense was that when many of the plaintiffs were active in wrestling, an entire network of territories existed, not just the WWF, and they performed (and got hurt) while working for many of them.

The Second Court of Appeals upheld the dismissal in 2020, and Konstantine's final attempt, an appeal to the Supreme Court, fizzled in 2021 when they declined to review the case. Konstantine dedicated years of his career to a case for which he did not earn a penny, and for which he had to raid one of his retirement accounts to pay $312,000 in WWE attorney's fees. Even now he feels the WWE is trying to milk an additional $75,000 out of him.

Despite the failure, Konstantine is proud of the things he did accomplish.

"It's become very apparent that there was this group of people that were tragically intertwined and didn't have a support structure," he says of his clients.

"They became alienated. A lot them didn't have a lot of family support. I think I related to that. I'm a bit of a loner. I come from a small family. No one gave a shit about us. I was guilty of getting too close [to my clients]. I got some of them on disability and I'd help them with more mundane things," he says.

To their credit, the WWE has made strides to improve wrestler health and safety. They banned high-risk moves like piledrivers, blading, and chair shots to the head, and in 2006 introduced a Talent Wellness Program.

Their touring schedule is also not nearly as grueling as it was in Bill Eadie's day, with around 230 live events per year instead of 900. As part of the Wellness Program, WWE has also implemented the ImPACT Concussion Management Program, which ensures that wrestlers do not return to action before they've passed a concussion management test and been cleared by a physician.

While Vince McMahon has not spoken publicly on this issue, an earlier iteration of Vince, a younger Vince, a pre-billionaire Vince, at least acknowledged some understanding of his responsibility for the welfare of his combatants. Buried on page 4C of the July 22, 1986, edition of *The Durham Sun*, a headline read, "Wrestling Mogul Knows the Ropes." Journalist Arthur O. Murray wrote, "McMahon also draws on Hollywood to answer criticism that promoters exploit wrestlers by not providing pension or insurance plans."

"There is no legal responsibility, but there certainly is a moral one," McMahon said.

That responsibility seems to have been forgotten over the years.

Of the sixty plaintiffs on the Bill Eadie case, eight of them have already died since the case was filed in 2016, including King Kong Bundy, "Mr. Wonderful" Paul Orndorff, and Road Warrior Animal. Although not all his clients submitted to have their brains studied should they die, six of his clients have been diagnosed with CTE postmortem, including Mr. Fuji and Jimmy "Superfly" Snuka. Which brings us back to this—why aren't those at the forefront of CTE research demanding an examination of dead wrestlers' brains?

When client Blackjack Mulligan was nearing death and desperately wanted to donate his brain, Konstantine contacted Chris Nowinski's group at the Concussion Legacy Foundation.

"I called Chris Nowinski and said I represented all these wrestlers. We're trying to coordinate studies and I'm in a position to help if any of my clients wanted to donate or pledged to donate should they die. I asked one of his staffers, 'How do we coordinate?' It was very obvious to me that there was something wrong because they didn't really seem to care," Konstantine says in a video on his website.

"Nowinski himself and his group are all financed by the WWE," he says.

Indeed, in 2016 the *Boston Globe* reported that since 2013 the WWE had agreed to donate $2.7 million to Nowinski's foundation. And yet during the time of the article, as various ex-wrestlers dropped dead, Nowinski's foundation did not study any of their brains. The CTE that Konstantine has found in his former clients was diagnosed through his collaboration with Dr. Bennet Omalu. Bennet's work gives Konstantine hope.

"If Bennet decides to publish a paper on this, some good will come out of this," Konstantine tells me.

I tried reaching out to Nowinski myself, writing to him on Twitter.

"I want to congratulate you on all the work you have done to raise awareness around the dangers of CTE, and would like to speak with you about your thoughts about CTE and professional wrestling. Could we please set up a time to talk?" I wrote.

"Thanks for the kind words, Brad, but I don't have the time right now," came Nowinski's reply.

I thank Konstantine for allowing me to ambush him and I get back on the Road. To reach the next Six Packer, however, I'll need to get on a plane. And shortly after that, Hulk Hogan and the Iron Sheik await to round out our journey.

I believe that wrestlers will eventually get their day in court. Perhaps Konstantine wasn't the right lawyer or didn't have the right combination of clients, or perhaps his strategy of multiple lawsuits wasn't the best approach. I believe wrestlers should be classified as employees, not independent contractors, given that wrestling has serious long-term health consequences. How soon those points get pushed to the extent that real, meaningful reform of working conditions occurs is up to people like you and me.

Do we care enough to demand change? Or is wrestling and its gladiators still too "fake" to warrant us taking them seriously?

MATCH 9

CONQUISTADOR #1/THE RED DEMON/MAC RIVERA/ JOSE LUIS RIVERA/THE BLACK DEMON/SHADOW #2/ JUAN LOPEZ/EL SULTAN VS. MARCELINO RIVERA

Puerto Rico

THINGS GET WEIRD ON ISLANDS.

For almost two hundred years, biologists have looked at islands as "living laboratories" for studying evolution. I know this because when I'm not chasing down ex-pro wrestlers, I'm one of those "island biogeographers." What makes islands so fascinating to scientists (beyond their tendency to inspire fruity cocktails) is their intrinsic isolation. That isolation, that separation from the mainland, the place from which you came, is why things get so weird—or unique, one might say—on islands.

The geological history of volcanic islands runs deep. Over millions of years, the chunks of land that today comprise islands rose, sank, collided, and moved horizontally and vertically according to the whims of plate tectonics. Now and again a seed or a spore or even a hardy pair of small insects washed up on shore in a freak storm and lived long enough to sprout or reproduce. Thousands of miles from their homeland, these new populations began the circle of life anew in these strange lands, surviving, reproducing, passing on genes—*evolving*—and, given a few hundred thousand or million years, these plants or insects eventually became entirely different species.

The island I'm on now—Puerto Rico—has its share of endemic creatures, three hundred of them according to the Nature Conservancy, animals and plants found nowhere else on Earth. These organisms were here long before humans' arrival, doing just fine before we showed up. But once people got to the island, they irrevocably changed the trajectories of these native species, snuffing some out of existence and forcing others into new habitats as we plowed over the land for crops like coffee and sugarcane.

Isolation does strange things to people as well. Puerto Rico's isolation has shaped a unique Afro-Taino-Euro-Latin culture in this American territory with its own peculiar customs and predilections. Among them is a love of professional wrestling, which arrived in the mid-twentieth century and eventually became known for its hard-core, brutal style. But before it grew extreme, before it was the site of a gruesome, real-life locker room murder, Puerto Rican wrestling inspired the future of the penultimate Six Packer, Jose Luis Rivera (the "s" in Luis is silent), who I've flown here to find.

On the night the Iron Sheik became WWF champion, Jose Luis wrestled in the opening match, representing his entire island nation. But while Puerto Rico is unquestionably a lush, beautiful place, I'll soon learn that it hides a darkness that Jose Luis is all too aware of.

*   *   *

THERE IS A KOAN IN THE ZEN BUDDHIST TRADITION THAT SPEAKS OF FOUR DIF-ferent types of horses: excellent, good, poor, and bad. Zen master Shunryu Suzuki said, "The best horse will run slow and fast, right and left, at the driver's will, before it sees the shadow of the whip . . . the fourth [worst] horse will run after the pain penetrates to the marrow of its bones."

Most people aspire to be the best horse, with its natural talent and instincts. But Suzuki warned us not to jump to this conclusion. In fact, it is often the bad horses that turn out best in the long run, for they have dealt with great pain and adversity and keep on running.

*   *   *

"I will send you the pin," Jose Luis texts me.

Driving in Puerto Rico is an exercise in reflexes and improvisation. Street addresses are of little use, and the numbering system, if it even exists, is erratic; GPS makes everything easier as people simply "drop a pin" for their location and the smartphone takes it from there. I swerve my black rental car around potholes while trying to decipher lane markers, and watch in wonder as people park on all sides of the street facing every possible direction. *If there's space, take it*, seems to be the policy.

Fresh rain stains the road from the capital city of San Juan as I drive through verdant tropical hills to the backdrop of an expansive blue sky.

Jose Luis, accompanied by an eleven-year-old boy, greets me on the street outside his home in Caguas, a city of 127,244 in the east-central part of the island. It's a blue-collar city, void of the tourism that drives much of the economy and stocked with all of the big-box stores that provide much of the island's employment. Retail service is the new agriculture—while crops like coffee are still farmed, the island's economy is no longer agrarian.

Jose Luis has been kind enough to take the day off from his job as a prison guard so he can show me around.

He walks me inside his suburban home, past three pet parrots named Cuca, Paco, and Lolo as well as a trio of dogs and into the living room, where I take a seat on a couch opposite a flat-screen TV.

"What do you want to do today?" he asks me in heavily accented, slightly broken English. It's unusual for him to have the chance to practice his English—although Puerto Rico is part of the US and English is taught in all the schools, in the non-touristy parts, it's rare to hear.

He is tall with long limbs and a physique that once was wiry but is now padded by his sixty-nine years. Short, close-cropped gray hair covers his flat head, and his small, dark brown eyes are bloodshot. A neatly trimmed mustache runs along his upper lip, his skin sun-kissed.

"I thought we could take a drive to the place you grew up, Mayaguez," I reply.

He nods, thinking, quiet. The boy who greeted me outside stands nearby, eyeing me curiously. He's big for his age, with a cherubic face and cheeks with handles. He's wearing a black Michael Jordan T-shirt.

"This is my son Yahir," Jose Luis says. Yahir gives me a soft handshake, but doesn't speak any English when I try to engage (sadly, I took French in high school).

Two more people enter the room: Yadira, Jose Luis's forty-six-year-old wife, and Richard, thirtyish with tan skin, an earring, and startlingly green eyes.

"We found him under a bridge when he was three. He now he lives with us," Jose Luis says, a smile at the corners of his mouth.

"Are you serious?" I ask, confused.

He laughs but doesn't respond, revealing a deceptively playful side.

Since none of them speak English except for Jose Luis, he translates my desired plan. Puerto Rican Spanish sometimes drops the last syllables of words, so "Caguas" sounds more like "Cawa."

While they negotiate, I walk over to a shrine in the corner of the room. On the top shelf is a figurine of the Virgin Mary holding baby Jesus, and below that sit the masks for all of Jose Luis's masked wrestling characters: Conquistador #1, Shadow #2, the Black Demon, and the Red Demon. Like Bill Eadie, Jose Luis spent much of his career with his face hidden. He's having more Conquistador masks made (his most popular character, a cult favorite of 1980s WWF aficionados), but added a design flourish to make it slightly different from the original. Even now, the specter of Vince McMahon's litigious corporate machine makes the Boys paranoid that he will come after them for trademark infringement.

Jose Luis hands me a Ziploc bag full of large buttons he's just had made for personal appearances at wrestling conventions.

"Take a couple," he says. The button shows all eight characters that he portrayed throughout his career (the non-masked personas of Juan Lopez, Jose Luis Rivera, Mac Rivera, and El Sultan round out the field).

A minute later, our agenda is solidified: we'll make the couple-hour drive southwest to the beach town of Mayaguez, with Jose Luis, Yahir, and me following Richard and Yadira in their lime-green Tacoma 4X4 with license plate "El Sultan."

The Road, the Boys' home away from home.

*   *   *

JOSE LUIS IS AN ENIGMA. VERY LITTLE IS PUBLICLY KNOWN ABOUT HIS LIFE beyond the matches he wrestled, and much of what is out there is inaccurate (his Wikipedia page says he was born on August 6, 1960; January 25, 1953, is the correct date). Last month the internet even claimed he was dead. His real name is Marcelino Alicea Rivera, although everyone today calls him Jose Luis, and that is how he introduces himself.

Unlike the other Six Packers, Jose Luis never achieved great success in wrestling, never sniffed main events or reached headline status. He was a utility player, or in the parlance of Kayfabe, a jobber, meaning his specialty was losing matches.

I remember watching him week after week on Saturday mornings as one of the "regular guys" without a gimmick, such as Barry Horowitz, who you knew were going to lose as they went up against the superstars. As a fan of underdogs, I remember thinking, "Just once, let Jose Luis or Barry win!"

Promoters like Vince McMahon crammed their TV shows with these one-sided "squash" matches as a tool to drive attendance to live events, which was still the cash cow of the wrestling business. Jobbers like Jose Luis made name talent like the Iron Sheik and Sgt. Slaughter look invincible; the only way to see one star fight another was to buy a ticket to the matches.

"Did it ever bother you that you had to do all those jobs?" I ask Jose Luis as we head down the highway. He's riding shotgun, with Yahir humming to himself in the backseat, occasionally chiming in with "Que?" when he wants a translation to know what we're talking about.

"No," he says.

I use a mix of follow-ups and awkward silences to push beyond his "yes"/"no" replies, and as the car ride goes on, he loosens up and volunteers more.

"When new people came in, Vince [McMahon] and [agent] Jay Strongbow told them, 'If you don't get a good match with Jose, you don't get a good match with nobody,'" he elaborates.

"I did a lot of things to make those people look good."

For Jose Luis, the pride was not in winning or losing, but in putting over the marquee talent, giving his body so that theirs could shine. And the gesture did not go unnoticed. In his 2019 autobiography, *Don't Call Me Chico*, Tito Santana described a time when the Boys passed the hat around the locker room, knowing Jose Luis had fallen on hard times.

"The boys were very generous when they heard the cause because they all liked Jose. In the end, I was able to give him $1,000 from the boys to help out for Christmas. His eyes teared up. This was something he never forgot," Tito wrote.

I'm curious about Jose Luis's family, where he came from, how he grew up.

"How many brothers and sisters do you have?" I ask.

"Twelve."

His father, also named Marcelino, worked on the docks in Mayaguez and as a driver for a sugarcane company, while his mother, Pura, grew up in the town of Arecibo.

"He stole her and brought her to Mayaguez. In those days, you tell your girlfriend, no matter she fifteen, sixteen, you take her home and you have your wife. That's what those old people did, you know, they take the girl to their home and that's it," he says without judgment.

His mom was a seamstress, while his father transitioned into driving a taxi when they settled in Mayaguez. They had seven kids together; Jose Luis's other five siblings are from his dad's first and third wives.

When Jose Luis was only fourteen, one of his older half-sisters who had gone to live on the US mainland came back to the island.

"She came to Puerto Rico and told my mom she wanted to take me with her to live in Paterson, New Jersey. She told her she would put me in school there," he tells me.

Jose Luis boarded a plane for the first time in his life and landed in a much different world. To learn English, he went back a few grades, working his way through the eighth grade before temporarily giving up. School wasn't for him—he'd much rather head into the city to explore. Every three weeks, he'd get a ticket for the WWWF shows at Madison Square Garden, where he and droves of other Puerto Ricans cheered on their hero, champion Pedro Morales. The wrestling he had seen on TV growing up in Mayaguez was nothing compared to these monthly productions in front of more than twenty thousand people. It became his dream.

After a brief return to Puerto Rico, Jose Luis settled back on the mainland, this time with much of his family in tow. His mother and older brother Jorge had relocated to Brooklyn, while his dad stayed behind in Mayaguez (his parents split soon after). He got his high school diploma at night and found work in a plastics factory. Then fate intervened.

"My brother Jorge met Pedro Morales in the YMCA in Brooklyn," he tells me.

Growing up in Mayaguez, Jose Luis and Jorge would watch wrestling on TV and then head to the park behind the school with their friends to act out the moves. Jose Luis could hardly believe he was now about to meet the most famous Puerto Rican wrestler of all.

Pedro Morales always liked to look out for his fellow countrymen, and after meeting the Rivera brothers, sent them to a local trainer to learn the craft.

Pedro also offered Jose Luis a piece of advice he took to heart: If you learn something, don't stay there. Keep moving.

"We went to this independent wrestling company in New York and Connecticut. We did live shows there on channel 41, the Spanish channel. I was there for three weeks, then they put me to wrestle," he says.

A clap of thunder snaps me back to the present, and seconds later pellets of rain explode on the windshield, the kind of sudden downpour that creates landslides on these island roads.

At only twenty years old, Jose Luis was in the wrestling business. He often tag-teamed with Jorge as the Rivera brothers, going by "Mac Rivera," an abbreviation for Marcelino ("Jose Luis" had not yet been invented). His memory for certain details around his wrestling career is astounding—for example, he remembers that his first match occurred on April 13, 1973. Some of the other Six Packers, such as Bill Eadie and Khosrow Vaziri, couldn't remember who they wrestled in their first match, let alone the date.

For the next three years, Jose Luis performed on as many wrestling shows in the New York/New Jersey area as possible while working full-time in the Keystone factory boxing up camera parts, mixing in the occasional trip to Puerto Rico to wrestle.

But he never forgot Pedro Morales's advice—don't stay in one place too long, keep on moving. When he heard there was work in the Dallas and Houston territories, he packed up and headed out, only to be rerouted to Tampa, Florida, to work for promoter Eddie Graham, part of the NWA (National Wrestling Alliance).

"I took a taxi to the hotel [near the wrestling office]," he tells me, raising his voice over the din of the rain.

"What's your name?" the promoters asked him when he showed up.

"Mac Rivera."

"Matt Rivera, great. We can use you," they replied.

Jose Luis shrugged and said nothing. Mac or Matt, he had a job.

But he kept on moving.

Following a brief stop in the Alabama territory, Jose Luis returned to the comfort of New York/New Jersey, where he picked up work wherever possible for independent promotions while driving a delivery truck. He had a brief stint as a jobber for the WWWF at their TV tapings, wrestling under the name Juan Lopez, but didn't catch his real break until January 1982. A couple of other jobbers, Johnny Rivera and Jose Estrada, invited him to come along to the WWF TV tapings in Allentown, Pennsylvania, on a Tuesday to see if he could get work.

"Superstar Billy Graham was talking to Lou Albano. I went to say hi to Billy, and he told Albano, 'Listen, this guy was with us in the NWA, he's a great worker, tell the Office.'"

As a former WWWF champion, Billy's word meant something. It earned Jose Luis steady work jobbing at TV tapings under the name Mac Rivera. After a few months, he approached Vince McMahon Senior to ask if he could go on the road to get more work.

"Take a look if you're in there," Vince Senior replied, jingling quarters in his hand and handing him the booking sheets for the next three weeks.

"Rivera, that's me!" he said, spotting his name throughout the book.

"Yes, that's you," Vince Senior replied.

Jose Luis became a regular on the circuit, making his Madison Square Garden debut on October 4, 1982, against Tony Atlas's best friend, S.D. Jones, in front of a (truly) sold-out crowd. "I was in the middle of the ring. I started looking around. I used to go there and watch the matches. I said to myself, 'Wow, the son of Marcelino Rivera, a taxi driver, in Madison Square Garden. Wow.'"

Jose Luis shifts in his seat next to me, and I wish I could look him in the eye as he tells this story rather than having to watch the road.

Seeing his opponent lost in the moment, S.D. came over.

"Amigo!" he said. Everyone called Jose Luis "Amigo."

"What happened?"

Jose Luis shook his head.

"Nothing, nothing. Let's go."

He'd end up wrestling in the WWF until 1991. That run of ten years rivals the tenure of all the other Six Packers, including Hulk Hogan.

Jose Luis, the jobber, the bad horse.

*   *   *

OUR WAITER, A PUERTO RICAN FROM BROOKLYN, PLACES A PLATE OF STEAM-ing red snapper with fried plantains in front of me as Jose Luis takes a sip of his piña colada. We've stopped for lunch at El Bohio restaurant in the resort town of Cabo Rojo. Jose Luis had suggested fast food, but I protested, want-ing to try some local authentic cuisine.

We're seated on a deck overlooking the Mona Passage of the Caribbean Sea. A school of ravenous tarpon thrash in the teal water just off the deck's edge, their silver six-foot bodies flashing as they jockey for food scraps.

"What's on that island?" I ask the waiter, pointing to a tiny nub of green land just offshore.

"Rat Island," he replies.

"They used to take tourists out there. Then [Hurricane] Maria came through. Fiona finished the job. They don't go out there anymore," he adds.

Remembering my own boredom as a kid when I was surrounded by adults, I engage with Yahir and ask Jose Luis to translate.

"What position do you play in baseball?" I ask the eleven-year-old.

His ears perk up. He seems excited to join the conversation.

"Right field and catcher. "

"Who are your favorite Major League teams?"

"The Red Sox and the Yankees."

"Why?"

"They have a lot of Puerto Rican players."

"I'm a Philadelphia Phillies fan," I volunteer.

His response cracks up Jose Luis.

"What did he say?" I ask.

"They're eliminated," he replies, referencing the Phillies' recent loss in the World Series. I mock glare at Yahir, who giggles.

"He has a YouTube channel," says Jose Luis, the proud father, explaining that Yahir's specialty is interviewing athletes and wrestlers.

"He'd like to interview you about your book at some point," he adds, and I promise to add it to our itinerary.

In early 1983, Vince Senior broke the most exciting news of Jose Luis's blossoming career: they had big plans to repackage him as a Puerto Rican babyface star in the mold of Pedro Morales. Pedro was getting on in years, and the population of New York Puerto Ricans needed a new hero to embrace.

"We have to change your name," Senior told him.

"Why? I'm Mac Rivera," he replied.

"No, no, no, *I'm* Mac, like McMahon," Senior asserted.

Senior, always a fan of ethnic gimmicks, wanted him to have a more Latino name.

"OK. What about I use Jose Luis Rivera?" Mac suggested, adding, "That's a Puerto Rican name.

"Look at it this way, Vince—there's three million people in Puerto Rico, and two million are named Jose," he explained.

"Yeah, let's go with it," Senior agreed.

But first Jose Luis needed a fresh start. The people knew him as jobber Mac Rivera; he would have to disappear for a while if he expected to get over for his big push upon his return.

"You go to Puerto Rico, you spend some time there. You come back as the Puerto Rican champion," Vince declared.

The plan was set. Jose Luis returned to the island.

Then things promptly went sideways. The local promoter, Carlos Colon, said he hadn't been told Jose Luis was coming in. They put him to work as a heel, without much of a push.

Six months later, Jose Luis traveled back to the mainland and approached Vince Senior at a Madison Square Garden show.

"'Vince, they used me as a heel. I was doing jobs for almost everybody. I want to come back.' I showed him my check for $595," he tells me.

"Well, that's OK for a match," Senior replied.

"No, that's for a week," Jose Luis said.

Senior was appalled.

"Fuck those people. You start December 26," Senior told him, the same card where Bob Backlund would defend his title against the Iron Sheik.

"Did you ever ask what happened to the plan, why they didn't push you in Puerto Rico?" I ask.

"No, I don't know," Jose Luis says.

"Why didn't you ask?"

"I don't know."

Jose Luis wasn't one to rock the boat.

Vince Senior at least was a man of his word. He started Jose Luis with a series of wins on television under his new name and babyface persona. At the December 26 Madison Square Garden show, he defeated veteran Rene Goulet in the opening match. Almost forty years later, he still remembers the finish like it was yesterday.

But a month later, his push was over. Vanished. Suddenly he was back to doing jobs, the plan to make him the next Pedro Morales scrapped. What happened?

"Somebody came to Vince, to the old man [Senior], and told him I was too young, I was green, and that I shouldn't get the job that Pedro Morales had. They hold me back," he explains to me.

"Who told him that?" I ask.

He pauses a long time, deciding whether he wants to share the name of the alleged snitch, something he has never done publicly before.

"Jose Gonzalez," he replies.

A chill goes down my spine.

"The Invader," I say, referencing his gimmick at the time.

"The Invader," he confirms. "That's what Jay Strongbow told me."

According to Strongbow, who was soon to become an agent in the Office, Gonzalez put down Jose Luis so he could get the push himself.

The chill I feel is because I recognize Gonzalez as the man whose altercation with fellow wrestler Bruiser Brody (real name: Frank Goodish) in the locker room in Puerto Rico in 1988 led to Brody's death. It's the reason why Tony Atlas's eyes got wide when I told him I was coming to Puerto Rico as part of my travels. An eyewitness to the stabbing, Tony had shared what had happened while I was with him in Maine.

Before the matches on July 17, 1988, in the city of Bayamon, Gonzalez called Brody into the shower area, as was customary for private discussions. A few moments later, Tony heard a scuffle and a loud moan. He rushed to the showers and saw Brody bent over holding his stomach and Gonzalez holding a knife. Many have speculated over the years that Gonzalez always resented Brody for not having properly sold for him in their matches earlier in his career.

Tony did everything he could to get Brody medical attention, but security thought it was just another wrestling angle. When he finally got him to the hospital, other stab victims filled the lobby. There was no sense of urgency around treating Brody, so Tony grabbed a doctor and literally dragged him over to Brody's body, where he instantly recognized the gravity of the situation. Before Tony left the hospital, the doctor assured him Brody would be operated on and that he was stable.

The next day Brody was dead.

What exactly happened is still unknown, but Tony believes Gonzales and his people somehow told the doctors not to prioritize treating Brody. Gonzalez eventually was charged with homicide (he claimed self-defense), but the case fell apart when the summons for Tony's and others' testimony were received *after* the trial was over. Gonzales was acquitted; Tony never stepped foot on Puerto Rican soil again.

While it appears Gonzales literally stabbed Brody in the front, he had figuratively stabbed Jose Luis in the back in 1984, ending his best shot at getting a major push with the WWF. Jose Luis returned to jobber status, along for the ride as Vince Junior expanded nationally.

But perhaps his jobber status was a blessing in disguise. While the finishes in wrestling were predetermined, your place on the card generally determined how much money you made. Jose Luis watched many of his colleagues further up on the card succumb to the temptations of the Road. Each town had the post-match hangout spot, be it the bar in the hotel or elsewhere.

"We're gonna party tonight," Hulk Hogan would tell him before the show. The Boys would hit the bars, and after a drink or two Jose Luis would Irish goodbye.

"Amigo, what happened to you last night?" Hogan would ask the next day.

"Ah, I went to sleep."

Today, Jose Luis is in generally good health, nearing retirement at a good government job with a nice house and a supportive family. His knees and one shoulder (dislocated in a match with "Mr. Perfect" Curt Hennig) still bother him from the years in the ring, but he's never had to deal with the pain of addiction like so many of the Boys.

"How did you stay in better shape?" I ask.

"Because I couldn't afford it," he replies with a chuckle.

"One time I was in the dressing room, and JYD [Junkyard Dog, real name Sylvester Ritter] told me, 'Amigo, come with me.' We went into a limo, and they give him an envelope and he gave them $200. I say, 'You pay $200 for that? Are you fucking crazy?'"

Two hundred dollars might have been Jose Luis's pay for one night. To see the entire amount go up someone's nose was unfathomable.

Money was tight. To save, he and Jose Estrada would bunk up and share rental cars with tag teams like the Hart Foundation and the British Bulldogs, four to a room and a car. The WWF only covered their airfare, so money they saved on hotels and cars made a significant difference in their take-home pay.

To this day Jose Luis remains grateful to Vince Junior for giving him a steady job and helping him in a pinch. When he was short on his mortgage payment one month, he drove over to the WWF office at 81 Holly Hill Lane and asked to speak with Vince.

"They gave me a $3,500 loan. I never paid it back. One time I said, 'Vince, I owe you some money.' He said, 'Mac, don't worry about it.'"

Vince always made time for Jose Luis and responded favorably to his ideas. But Jose Luis was also never a threat to Vince's power or control; he was an undercard guy who just wanted steady work.

After three years of preliminary matches as Jose Luis Rivera, in 1987 he wanted to create a character to join the menagerie of gimmicks on display by the red-hot WWF. When the original iteration of the tag team Demolition flopped because the fans recognized Randy Colley as Moondog Rex, Vince promised to find a new, high-profile spot for Colley. The Office quickly put together a new team called "The Shadows," comprised of Jose Luis and Randy under masks. The Shadows were generic heels wearing black bodysuits and gray masks from "Parts Unknown," home to so many of wrestling's bizarre characters over the years. But without a buildup or push, the Shadows quickly fizzled, and Colley quit.

Jose Luis had an idea to create a new Latino tag team with his buddy Jose Estrada, given the popularity of ethnic gimmicks. He mentioned it to Vince, who gave his approval and the simple guidance of wanting shiny costumes.

"He wants something shiny, we'll do gold," he told Estrada, envisioning head-to-toe gold outfits.

"We went to people in New York to do the measurements and they made the boots, all the gear," Jose Luis tells me. Given the WWF contracts at the time, Jose Luis and Jose had to pay for all of that out of their own pockets, about $1,700.

"We needed a name. Estrada told Vince 'Solid Gold.'" Vince didn't bite. But one of his Office deputies, Howard Finkel, said, "I've got a name."

The Conquistadors were born.

"What the heck is a Conquistador?" Jose Luis asked Howard.

It fit the all-gold look. Jose Luis embraced it, and for the next few years he and Estrada enjoyed moderate success as a heel tag team.

Always the loyal soldier, Jose Luis sometimes pulled double duty at events, wrestling once under a mask with the Conquistadors and then again as Jose Luis Rivera. He sprinkled in a couple of other masked characters, the Red Demon and the Black Demon. Although he had a long run, the ride stops for everyone, and in May 1991 Vince came to him and said he couldn't use him as a regular anymore.

Jose Luis had an opportunity to wrestle with another promotion in Puerto Rico. He returned to the island, this time for good.

*   *   *

UP TO NOW, I'VE FOCUSED ON FILLING IN THE BLANKS IN JOSE LUIS'S WRES-tling career. But all that time that he was following Pedro Morales's advice to keep moving, bouncing from territory to territory, he had a family life as well. A somewhat complicated one at that, as I learned from his daughter Johanna during a visit to Hillsborough, New Jersey, several months ago. My time with her raised as many questions as answers, which I plan to bring up with Jose Luis during my stay here.

Johanna asked to meet at a Starbucks near her home. She had curly hair and dark eyes and wore jeans and a black tank top. Her fingernails were painted bright red.

"Were you close to both of your parents?" I asked her.

"I was closer to my mom. Because her and my dad separated when I was young. I lived with her because I was closer to her. I was talking to my dad here and there," she says.

"Do you know why they separated?"

"No, not really," she replied. "I didn't want to pry."

Her parents had met shortly after Jose Luis moved to Brooklyn. He was nineteen, and Carmen, her mom, who was also from Puerto Rico, was eighteen and living with some mutual family friends. They hit it off, and while she and Jose Luis never married, they soon had a son, Jorge. Five years later, in 1978, Johanna was born. By this point they had moved to Paterson, New Jersey.

Jose Luis later met another woman, Ana, who he ended up marrying and having two more kids with. It was hard for Johanna and her brother Jorge to accept that their dad lived so close with a whole new family. When he wasn't on the Road, that is, which was most of the time.

"Whenever he was home I would go to his house and stay over. But it was normally him on the Road," she told me.

She watched him wrestle on TV, and even though Carmen told her it was staged, Johanna worried about him.

"It was exciting, but I used to get frustrated when they hit him because I thought it was real," she told me.

"Plus your dad was a preliminary guy, so he lost a lot and was always getting beat up," I said.

"That's what I told my mom!" she replied.

She finally had to ask her dad if they were hitting him for real.

"Yeah," he replied, always wanting to protect the business.

The look on her little face startled him.

"No, no, no, no," he backpedaled. "It's not real, we trained for it," he reassured her.

She accompanied him to Madison Square Garden a few times, meeting Hulk Hogan and the Iron Sheik. While her brother Jorge loved it, she did not share in the awe.

"It was just weird. That's all I can remember," she said.

"How would you describe your relationship with your dad?" I asked her.

"I was angry with him for a while. Because he got married and had children and I felt he'll just forget about his other two [kids]," she replied, not pulling her punches.

In her late teens and early twenties, her anger intensified, and they became somewhat estranged. The birth of Johanna's first daughter, who's now nineteen, thawed things a bit, but it wasn't until Carmen was dying of breast cancer that things really changed.

"When my mom was sick, she would tell me, 'Whatever you have, whatever you feel toward him [Jose Luis], just let it go.' She said, 'I know I'm gonna die, and I need you to build your relationship with your dad.'"

And so she did. Her brother Jorge had his own reconciliation process with Jose Luis, beginning when the former moved to Puerto Rico. They bonded over wrestling, with Jose Luis starting up again with a local promotion and Jorge kicking off his career.

"He passed away ten years ago," she said about Jorge. I didn't pry about what happened, figuring I would ask Jose Luis himself.

It was clear to me in our hour together just how much Jose Luis means to Johanna, how strong their relationship has become. I had found her through an internet search—in 2019, she posted a GoFundMe to raise money to defray the costs of her dad's knee replacement, which his insurance did not entirely cover. He didn't want her to do it at first—wrestlers don't like feeling vulnerable—but she persisted, and she was able to raise almost a thousand dollars from fans.

"He's a very quiet person. You have to talk to him in order for him to talk to you. He's a big teddy bear. He's very lovable. He's a jokester. I cannot have a conversation with him because it always turns into a joke with him," she told me.

"He's a good person."

*   *   *

IT DOESN'T TAKE LONG FOR NATURE TO RECLAIM WHAT'S RIGHTFULLY HERS, especially here in the tropics where the sunshine and rainfall are plentiful.

A few blocks away from the house where he grew up in the seaside town of Mayaguez, vines and dense vegetation crawl up and through the classrooms Jose Luis once attended. The concrete walls of Escuela Sabanetas Mani, his elementary school, are painted a vibrant tropical blue. While the school closed five or six years ago, locals still keep their horses on the grounds to avail themselves of the water that the government never shut off. A chain-link fence surrounds the school, and the buildings themselves have begun yielding to the vicissitudes of time, the roof having blown off, the scaffolding exposed.

A young Jose Luis and his six siblings wore paths around these parts, wrestling in the park, playing cops and robbers, growing up outside. Feuds at school developed into rock-throwing fights that often landed Jose Luis in trouble at home.

Following our lunch stop in Cabo Rojo, we pull up in front of the family home, painted red with stone tiling and an open garage with several metal folding chairs in a little circle. The house has changed considerably over the years. When Jose Luis was growing up in the 1950s, nine people crammed into just three bedrooms, five boys in a single room. Concrete extensions and renovations modernized the house over the years, and the family still resides there.

Jose Luis's older brother by two years, Jose Alberto, greets me and tells me he still lives here. He speaks good English, having also lived in Paterson, New Jersey for a spell. His complexion is a much darker shade of brown than Jose Luis's, and he has the weathered skin of someone who's rarely indoors. He and Jose Luis quickly fall into the pattern of big brother/little brother.

"Did you guys fight a lot as kids?"

"Yeah!" Jose Alberto exclaims, as if the question is ridiculous. We sit in the metal folding chairs while someone breaks out a case of Michelob Ultra, a popular beer in the Rivera family.

Everybody had a pet name growing up—Jose Luis was "Chiqui," Jose Alberto was "Bimbo," and Jorge, who broke into wrestling with Jose Luis and who just passed away a month ago, was "Cholo."

Jose Alberto shares his brother's sense of humor, a mix of deadpan and self-deprecation.

"He wasn't easy," he says when I ask about Jose Luis as a kid.

"He didn't stay still too long," he adds.

I'm curious about their parents. What made Jose Luis want to leave the island for New Jersey, sight unseen, at age fourteen?

"My mother was quiet, a good mom. My father, he used to drive taxis. He was always in the street. He used to drink, play dominoes, things like that. I was the one that always liked to be with him," Jose Alberto says.

I get his drift. Their father only visited Jose Luis on the mainland once, saw him wrestle just one time. After he split with their mother, he met another woman and sired two more kids, but that relationship fell apart as well. He was diabetic and in poor health, and died in 1991.

"When he got sick, he was living here alone," Jose Alberto explains. It was Jose Alberto who was always closest to their father, helping to take care of him at the end when he had no one else.

Jose Alberto never cared for wrestling—that was something Jorge and Jose Luis did together. He preferred the blue-collar life here in Mayaguez, working on the docks.

Around the time of their father's passing, Jose Luis was finishing up with the WWF and looking to make his next move. A local promotion lured him back to the island for a short time, but he got hurt and the company sold. He was nearing forty years old with decades of earning still in front of him. A promoter in Brooklyn offered him $900 per weekend, but that would mean moving back to New York or having to fly back and forth every week. The alternative was much less pay (but which would go further here) to work as a correctional officer, helping to break up fights in one of the island's rougher prisons. Jose Luis chose the latter and continues in that job to this day (although he's since transferred to the hospital, where fight-quelling isn't one of his job duties).

"When they got a fight or whatever, have a brawl or something, we go in and finish everything," Jose Luis says. He'd have to break up fights knowing that guys had knives and other weapons and he had little more than a baton.

Although his work was both hard and dangerous, being back in Puerto Rico gave him a chance to reconnect with his oldest son, Johanna's brother Jorge. Unlike Johanna, Jorge was starstruck when accompanying his dad to shows at Madison Square Garden as a kid, forever treasuring the T-shirt Hulk Hogan gave him off his back in the locker room. Jorge got into wrestling as an adult and learned from his dad, who would still wrestle on the occasional show.

Then ten years ago things took a tragic turn, something Johanna had alluded to back in the Starbucks in New Jersey. Without going into great detail, Jose Luis now recounts how Jorge died.

Jorge was dating a woman who some people were after (Jose Luis never specified why). At six thirty on the night of his death, Jorge told Jose Luis these guys were going around town with baseball bats looking for his girlfriend.

"Jorge, they're going to kill you!" Jose Luis recalls saying, pleading with him to stay safe. After midnight, the group found Jorge and his girlfriend; they shot her four times and she survived. Jorge did not.

Jose Luis doesn't elaborate and I don't press him. The violence that he witnesses every day at work cost him his oldest son.

*   *   *

I take a couple of much-needed days of rest and relaxation before linking up with Jose Luis again.

It's a Tuesday evening and we're back in Caguas. Jose Luis drops me a pin, and I pull into a crowded parking lot serving a cluster of restaurants. Luckily, Yahir is out front, and as soon as he spots me, he excitedly yammers in Spanish while leading me to the back of one of the restaurants.

I come upon the trio from a few days ago—Jose Luis sipping another piña colada, Richard plowing through the ubiquitous Michelob Ultra, and Yadira, with her hair pulled back and wearing a T-shirt that says "Baby Girl."

They've already got their food, a delicious mix of BBQ ribs, fried plantains, mozzarella sticks, and some mysterious fried orange balls that taste surprisingly sweet. Tinny Puerto Rican pop music blares a few decibels too loud from unseen speakers.

I take a seat next to Jose Luis, who looks weary but content. When he's not at work, much of his time is spent shuttling Yahir to baseball practices, being a dad a fifth time over, but now with a lot more time on his hands.

I tell him about meeting Johanna and hearing her side of their estrangement and reconciliation. He raises his eyebrows and nods.

"How would you describe your relationship with Carmen?" I ask him, referencing Johanna's mom.

Through a mouthful of ribs he replies, "It was great at the beginning. Then I fucked up."

I laugh, startled by his candor.

"You fucked up."

He nods.

"What did you do?"

"You know," is all he says in response, a guilty look on his face.

I connect the dots.

"Other women."

"Yeah."

"Did she break up with you?"

"Yeah."

Jose Luis's next partner was a woman named Ana. I see Yadira and Richard snickering in the background—perhaps their English isn't so bad after all.

"Why are they laughing?" I ask.

"She hates her," Jose Luis replies, referring to Yadira's dislike for his ex.

Ana and Jose Luis had two kids together before divorcing in 2009. When I ask when they were born, Jose Luis stumbles, asking Yadira and Richard for help. (No such help was needed when I asked about his matches in Madison Square Garden.)

I also get his origin story with Yadira, which may be the most incredible tale of all.

"I met her by phone in 2006," he says.

"Like on a dating app?" I ask.

"No, no. She just called and I said, 'This is a wrong number,'" he replies.

"Wait. A wrong number? That's how you met her?" I say.

By chance, they had both recently traveled to Orlando, and by chance, she dialed his number looking for someone else. They began chatting and hit it off. They continued the "phomance," and finally after about a month they made plans to finally meet in person. Jose Luis had only seen a photo of her.

"Then the conversation stopped. She never called, never answered. Somebody sent me a message: 'She had a little accident,'" he tells me.

The little accident wasn't so little. Yadira, who worked at Walmart, had fallen off a second-floor platform while retrieving something and landed on her head. She was in a coma for six months.

The doctors were pessimistic she would survive, let alone fully recover, and she claims Walmart did little to help with the medical costs. Jose Luis took out loans to help pay for her treatment. This whole time he still had never met her.

Yadira recovered at home in bed, but didn't want Jose Luis to see her for the first time weak and hooked up to a machine. Finally, she relented.

"You come to the porch and wait for me," she told him. He did as he was told, they met, and went for a short trip to the beach. He came to visit every weekend from that point forward, eventually getting an apartment for them to live in together.

She made a full recovery, and a few years later, Yahir was born, who is now leaning over a bowl of vanilla ice cream as the meal moves on to dessert.

I'm still curious why Jose Luis chose to be a prison guard following his career in wrestling, given the danger and brutality of that job.

"My idea was to get a weapon," he replies.

"It was getting hard by that time to get a weapon. One of my friends told me, 'Listen, you go to corrections, and they *give* you one!' I planned to work there for one year. Next summer will be thirty years," he says.

"Why did you want to have a gun?" I ask.

"Because Puerto Rico is not too easy. I don't got no problem yet that I have to use it. It's still very bad," he says.

He reveals that even the other day, on our trip to Mayaguez, he was armed the whole time. I have no idea where he was hiding the gun, but clearly he's learned that on this island, you don't take any unnecessary chances.

Finished with his ice cream, Yahir stands behind his dad, clinging to his back, anxious to go. A waitress brings out a slice of cake with a lit candle to the neighboring table, which erupts into a local version of "Happy Birthday."

Much to my surprise, Jose Luis joins in, smiling and singing along.

Tomorrow he'll get up and do it all again, clock out at the prison, take Yahir to baseball practice, watch some TV with Yadira and Richard. He'll take a few more steps toward getting his new wrestling promotion off the ground; he's already got his promoter's license, and just needs to get the talent assembled. His idea is to feature "old school" wrestling, the way it used to be.

The bad horse, assembling his stable.

PART IV
THE FINISH

MATCH 10

HULK HOGAN VS. TERRY BOLLEA

I am a real American

Fight for what's right, fight for your life

—"Real American," Hulk Hogan's entrance song

FOLLOWING THE IRON SHEIK'S VICTORY OVER BOB BACKLUND IN MADISON Square Garden on December 26, 1983, Khos and Caryl returned to their hotel room at the Ramada in Midtown. From the dusty streets of Damghan, Iran, Khos had risen to the very pinnacle of pro wrestling in the US, winning the WWF championship. But there was hardly time to celebrate.

The next morning Khos was gone early, off to the next town. Before flying home to Atlanta, Caryl afforded herself a few small indulgences while she was in the big city. She ate breakfast at the hotel restaurant, where The Rock's grandmother, Lia Maivia, herself a wrestling promoter, filled her ear with advice on how her life would change now that she was married to the world champion. She followed that up with a shopping spree at Macy's, where she picked up her first-ever Gucci makeup bag and two beautiful robes, souvenirs of the biggest match of her husband's life.

Meanwhile, Khos drove to the local high school in Lancaster, Pennsylvania, where he would defend his title for the first time, against "Chief" Jay

Strongbow (actually an Italian from New Jersey named Joe Scarpa). But what Khos didn't know was that while he and Mr. Fuji and the Invader and others were working this small-town show, almost a thousand miles away, Vince McMahon had already moved on to the future, leading a TV crew to the Chase Park Plaza Hotel in St. Louis.

For decades, the Chase had hosted *Wrestling at the Chase,* a TV program that had become an institution in St. Louis under the guidance of local promoter Sam Muchnick, the longtime president of the WWF's rival, the National Wrestling Alliance (NWA). Muchnick held the squabbling NWA territorial lords together for many years, but following his retirement in 1982, the existing cracks widened. Muchnick's disciple Larry Matysik fell out with Muchnick's successors in St. Louis and started his own promotion. In 1983, Matysik then made a deal with Vince McMahon that he would come to regret: he closed his promotion and agreed to partner with Vince on all WWF shows in St. Louis. According to Matysik, a week later Vince pushed him out and asserted 100 percent control, something he could do because he had also acquired the precious TV time slot for *Wrestling at the Chase.* Vince kept Matysik on as an employee, but there would be no "partnership." It was just another in the long list of aggressive moves that define Vince's legacy.

"Wrestling is a rotten business, with rotten people, and the only way you succeed is to be more rotten than the other guy," Matysik says Vince told him around this time.

On December 27, WWF cameras rolled for the first time at the Chase Park Plaza Hotel, capturing the debut of a blond explosion named Hulk Hogan. From the moment he emerged from behind the curtain, Hulk had an emotional hold over the audience, generating a hysteria that was simply dubbed "Hulkamania." While other babyfaces strode to the ring giving high-fives, Hulk would spin 360 degrees with his massive arms extended, pointing to the crowd and speaking to them with expressive green eyes in a way that convinced each of them *he pointed at me!* He was the manifestation of all their hopes and dreams but also their fears and pain, almost messiah-like in his vulnerability and willingness to take on their burdens. He didn't just wrestle for them, he *was* them.

Terry Bollea was the man in the Hulk costume that never came off, the son of a pipe fitter and secretary from Port Tampa, Florida. Before he was a wrestler, he was a rock-and-roller, touring the Southeast with a band called Ruckus. While others had a leg up on Terry when they began wrestling because of their athletic backgrounds (Terry's sports career ended with Babe Ruth League baseball), Terry had them all beat when it came to the entertainment side of the wrestling coin, the charisma and stage presence, because of his past as a rock star. It didn't hurt that he was six foot five and a half and over three hundred pounds, with biceps that pushed twenty-four inches.

Vince had successfully poached Terry from the AWA following the Trojan horse maneuver detailed in Chapter 5. He had sent photographer Steve Taylor to meet Terry backstage at an AWA show, where Steve passed him Vince's business card; this led to a secret meeting in Minneapolis where Vince laid out Terry's future: come to the WWF and you will be our champion, the world's first million-dollar wrestler.

But the rest of the Boys weren't cut in on the plan. Khos was just getting settled as the new champion and hoping to hold the title for as long as possible. And before losing the title to Khos on December 26, Bob Backlund had been told by Vince that he would get a rematch on January 23 at Madison Square Garden and would win the championship back at that event.

Ironically, the biggest obstacle to Vince's plan of Hulkamania-led world domination was his own father.

Vince Senior had reluctantly watched from the side as his son, now the owner of the company, began expanding nationally in 1983. Junior was a disruptor, pissing off Senior's friends with his invasions of their territories and airwaves. And now Junior wanted to anoint a musician/bodybuilder as the future of the wrestling business.

At a TV taping in early 1984, Junior informed Backlund that he would not, in fact, be getting the championship back, and that instead it would go to Hulk Hogan. Backlund was devastated and appealed to Vince Senior, who asked Junior to reconsider his grand plan. But there was no going back.

It's unclear when exactly Khos learned that he would lose the title to Hulk, but even if he wasn't told directly before arriving at Madison Square Garden on January 23, he could read between the lines. Hulk was clearly the chosen one, and Khos had served his purpose as the transitional champion between babyfaces.

But it almost didn't happen.

About a week before the big show, Khos got a call from his old trainer, AWA promoter Verne Gagne. Livid at Hulk's defection from his territory, Verne proposed a screw job: he offered Khos $100,000 to break Hulk's leg for real during the match and take the WWF title to Minnesota.

Khos was torn. One hundred thousand dollars in 1984 was a lot of money (actually, in 2022 that's a lot of money, at least to me), and he owed his start in professional wrestling to Verne, who had trained him. But Vince Senior and Junior were the people who had made him the world champion. (Interestingly, the viciousness of breaking someone's leg didn't play a huge role in Khos's calculus, which tells you something of the barbarism of this business.)

Just three days before the show, Khos again defended his title against Chief Jay Strongbow, this time at the Pittsburgh Civic Arena. Sgt. Slaughter (Bob Remus) was also on that card, wrestling against Jimmy "Superfly" Snuka. Following the matches, Bob got a knock on his hotel door.

He was surprised to see his friend Khos standing there, his face twisted with anxiety.

"Mr. Sergeant," Khos said, always very formal with his buddy, "can I talk to you for a minute?"

Khos trusted Bob, knew that he had a good head for the business. Bob knew Verne just as well as Khos did; both of them had endured his training camp in that shit-stained barn on Lake Riley back in Minnesota.

Khos laid out Verne's proposal and his conundrum about what to do while Bob listened patiently, nodding his head.

Finally, Bob spoke: "Khosrow, don't do it. You're going to make a lot more money than $100,000 working for Vince."

Khos thanked his friend for his time and went back to his room to call Caryl; she wouldn't be coming to Madison Square Garden to watch this time.

On the syndicated TV shows the weekend before the Monday card (Madison Square Garden cards were almost always on Mondays), "Mean" Gene Okerlund interviewed Hulk about his upcoming match with the Iron Sheik, sixty-two seconds of classic raving, rambling Hulkamania hyperbole. A few excerpts, all spoken in a single breath:

I've been hangin' and bangin,' the twenty-four-inch pythons have felt the electricity, the power, like they've never felt before.

It's the fact that these Iranians, the fifty-two people, the 444 days in captivity, the oil embargo, the cartel, putting that six-shooter to the head and holding up the United States.

If a thousand demons and wizards were to chain the Hulkster down, I would break the chains that bind me in the center of the ring, Madison Square Garden, the pinnacle of professional wrestling, and put the Sheik in his place.

Exhale.

When Terry Bollea showed up at Madison Square Garden three days later, he could hardly believe his good fortune. Just five years prior he had considered quitting the wrestling business for good, tired of driving five hundred miles to make fifty dollars a night as he bounced around the territories. Now he was about to inherit the brightest torch in the wrestling universe.

Unlike the slow-paced championship match between Bob Backlund and the Iron Sheik the month before, the match between Hulk and Sheik was a dizzying and frenetic five minutes and thirty-five seconds. At its denouement, the Sheik locked Hulk in the camel clutch, the same move that had forced Backlund's involuntary submission less than a month prior. But this time the Hulkster "broke the chains that bound him," rising to his feet with the Sheik still clinging desperately to his back, then rammed him into one of the turnbuckles. The Sheik flopped to the canvas. Hogan hit the ropes, leaped, and dropped his mammoth right leg across the Sheik's throat, his patented finishing maneuver.

With Hulk hooking the Sheik's left leg, referee Jack Lotz slapped the canvas three times, and Hulkamania truly ran wild.

*   *   *

I HAVE A CONFESSION.

Despite generally being a fan of the underdogs and not the superstars, I couldn't help but fall for Hulk Hogan. Why this bald, Fu Manchu'd, hot

dog-skinned brawler with hair extensions had such a hold over me and millions of other Hulkamaniacs cannot be scientifically defined.

Hulk and his following are acts of faith.

Literally, such acts are tattooed on him. "I am that I am" runs in cursive
across his right forearm, a derivation of Exodus 3:14. Across the top of his
back in large block letters, it reads "Immortal."

Although he was initially billed as "The Incredible" Hulk Hogan (before
litigation from Marvel Comics ended that), by the time of my adolescence
he was referred to as "The Immortal" Hulk Hogan. He no longer needed to
be champion to be considered one, reaching that rarefied air of greatness.
In terms of sheer star power, he is the G.O.A.T. (Greatest Of All Time) in
the wrestling business (The Rock may be a bigger star overall, but Hogan
is the bigger *wrestling* star). Just this year, more than three decades past his
prime and almost ten years since he wrestled his last match, a survey by a
University of Kansas professor found Hulk Hogan to be the most frequent
response when 503 adults were asked to name a single pro wrestler.

Gun to my head, I would always choose the Iron Sheik over Hulk as my
sentimental favorite, but Hulk stands out at significant benchmarks of
my life. I was far from alone—an entire generation of wrestling fans grew
up worshipping the man who stood for everything good in the world. His
"Four Demandments" of "train, say your prayers, eat your vitamins, and
believe in yourself" fit perfectly with the moralistic vibe of Reagan's 1980s,
the pop culture that implored us to "Just Say No." Before matches, Hulk
would cross himself after tearing off his T-shirt, and afterward ever trium-
phant, he would lay the championship belt on the mat and point to the "big
Hulkster in the sky."

At age six, I stood on a railing at the Providence Civic Center's
closed-circuit screening of WrestleMania III, flexing in sync with the Hulk
during his post-match posedown. My dad stood quietly to my side, both
amused and baffled by his son's adulation for the absurd character on the
big screen.

At age twenty-one, I pasted a blond Fu Manchu to my upper lip and
donned a red-and-yellow Hulkamania shirt as part of my fraternity's costume tradition for our weekly beer frisbee games.

At thirty, the night before the biggest test of my academic life, the quali-
fying exam for my PhD, I plugged in Hulk's WrestleMania X8 match against

The Rock for inspiration. By this point Hulk was well past his prime and wrestling as a heel; the nostalgia-obsessed crowd turned him back into a babyface that night with their insistent cheers, a truly awesome display of wrestling's populist nature.

Well into adulthood I believed in Hulk Hogan *because* the character was absurdly simplistic, providing welcome relief from the anxiety produced by a world painted in so many shades of gray. And so I was devastated when the news story broke in 2015 that Hulk had been caught on tape making racist statements. The tape was leaked to the press during his lawsuit against the media company Gawker, who had published a portion of a sex tape involving him. Hulk had been unknowingly taped in the bedroom back in 2007 using the N-word, and the story led to his immediate cancellation—he lost endorsement deals and was expelled from the WWE Hall of Fame.

As a fan, I had fallen into the trap that so many of the Boys themselves fall into—I had believed that Hulk Hogan was real, and not just the comic book creation of Terry Bollea. I had to remind myself that Hulk Hogan didn't say the N-word, Terry Bollea did. Unless, of course, they had become one and the same.

So just who is Terry Bollea?

*   *   *

$39 TICKETS TO DISNEY WORLD! RON JON SURF SHOP 245 MILES! FIREWORKS!
Welcome to Florida.

This state, an erstwhile-swamp-turned-tourist-trap, has the vibe of an airport terminal mixed with Bass Pro Shops. But it's sunny and hot, and that's enough to make it one of the country's most popular destinations.

Many ex-pro wrestlers, drawn by the beach and sated by the panoply of strip clubs, call the St. Petersburg–Tampa area home. A long barrier beach stuffed with kitsch (think miniature golf courses and mediocre candy shops) extends along the western shore of the Pinellas Peninsula, with St. Pete on its southeastern flank. Across Tampa Bay is the city of Tampa itself, a former cigar town, and at its southern end is the neighborhood of Port Tampa, where Terry Bollea grew up.

I've got the address 3106 West Paul Avenue scribbled in my notebook, and I slowly drive the streets of Port Tampa in search of Terry's childhood home. The area is blue-collar-on-the-rise, with old houses being torn down and freshly built for the nouveau riche. When Terry's family moved here shortly after his birth in Georgia in 1953, Port Tampa was its own town (it would be annexed by Tampa in 1961), a cluster of streets just north of Mac-Dill Air Force Base where kids rode bikes and skinned knees. Everyone was a Cincinnati Reds fan, given there were no Major League teams in Florida and the Reds trained in Tampa. Segregation was still in full force, despite the *Brown v. Board of Education* ruling in 1954 that ordered all public facilities in the country to be integrated. Florida and Tampa were very slow to catch up. In 1959, Black parents sued Hillsborough County (of which Tampa is a part) to integrate the schools, but Judge George Whitehurst denied the request.

Terry Bollea is far and away the most famous Six Packer and arguably the most famous wrestler of all time, and so plenty has been written about his life. Most of what is known about his childhood comes from his two autobiographies. But those treatments have introduced as many questions as answers, due to a combination of Terry's faulty memory and his tendency to stretch the truth. As is the case with so many of the Boys, the line between work and shoot, myth and reality, hasn't mattered much to Terry's livelihood. In fact, it's likely been advantageous to feed the myth, and for the most part, doing so has been benign. For example, Terry has claimed that he wrestled on more than 365 days per year and that André the Giant weighed almost seven hundred pounds when he slammed him at Wrestle-Mania III. These were exaggerations that simply added to the aura of Hulk Hogan, even if they were not literal truth.

"I dread it every time I see him do an interview," his close friend and former boss Eric Bischoff told me back in Cody, Wyoming.

"Because he doesn't know. He just gets all worked up. He goes into promo mode. When he sees a camera, and there's a red light on it, he's Hulk Hogan."

Given how exhaustively the rest of his life has been covered elsewhere, two things interest me most: his music career pre-wrestling, and how he broke into the wrestling business. On the latter, he has told the story of his initiation into wrestling many times, how trainer Hiro Matsuda broke his leg on day one to teach him respect for the business and how he came back ten weeks later, impressing Matsuda with his toughness and commitment. But did Matsuda really break his leg? Or is this a bit of the Kayfabe magic?

I also would like to get an audience with Terry himself, which I know is a long shot. He has grown more reclusive in recent years, wary of public attention after a string of scandals and still smarting from having been booed last year right here in his hometown at WrestleMania. He runs a karaoke bar and shop on Clearwater Beach, and so I know if all else fails, I can drop by.

*   *   *

I PARK THE FUSION A FEW BLOCKS AWAY FROM TERRY'S CHILDHOOD HOME SO I can stroll the neighborhood. The cicadas are out, providing the soundtrack of the South, the grass perpetually wet from the region's spastic but inevitable thunderstorms. While the nearby main drag of West Gandy Boulevard teems with new retail and development, only a few blocks to the south, streets like West Paul are palm-lined and so narrow that many cars are parked on the adjoining grass. Walking the block I straddle the past and the future—a brand-new, two-level home with plaster walls and a gray-brick driveway is right next to a sagging one-level home begging to be torn down.

The Bollea homestead sits back a ways off the sidewalk, a small, single-level wood-frame home built in 1949. Trees obscure the view of much of the front of the house, which is painted white with a roof of black asphalt shingles. According to Terry's autobiographies (2002's *Hollywood Hulk Hogan* and 2007's *My Life Outside the Ring*), he had a simple and generally fulfilling childhood behind those walls, where his mom, Ruth, made minute steaks on Fridays for dinner and his dad, Peter, built a pitching mound in the spacious backyard. On Tuesday nights, the family sometimes made the trip to the Fort Homer Hesterly Armory to watch Championship Wrestling from Florida.

I know the Bollea family sold the home in 2004, but I have no idea who lives there now. I creep around the side of the property, where there's a carport, but don't see any cars parked. The air conditioning sounds like it's running inside, so I take a chance and knock on the front door. Hard footsteps and a deep voice sound from inside, and a moment later, a man with neatly parted white hair and darker eyebrows opens the door, cradling a cell phone. He's smartly dressed, with a blue Lacoste polo tucked into khaki shorts.

"Hi, my name's Brad Balukjian, and I'm a writer. Do you know that Hulk Hogan lived here?"

The smirk on his face indicates this isn't the first time this has happened.

"I saw you lurking around," he replies with a British accent. "I thought you might be wanting to buy the place. Every day I get a call about this house. My neighbor just sold for a tear-down. I'm getting offers of $450,000," he says. Not because it was Hulk Hogan's house, but because real estate is as hot in Port Tampa as the weather.

His name is Stephen, and he's in between work calls. He's worked at Bank of America for twenty-three years.

"Want to come inside?" he asks.

I'm grateful for the blast of air conditioning that whisks the sweat from my brow.

Stephen's done a lot of good work with the place. It's tastefully decorated in modern style; he replaced the linoleum floor and shag carpet with hardwood floors.

"It was filthy," he says of the state of the place when he bought it from the Bolleas, who continued living here long after Terry became a megastar.

He walks me down the hall, past his own bedroom ("Sorry, I didn't make my bed"), and then points to a small space being used as an office.

"That was his [Terry's] room," he says.

Although Terry's parents added a third bedroom in the 1980s, during his childhood there were only two bedrooms, one for them and the other for Terry and Allan.

Terry is known for calling everyone "brother," bookending his sentences with the term. But as much as he overuses the word, there is, in fact, only one person to whom it truly applies: his older brother, Allan.

It must have been quite a sight, these two behemoths sharing a bedroom. Terry was already six feet tall and weighed 196 pounds at age twelve, and while Allan wasn't as tall, he was a big guy.

Terry had a complicated relationship with Allan; while they were close, Terry doesn't remember a time when his brother wasn't in trouble. It started with bar fights and escalated from there; for a while Allan disappeared completely, on the run from the authorities, resurfacing here and there at wrestling shows to ask Terry for money, to which he obliged. Allan was on borrowed time, and in 1986, Terry got the call he always feared was coming—Allan had overdosed and passed away. In his books, Terry says this is when he himself quit using cocaine cold turkey.

After peeking into the bedroom, Stephen leads me to the backyard, which is beautifully landscaped. A yellow-and-black butterfly flits by. I picture Terry back here as a kid, playing catch with his dad. Baseball and bowling were his favorite sports, and he was really good at both. He could crush the ball in Little League; stories still circulate about him pounding home runs over the stadium lights, Paul Bunyan with a bat. But Terry was also overweight; "When I say I was big, I don't just mean I was tall. I mean I was fat," is how he once described himself.

To some degree, you're always the person you were when you were eight, ten, twelve years old. On the outside, Terry wouldn't be fat for long—in his junior year at Robinson High School, he started working out at Hector's Gym and completely reworked his body. He sprouted like a beanstalk after a Tampa rain, peaking at six foot five and a half and 250 pounds. For the rest of his life Terry would watch his body like a night sentry, never forgetting on the inside what it felt like to be called "Fat Head" and teased by his classmates.

In fact, according to those who know him best, Terry is still that shy, sensitive kid from Port Tampa, even if that side is rarely on display to the public.

"Would you say Terry's a sensitive guy?" I ask one of his closest friends, former wrestler Brian Blair, later that day at Blair's home. Blair would become most famous as B. Brian Blair of the Killer Bees tag team in the WWF.

"Yeah. He doesn't show it on the outside. But yes. His mother and father were the salt of the earth. I remember when he found out Allan died, it ripped his heart out," he says.

"Terry is one of the most real guys. He's a very loyal person. I couldn't ask for a better friend," Blair adds. He and Terry still hang out regularly, sharing a passion for shooting guns.

Eric Bischoff echoed Blair's sentiments.

"Terry Bollea is one of the kindest, gentlest, and generous people I've ever met. He's just a kid from Florida," he told me.

Even his tendency to stretch the truth, to blur the line between Terry Bollea and Hulk Hogan, may be borne from his deep-seated desire, almost craving, to please people. When I asked Eric why Terry tells such tall tales about his time in wrestling or if he's even aware that he's doing it, Eric said, "He's telling the story that he thinks fans want to hear."

When Terry hit it big and became wrestling's biggest star, he did his best to take care of his friends, helping to get them jobs with the WWF and WCW (World Championship Wrestling). The requests and demands on his time were impossible; many took advantage of his generosity, part of why he has become so guarded and reclusive now.

As I prepare to leave Terry's childhood home, Stephen walks me to the door and tells me about the time Terry's VH1 reality show, *Hogan Knows Best*, came here to film, around 2007.

"Everything went pear-shaped after that," he says.

*   *   *

PEAR-SHAPED INDEED. EVEN NON-WRESTLING FANS COULDN'T HELP BUT BE aware of the unraveling of Hulk Hogan that began in 2007.

It started with his son Nick's car accident. An aspiring race car driver, the seventeen-year-old decided to make Clearwater's streets his personal track. His Toyota Supra jumped the curb and slammed into a palm tree, and as a result, his passenger and friend John Graziano, who wasn't wearing his seatbelt, is paralyzed to this day. Nick ended up spending 166 days in jail for a reckless driving felony, and Terry settled a civil suit with the Graziano family for an amount rumored to be around $1.5 million.

In the midst of that debacle, Terry's marriage to Linda Claridge was falling apart. They had met in Los Angeles in 1982 and married a year later, shortly before Terry's match with the Iron Sheik. Unlike most of the Boys' romantic partners, Linda joined Terry on the road, and for several years they ran wild together, enjoying the ride. They had two children together, a daughter, Brooke, and Nick. But Linda's suspicions of Terry having affairs and the strain of the fame that came with their celebrity chipped their bond down to a nub. She filed for divorce in November 2007, resulting in a settlement that eventually cost Terry about 70 percent of the couple's assets.

Terry hit rock bottom. His body was wrecked from the years in the ring—starting in 1998, he had his knees replaced, his hips replaced, and as of this year he has had at least ten back surgeries that the public knows about. He began washing down fistfuls of pain pills with handles of Tito's vodka. At one point he put a gun to his head and considered pulling the trigger. The physical pain was barely tolerable; the emotional pain was not. His wife was gone, he was feuding with his daughter, Brooke, and his son was heading for jail. And he could no longer do the one thing, maybe the only thing, Terry Bollea always knew he did better than anyone: perform.

It's around this time that the infamous sex tape with the N-word on it was made. Estranged from Linda, he crashed with his buddy Todd Clem (better known as radio shock jock Bubba The Love Sponge) and his wife, Heather, who had an open marriage. Terry slept with Heather with Todd's blessing. What Terry did not bless, however, or even know about, was that Todd was secretly videotaping his encounters with Heather. Five years later, a copy of the tape was leaked to Gawker, which published an excerpt along with some commentary. That move would end up being Gawker's undoing, as Terry sued them (secretly backed by billionaire Peter Thiel, who would later step forward to reveal his involvement and motivation) into bankruptcy, recovering $31 million of the $140.1 million awarded by a Florida state jury in 2016.

Much worse than the sex, however, were Terry's words on the tape. He was upset with his daughter, Brooke, and began discussing her boyfriend, who was Black. In so doing, he used the N-word multiple times as part of a racist rant. Terry had no clue this footage existed until the people behind the leak of the sex tape allegedly tried to blackmail him with it in 2012. While Terry cooperated with the FBI to thwart the alleged blackmail attempt, in 2015 the N-word tape leaked anyway.

Mortified, Terry launched a media apology tour, taking responsibility for his actions and pleading for forgiveness. If such a tape had leaked in 1984, it would have surely done serious damage to his career, but in 2015, the scandal threatened to bury Hulkamania forever. According to a 2010 study by National Media Inc., wrestling fans were now more progressive than most sports audiences; such bigotry did not go over well.

"Are you a racist?" ABC's Amy Robach asked during one of his interviews.

"No I'm not. I never should have said what I said. It was wrong. I'm embarrassed by it. But a lot of people need to realize that you inherit things from your environment. Where I grew up was South Tampa, Port Tampa, and it was a really rough neighborhood. Very low-income. And all my friends, we'd greet each other saying that word, we teased each other with that word. The word was just thrown around like it was nothing," Terry replied.

"Is it fair to say that you inherited a racial bias?" followed up Robach.

"I would say that is very fair. But you can break the cycle. That's what everybody needs to know. You can break the cycle and become a better person."

Although he led off the interview denying that he was a racist, Terry ended up admitting that he was prejudiced, with the caveat that that prejudice was essentially not his fault, but the fault of the times and his surroundings. He had made his case.

For decades, Hulkamaniacs like me needed Terry Bollea to be Hulk Hogan, needed someone larger than life to look up to and believe in. Now, Hulk Hogan needed us to believe in Terry Bollea and the power of redemption.

For the past several years, Terry has maintained a generally low profile. He was quietly reinstated into the WWE Hall of Fame in 2018 and has made a handful of public appearances for the company since then. He rarely talks to the media, which is why Eric Bischoff was skeptical that he would meet with me. His victories in lawsuits against Gawker and the Laser Spine Institute (a reported $10 million settlement for allegedly botched surgeries) restored his wealth, and following a second divorce, he reportedly has found happiness with his new squeeze, Sky Daily. His back surgeries have limited his mobility at times, but he's battled back, Hulked Up, made the superhuman comeback he was always known for in the ring, and while he still deals with pain, he's mobile once again.

"Hulk's getting better at being comfortable with Terry Bollea. He's discovering who that guy is, finally, now that he's in his late sixties. He's adjusting to this day to it. It was really hard on him to go from being Hulk Hogan to being Terry Bollea," Eric Bischoff told me.

*   *   *

ANTHONY BARCELO IS STILL ROCKING.

He opens the windows of his apartment in a teal-colored complex called Ridgewood in the nearby town of Seminole as I take a seat at the kitchen table.

He's a one-man band, playing covers, originals, whatever the people want to hear, crooning on the beach, a soft rocker.

"I'll be at the American Legion, Post 273," he tells me about his gig later today. "I do a lot of corporate events, private parties."

He's got a handsome face with dyed dark hair pushed up in spikes. The Florida sun has been kind to his sixty-eight years. He's dressed for the beach, with board shorts, a visor, and a Led Zeppelin T-shirt. Two small hoop earrings dangle from each ear.

"We lost touch for twenty years or so," Anthony tells me when I ask about his former bandmate Terry. "And then out of the blue, a few months ago one of my keyboard players was playing at the Sandpearl in Clearwater and saw Terry having dinner there. He asked for my number, and then he called and said, 'Man, come over here, come to my club, we'll do karaoke.' We talked and laughed, all that good stuff," he says.

He hasn't been yet, but says he'll go soon, once he's not so busy.

Anthony, short and slight with an angular face that drove women in the audience crazy, and Terry, a shy giant with a hairline already receding in his twenties, were an unlikely pair. In 1972, when Terry was nineteen and Anthony was eighteen, Terry saw him in a music store and said that he and his buddies needed a singer to form a new band. Terry was on bass. Along with a drummer, guitarist, and keyboard player, the band Koko was born.

"We played every weekend. We played the local clubs in the Tampa Bay area, and we had an agent that would send us to the University of Florida in Gainesville, and we'd play all the frat houses and sororities," Anthony says. They played mostly covers—Steely Dan, the Doobie Brothers—and mixed in some originals. It was the era of live music, before DJs and electronic music hit it big.

"What was your impression of Terry when you first met him?" I ask.

"Extremely talented musician. He was a really good bass player, man, he could hang with anybody. That guy could really play. He studied music at USF, that was like his minor," Anthony replies.

Terry earned his associate's degree from Hillsborough Community College, then majored in business and minored in music at the University of South Florida in Tampa. He had a knack for numbers and good business sense, but college wasn't really for him. He was all in on his music career.

"What was your impression of him personally?" I follow up.

"Very, very gentle, quiet. Never seen him raise his voice at anybody," he replies, describing the same man who for decades ranted in America's living rooms about "hangin' and bangin'" and in one particularly memorable promo, promised to load Donald Trump and his wife and kids and all the little Hulkamaniacs on his back and backstroke them to safety from the bottom of the Atlantic Ocean (look up "Hogan Promo at WrestleMania IV" on YouTube—worth all two minutes and twenty-five seconds).

"He had to be at least six foot five. And back then, we were wearing platform shoes. I'm five eight, so I was over six foot tall. And he, man, he looked like a wall. And that bass looked like a ukulele on him," he adds.

Koko's look was right in step with the 1970s—Terry raided his mom's jewelry cabinet and closet to accessorize his stage costume with earrings and funky hats.

About a year later, at the end of 1973, Anthony and Terry shook things up and shifted personnel. Out of the ashes of Koko (and another short-lived band named Bandit) emerged what would be their most successful band, Ruckus. Larry Stovall was on drums, Dan Chapman on keyboard, Gary Devriend on guitar, Anthony on vocals, and Terry on bass. For over three years, Ruckusmania ran wild.

"We played all the big clubs, the Flying Dutchman, the Aurora Ballrooms, we played all the big rock clubs," Anthony says.

Ruckus lived up to its name, touring as far west as Alabama and north to the Carolinas, repped by MCA. Terry dropped out of USF and put all his eggs in the rock-and-roll basket. They made a living touring full-time, and while it wasn't glamorous, they were living the dream. Terry, ever conscious of his body, would load his weights into their sixteen-foot International Lodestar truck along with all the band's equipment, and then set up a mini gym in their hotel rooms. The band split between riding in the Lodestar and Terry's Ford van.

Anthony and Terry made a pact to see just how far this music thing could take them, fingers and toes crossed for that elusive record deal that would signal they had truly arrived. When they needed extra money, Anthony's dad got them into a labor union working construction, Local 1207.

"Me and him were out there in the hot sun helping to build University Square Mall," Anthony recalls.

When Terry later became the Babe Ruth of wrestling, Anthony wasn't surprised. He had seen his friend developing the skills that made him so charismatic in the ring during his time as a musician.

"I mean, you couldn't help but look at the guy. He's just a freak of nature, just so big. He knew how to work the crowd. He knew how to talk to the people. He had just a commanding presence on stage," Anthony says.

While the lead singer is often known to be most proficient on the mic, Anthony says Terry, the bass player, had a better gift of the gab than he did.

"We were driven together. We put these bands together. From Koko to Bandit to Ruckus, we did this together. It was us," he says, his voice still full of feeling forty-six years later.

That feeling is why Anthony was so devastated when Terry called it quits toward the end of 1976.

"We were in Atlanta, we were broke, the truck broke down, and we were freezing on the side of the road. Our agent had to send us money so we could fix the truck. So Terry, the guitar player, and the keyboard player said, 'No, we'll eat these crackers, the money we've got we're putting in gas and we're driving back to Florida. We're going home.'"

Anthony and the drummer stayed behind to wait for the money from the agent, and Ruckus never played again.

"I was sad, I was mad at him. I was sad, you know, because he was my friend. You know, man, we went from '72 all the way as far as we could go. And I knew it was at an end. I didn't know what I was going to do."

Terry came home, sold his bass, sold his van, and hit the gym harder than ever, adding the steroid Dianabol to his diet. He quickly put on about fifty pounds of bulk and muscle, blowing up to 320 pounds. Hulk Hogan was born.

Anthony kept on rocking, to this day.

Before he leaves for his American Legion gig, he tells me if I want to know more about Terry's early life, I need to talk to a cat named Danny Brazil. He gives me his number, which I pocket for later. But first I need to see the guy who helped break Terry into wrestling.

*   *   *

DOWN A LONG DRIVEWAY TEEMING WITH PLANT LIFE IN THE SUBURB OF Odessa, I find Gerry Brisco riding a lawnmower. He's recovering from

COVID, which scuttled his plans to attend the recent induction ceremony at the National Wrestling Hall of Fame in Waterloo, Iowa, but he already feels well enough to meet.

"We'll find some shade," he says, walking me to the back of his property, which sits on a beautiful lake dotted with lily pads. He puts cushions on some white plastic chairs and hands me a bottle of water, and we sit under a large tree dripping with Spanish moss. A long wooden dock with several cabanas extends straight out into the lake.

Gerry, seventy-six, was a standout amateur wrestler who competed at Oklahoma State before turning pro with his brother Jack. While Jack's peaks exceeded his (Jack was NWA champion in the 1970s), Gerry had a long and successful pro wrestling career that extended long beyond his retirement from active wrestling. He served as one of Vince McMahon's lieutenants, working as a road agent all the way up to 2020.

In the mid-1970s, Gerry wrestled for Championship Wrestling from Florida, based here in Tampa, and was also a part owner. Well before they met, Gerry kept a watchful eye over Terry, like Obi-Wan Kenobi keeping tabs on a young Luke Skywalker in the Tatooine desert. Terry was a regular at the Tuesday-night wrestling shows, and standing in the tenth row, his mop of blond hair towered over everything else. Gerry and his brother Jack would look out at the crowd during their bouts and wonder, "Who is that guy?"

"We were coming into town one time wanting a cold brew. We'd heard about this bar called The Other Place. We had no idea Terry was playing in a band there," he says, sweeping a hand through his dark hair, wet with sweat.

Gerry and Terry had a mutual acquaintance, a bartender named Theresa who lived next door to Terry.

"Who is that guy?" Gerry asked her, pointing to the behemoth with the bass on stage.

Theresa agreed to pass a message to Terry that Gerry wanted to speak with him. In between sets, Gerry and his brother Jack sat down with Terry.

"We always see you at the Armory," Gerry began. "Have you ever thought about getting in the [wrestling] business?"

"Yeah, how do you do that?" Terry asked.

The stage was set. When Ruckus broke up, Gerry set up a tryout for Terry with one of the promotion's trainers, veteran grappler Hiro Matsuda.

"Here's where the rumors get kinda convoluted. I know Brian's [Blair] got his theory of it, but my brother and I were actually there in the building and saw the deal," Gerry says as a trio of giant sandhill cranes walks past us.

Blair had shared his version of the story, which he almost certainly got secondhand from Terry. In that version, Terry goes into his tryout with Matsuda, who breaks his leg trying to teach him a lesson in humility and puts him in a cast for the next ten weeks.

Undoubtedly Matsuda and promoter Eddie Graham's other enforcers were not above such brutality. It was common for local toughs to come down to the wrestling offices wanting to be wrestlers. Gerry shares one incident where a sheriff's deputy had a tryout; Graham's enforcers beat him up so badly that he checked into Tampa General Hospital. Hillsborough County sheriff Malcolm Beard came down to the offices to confront Graham.

"Eddie, what are you doing to my guys?" Malcolm asked.

"Well, he wasn't your guy, he stepped in *my* ring," Graham responded.

According to Gerry, Terry came down for his tryout and got in the ring with Matsuda. Although Terry never wrestled as an amateur, he was huge and strong and naturally athletic. Matsuda locked up with him amateur-style and started out easy, telling Terry to try and pin him, while Gerry and Jack watched at ringside.

"Terry was doing really good, we were really shocked at his skill level. So Matsuda said, 'OK, I'm gonna take it up another level.' Matsuda starts working down toward [Terry's] ankle. He kinda takes an ankle lock. I couldn't hear the snap, Matsuda said he heard a snap, but the bottom line is he wrenched Terry's ankle so he couldn't stand up anymore," Gerry recounts.

Despite the snap, Terry's ankle (or leg) was not broken, Gerry clarifies.

"He did not break the ankle; he put it in a position where it was severely sprained and swelled up," he says.

In Terry's first book, Terry says he was so hurt he had to wait for his dad to get off work to pick him up and drive him home. In his second book, his dad drove him to the hospital first. According to Gerry, he and Jack taped it up and Terry drove home on his own. Gerry worried they'd never see him again, but a couple weeks (not ten) later, Terry returned with his ankle wrapped in a high-top shoe.

"I'm ready to go," he told Gerry and Matsuda.

"Matsuda really appreciated his courage to come back again," Gerry says. From then on, Terry had their respect. While Matsuda put him through the ringer, he taught Terry the craft. Gerry knew he would become a big star one day, and did his best to give Terry the experience he needed.

"We'd always known the place for Terry to eventually end up was Vince McMahon Senior, 'cause that's where all the big guys went. And we knew he was too big for this territory," Gerry tells me.

To get him ready, Gerry and Jack mined their contacts in the territories and sent Terry to the Pensacola/Alabama, Memphis, and Atlanta promotions. Terry quit once early on, frustrated by his lack of bookings and paltry pay, and even took off for a year to Cocoa Beach with his buddy Ed Leslie (the future Brutus "The Barber" Beefcake) to help run a bar and gym. But wrestling was in his DNA.

"When you think you're ready, let us know," Gerry had told Terry. "Jack will get you booked in New York. He'll call Vince Senior."

In late 1979, that day arrived. Gerry remembers the day vividly.

"My brother was over. It was a Friday night, we're having a couple of beers and playing pool. All of a sudden we get a knock on the door, and it's Terry and Eddie Leslie.

"Come on in," Gerry said. "What's up?"

"I'm ready," Terry replied.

"So Jack picks up the phone, calls Vince. And Vince takes Jack's word. 'Tell him to come on up, I'll take care of him,'" Gerry recalls.

With only a few bucks to his name, Terry made the move north. On December 17, 1979, he made his debut in Madison Square Garden. The rest, as they say, is history, brother.

*   *   *

DANNY BRAZIL'S PHONE NUMBER IS BURNING A HOLE IN MY POCKET, SO I GIVE it a ring and arrange to drop by his place on Treasure Island, a stretch of barrier beach demarcated by a sign featuring a peg-legged pirate.

Danny Brazil is the real-life Danny Brower (Brazil was his wrestling name), who not only grew up with Terry Bollea but also played a role in the federal government's case against Vince McMahon for alleged steroid distribution in 1994. Although Danny was never called to testify, his name was invoked multiple times during the defense's questioning of Terry, who was a witness for the prosecution. Somehow (and this greatly undermines my faith in our legal system) Danny was incorrectly referred to as "Dave Brower" throughout the trial in all its official documentation.

A split second after I knock on the door, Danny whisks it open with a big grin, revealing yellowed teeth. He welcomes me as if we're old friends. Four hours of breathless, mostly one-sided conversation ensue in which I learn more about Terry Bollea than I thought possible and which leave my head spinning.

"You drove here from California?" he asks, motioning to a couch for me to sit down. "That's pretty cool."

Across from the couch, a small tube TV with two VCRs underneath displays 1980s NASCAR races, the volume turned down low. Next to me on the couch is a weightlifting belt lying next to a recently used Walkman with headphones. In the corner of the room, a large white cage houses a macaw noshing on rabbit pellets, which every so often pierces the air with a screech.

"It's a rescue of a rescue," Danny says without further explanation.

In another corner of the room, a bright MOLSON sign lights up a desk, and the walls are covered with framed paintings of fish and torn, faded wrestling posters advertising Danny's old matches.

"Can I interest you in some Yoo-hoo or some coffee?" Danny offers. He's slight, with a mane of shock-white hair escaping from the edges of a black NBC Sports baseball hat and tumbling to his shoulders. He's wearing shorts with white athletic socks hiked up high and an untucked black polo shirt.

A few minutes later, he emerges from the kitchen with a pot of boiling water, pours some into a cup, and stirs in a packet of Nescafé.

"I've got some hazelnut creamer," he says, handing me the mug.

"The 1980s, it was a great time," he says as we settle in.

Danny, a year younger than Terry, met him when they were kids, at the Pinarama bowling alley in Port Tampa.

"I was eighth grade, he was in ninth grade. I thought I was a pretty hot-shot guitar player. We're at the pinball machines and we're talking about guitars and all that. And he said he had a Bandmaster. And I'm like, 'You've got a Fender Bandmaster?' Next thing I know we're over at his house," Danny says.

They were hitched together from there, bonded by their obsession over rock music and guitars, spending hours after school together at Terry's house on West Paul Avenue.

"His mom was like a second mom. She would pick me up and drop us off at Monroe Junior High. And we'd ride the bus and screw around with the guitars and go to lessons. Then my dad would pick us up and bring him home," Danny recounts.

They'd pool their time for lessons at Arthur Smith's Music Company studio, and their eyes got big when Terry's dad bought him the coveted Guild Starfire guitar.

As they entered their teenage years their jam sessions got more serious. Eventually they joined with friends to form their first band: Plastic Pleasure Palace. Danny was the bassist, so Terry played guitar, Chet Yokum was the drummer, and Jack Nugent sang. When that group morphed into Infinity's End, personnel got shuffled and Danny ended up in a roadie role. Although only fifteen, sixteen years old, they were playing fraternity parties on college campuses.

What was a young Hulk Hogan like?

"He just wanted to do everything," Danny tells me over the cries of his caged macaw.

"I go over his house, he's fourteen years old, and he's already talking about playing in Johnny Winters's band. He wanted to climb Mount Everest. He wanted me to go with him," he adds.

Even at fourteen, bits of Hulk Hogan were peeking through. The man who would one day slay giants and save America was talking about climbing Everest in the ninth grade.

Danny was significantly less ambitious. When he and Terry parted ways as Terry's music career took off a few years later, Danny was thrilled to drive the tractor picking up balls at a driving range.

"Take a look at this," he says, handing me a bound volume. "Robinson High, 1971" reads the yearbook. I flip through, finding Terry's senior photo, his straight hair longish and parted, perhaps the last time he didn't sport a Fu Manchu. On another page, in chicken scratch cursive, I find Terry's tribute to Danny, part of the time-honored tradition of signing each other's yearbooks: "Dan, Your [sic] crazy as shit, stay that way. Terry Bollea."

I bring up the recent controversies in Terry's life. In explaining his racist comments on the sex tape, Terry had invoked the influence of his childhood environment. Danny grew up in that same environment. Was it the way Terry described?

"I can remember, at the Armory and the fairgrounds, there were colored bathrooms and white bathrooms, colored water fountains and white. Port Tampa had a Black section. And growing up, we all got along," he says. According to Danny, Port Tampa was such a poor area that class divided people more than race; the poorer kids, Black or white, clashed more with the wealthy kids as busing integrated the schools. That being said, he recalls an incident in high school that stayed with him for a long time. At a football game, he and Terry were jumped by about ten Black guys and ended up in a brawl.

"Why did they attack you?" I ask.

"No reason, just out of the blue," he replies. "I watched him [Terry] get his ass beat." Terry's dad witnessed the incident and was freaked out, according to Danny.

Danny discusses the fight's impact on him: "You know, that leaves impressions on you. Speaking for myself, that made me wary. There was a big thing a couple years ago, 'Oh, he's [Terry] a racist.' He's dealt with so many Black people over the years and I've never seen one sign off any racism. He took so much grief. Bullshit," he says.

"Terry said that growing up, that [the N-word] was a word that everyone used all the time," I say.

"I would say yeah!" Danny agrees. "But not in a malicious way. It was affectionate."

As Terry's music and later wrestling career took off, he and Danny fell out of regular touch. Danny ended up owning and running a series of Goony Golf miniature golf courses and later met a woman to settle down with. He was deeply in love, which made what happened next so devastating: he says she betrayed him and disappeared into the night.

Enter Terry Bollea, who saved Danny's life without even knowing it.

June 16, 1981, is a date forever seared into Danny's brain. He had been up for several days on a bender, snorting every last grain of cocaine he had and chasing it with booze. The supposed love of his life was gone and he didn't see much worth sticking around for.

"I ended up on the Skyway [the bridge connecting the Pinellas Penin-sula to the main part of Florida]. There were two spans, and one of them got torn down by a big ship. Well, in 1981, they hadn't torn it down yet, and you could drive out on the St. Pete side. People would fish off it. I'm in a white Volkswagen, and I was just gonna drive off the fucking thing. That's how fucked up I was. I remember sitting there and next thing I know the sun's coming up and there's birds hitting the water and I'm crying," Danny recounts.

He's not sure what stopped him from stepping on the gas, but he returned home and crashed, wondering if the next day he would go through with it.

Terry was back in town, fresh from a lucrative tour of Japan, and getting ready to wrestle a few matches for the Florida territory. He had done well in his first run in the WWF and became an instant hit in Japan, where they called him "Ichiban," meaning "number one." He wasn't yet a national star, but the pieces were coming together.

When Terry was back in Tampa he would sometimes stop by Danny's place to catch up. The morning after Danny's near-suicide, he and Ed Leslie (who had also started wrestling) came blowing in in Terry's Lincoln Town Car, throwing open Danny's door and dragging him out of bed. Danny wanted none of it, told them to leave him alone, but there was no arguing with his childhood friend.

"They dragged my ass to this gym in North Tampa. They about killed me. But they showed me what to do. And they were telling me, 'If you get your ass in shape you could do this stuff.'"

Danny, who's only about five feet ten, had ballooned to 260 pounds. Terry showed him his strict training and dieting regimen and gave Danny the spark he needed to pull out of the darkness. Terry went off to become the biggest star in wrestling, while Danny trained with former wrestler Boris Malenko and began cutting his teeth in the territories, just as Terry had done a few years prior.

Danny Brazil was no Hulk Hogan, so while he got work, the highest he got was as an occasional jobber for the WWF. He and Terry had fallen out of touch again, so Terry was shocked to see his old friend show up as talent at a TV taping in Tampa in late 1988. While there, Danny met Vince McMahon, who was fresh from filming a movie with Terry called *No Holds Barred*. After having been WWF champion for over four years (ever since he defeated the Iron Sheik), Terry was tired of the Road and hoping to make a transition to Hollywood, essentially what The Rock would successfully do over a decade later. Vince, who always saw himself as an entertainment mogul first and a wrestling promoter second, was happy to facilitate Terry's transition. When Vince met Danny and saw that he was someone Terry could trust, someone who had known Terry since the ninth grade, he had an idea: have Danny work as Terry's road manager, someone to help him with the crush of publicity that was coming with the upcoming release of the movie.

Following WrestleMania V in April 1989, Danny hit the road with Terry. For the next nine months, they rode in limos and in first class on planes. Unlike the rest of the Boys, Vince paid for Terry's (and Danny's) transportation and hotels; the only thing he didn't cover was meals (a substantial cost, as Danny tells me a typical post-match meal for Terry was six or seven tuna fish sandwiches).

Danny hands me a crate full of old booking sheets, hotel receipts, and travel itineraries. I had heard about the demands on Terry's time at his peak, but now that I see a typical day written down, it truly sinks in.

"I used to think, in some shape or form, that Terry's almost superhuman," Danny says. "I used to get a pack of plane tickets every three weeks. All our flights were the first flight out in the morning. Part of my job was, if something happens, prevent a situation from turning into an incident."

Not only did Terry have to wrestle, but he had to make countless media and community appearances. He could be moody and fans could be demanding, so Danny was there to defuse any potential problems. Generally, however, Terry went above and beyond with his patience and generosity with fans. He was the most requested celebrity of the 1980s for the Make-A-Wish Foundation, which specializes in granting wishes to critically ill children.

"What's in his heart—I would see some of these things with kids. He wouldn't let the press in. To spend time with kids and to be upbeat, then cry his eyes out for twenty minutes, then tear the house down. If he had the time or the opportunity to do something, he would do it, of his own accord," Danny tells me.

Danny and Terry were close, so close that Terry had his steroids shipped to Danny's house and taught him how to inject. And while Danny grew even closer to Terry, he witnessed Terry and Vince McMahon drift apart.

Terry and Vince were the symbiotic duo that put the WWF on the path to end up where it is today. Arguments of who was more important are futile—they both deserve equal credit. Vince needed Terry to be his horse, and Terry needed Vince to steer the ship. In the process the two became best friends, almost brothers. They shared an indefatigable work ethic and boundless ambition, qualities that sometimes led them to fight like brothers. But by 1989, the relationship was strained. *No Holds Barred* had flopped at the box office, Terry was beat up physically and mentally, and Vince was pivoting to a new upstart, the Ultimate Warrior, as his new horse.

"Vince and Terry were at each other's throats a lot," says Danny, who witnessed all the backstage politics firsthand. Two days before Christmas in 1989, Vince pulled Danny aside. "I'm gonna have to let you go. We're going in a different direction," he said without further explanation. A few months later, at WrestleMania VI, Hulk followed Vince's marching orders, losing the title to the Ultimate Warrior and passing the torch.

When the box office dropped with Warrior as champion, Terry was there to pick it up and give Vince an "I told you so." By WrestleMania VII Terry was champion again, but business was headed downhill.

Late 1993 was the last time Danny talked to Terry.

The feds were after Vince for alleged steroid distribution, and Terry was temporarily out of wrestling, on the outs with Vince. In 1994, the *United States v. Vince McMahon* hit the courts, with Terry lined up as a witness for the prosecution and Danny for the defense. Although they were on opposite sides, neither Terry nor Danny planned on giving testimony that would damage Vince. The case itself was fairly weak—of all the things to pin on Vince, forcing his wrestlers to do steroids was not going to stick. Although Vince created a culture where steroids were commonplace, those who were there say that he never directly pushed them on the talent.

But Vince didn't know what Terry was going to say under oath and feared the worst. Terry was equally concerned, unsure if Vince's legal team was going to try and throw him under the bus in some way. Terry discussed this in his second book (published in 2009), a portion of which I now read aloud to Danny:

I still had this instinct that Vince was somehow going to flip the whole case and blame it on me. I had no idea how he would do that, but I just thought it would be an easy way out if he pointed a finger at Hulk Hogan and let the media run wild. My instinct was right. As I walked into that courtroom, I looked over and saw my mule—the guy who used to carry drugs and steroids for me on the road—sitting right next to Vince and Vince's attorney. *Why is he here?* I wondered. If my testimony hurt Vince, I have no doubt that they would have used my mule to tell every tall tale in the book about my steroid use and how I was running them all over the country, or selling them, or forcing them on my opponents. This mule must have been there as a backup to crush my credibility. That would have meant the end of my career. Forever.

Danny stares at me, his eyes bugging out of his head.

"MULE!" he almost shouts, the wheels spinning in his head.

After all they had been through together, it stung to be reduced to a beast of burden. But it also helped explain an awful lot. When the trial was heating up, Danny had tried to call Terry to reassure him that he wasn't going to say anything to hurt him. Terry, beyond paranoid as he watched his legacy tainted by steroid revelations (made worse by his overt lies on the *Arsenio Hall Show* about his use), picked up the phone but refused to talk, pretending it was a bad connection.

"That just explains so much," Danny says. Now that he's heard Terry's side, he understands why Terry refused to talk to him, that he was terrified that Danny had flipped on him.

"Mule!" he repeats, shaking his head.

There was also a bit of Kayfabe in Terry's recollection of the courtroom. Although Danny was a potential witness for the WWF, he was never called to testify and never sat in the courtroom, let alone right next to Vince.

I finish my Nescafé coffee and get ready to go.

"What do you do for work nowadays?" I ask.

"I guess, well, I'm retired. I'm not supposed to be here now," he says, telling me about a terminal thyroid cancer diagnosis two years ago. Thirty-nine radiation treatments and nine bouts of chemotherapy later, his prognosis looks good. He doesn't take a single day for granted. Mentally, physically, he's been through the wringer, just like Terry.

"Would you like to get back in touch with Terry?" I ask on my way out.

"Yeah," he says, nodding, his mood reflective.

"I'd like to tell him thank you for the ride."

*   *   *

WHILE TERRY'S FRIENDS AND FORMER COLLEAGUES HAVE BEEN ENORMOUSLY helpful, I still want to talk to the Hulkster himself. My chances don't look good, however. Despite Brian Blair having put in a good word for me and the WWE giving me clearance to talk to him (he is still under contract with them), my phone is not ringing. So it's on to Plan Z, a visit to Hogan's Hangout on Clearwater Beach.

The bar and restaurant is on the main drag of Mandalay Avenue, surrounded by beach shops and cafés. Monday nights are karaoke night at Hogan's Hangout, and Terry is known to personally stop by. I arrive early and grab a spot at the bar to watch the crowd file in, ordering up some calamari and a Summer Shandy. A small stage is set up toward the back of the ground floor, and sitting on a stool, looking eerily similar to his wax likeness in the nearby Hogan's Beach Shop, is legendary wrestling manager Jimmy "Mouth of the South" Hart. Jimmy is a longtime buddy of Terry's and apparently still helping him out. Pushing eighty years old, his dark brown pompadour, mustache, and black sunglasses seem frozen in place as he holds a clipboard.

Large TV screens above the stage show vintage Hulk Hogan matches; I watch as he drops his leg over the Iron Sheik's body on that fateful night in 1984. The DJ starts spinning and warming up the crowd, but no sign of Terry yet. Hulkamaniacs of every size, shape, and color begin filling the bar, many dressed in Hulk attire.

Karaoke kicks off with a father and son singing "The Humpty Dance," the young towheaded kid wearing a Hulkamania T-shirt. Jimmy Hart, never taking of his sunglasses, silently sways on his stool.

Mike, here for his fortieth birthday, is next, wearing a red-and-yellow feather boa (Hulk's colors) and a Hulk tank top, and sporting a tattoo of Hulk's face on his left bicep.

While the acts go on, I look at my phone and read a recent news article that Vince McMahon has announced his retirement from the WWE. Although he is still the majority shareholder of the company, the heat from his nondisclosure agreements with various former employees (relating to allegations of affairs and sexual misconduct) was enough to push him out as CEO. He took to Twitter, saying, "At 77, time for me to retire. Thank you, WWE Universe. Then. Now. Forever. Together."

It was a move no one thought possible. Vince would retire when he dies, was the conventional wisdom. Even now, many are skeptical that he will actually, functionally step down.

In that infamous *Playboy* interview from 2001, Vince wrapped up by saying, "When it's time for me to go, I would like to be devoured by the biggest, baddest carnivore that ever walked the face of the earth."

Little did he know that those carnivores would be the women he employed in the Office.

About half an hour into the karaoke performances, several heads turn, necks straining to see the back door. And then he emerges, the Immortal Hulk Hogan.

He looks to have shrunk to about six feet three (the back surgeries took their toll), and he walks gingerly to the stage next to his girlfriend, Sky, and her young daughter. His head is still enormous, the Fu Manchu beautifully intact, red sunglasses perched atop a black bandana.

"Ladies and gentlemen, please welcome to the stage, Hulk Hogan!"

He looks out to the crowd, his eyes expectant, and gives one ear-cup for old times' sake, and the crowd loves it.

He grabs the mic.

"What's up, maniacs? Wow, it's starting to get real crazy in here on Mondays," he says to another eruption of cheers.

For the next couple of hours, he sits on a stool on stage next to Sky, watching his fans perform. Now and again he gets up and grabs the mic to rev up the crowd, putting over the singers and reminding everyone to tip their bartenders. If you sing, you get to shake his hand and grab a selfie. I briefly consider putting my name in to perform something like Pat Benatar's "Hit Me with Your Best Shot," giving me the opportunity I've been so craving, a chance to meet the Hulkster. A younger, more eager version of me would have done it, done it for the story, but I don't feel so compelled.

Down the road at Amalie Arena in Tampa, 8,955 fans are cheering the babyfaces and booing the heels at the WWE's *Monday Night Raw*. Maybe in another universe, where Terry never got divorced and his son, Nick, never got in the car crash, and Terry never said the N-word, he'd be performing at that show, flexing to his thousands of adoring Hulkamaniacs.

But I'm not so sure he'd be any better off for it. Because that Hulk Hogan would never have been tested the way this one has. As he fist bumps and flexes on stage with each karaoke participant, a look of peace creeps over his face. He's still in his element, still on a stage, but the crowd of a hundred or so here bears more resemblance to the crowds he and Danny Brower and Anthony Barcelo played in the days of Infinity's End and Ruckus.

Hulkamania may not be what it once was, but Bolleamania is running wilder than ever, brother.

THE MAIN EVENT

JAVANMARDI

I'VE GROWN UP SINCE LAST I WAS IN FAYETTEVILLE, GEORGIA. Seventeen years ago, when I came to this family-oriented suburb of Atlanta, I was full of confidence. At twenty-four years old, everything that I wanted had fallen into place in my young life. I applied to only one college and got in, and when I didn't like any of the options for a major, I invented my own. I dreamed of working at *Islands*, the magazine I had read since I was ten, and quickly got a full-time editorial job there, where I also fell in love. There was no doubt in my mind that the Iron Sheik biography would also be a success.

As I return to Fayetteville in middle age, I've been sobered by the inevitable checks and balances of life. My relationship failed; *Islands* went out of business; just last year I finally graduated past having roommates and got my own apartment. At forty-one, I also realize I'm the same age that Khos was when he won the WWF championship from Bob Backlund.

I'm sitting in my Ford Fusion at the end of the long driveway to 160 Camelot Drive, the large house in Fayetteville where I rented a room while working with Khos. I never imagined I'd be back here among these lush low hills, reliving an experience that started so full of promise and ended in disaster.

The lawn is enormous and perfectly trimmed, and the house hasn't changed a bit, a red-brick Colonial with bright blue shutters and several cars parked in the driveway. I wonder who lives here now, if it's still a crash pad for pilots at nearby Hartsfield-Jackson airport.

The town has changed considerably since 2005. As the county seat, Fayetteville has always been the focal point of Fayette County, but the Downtown Development Authority recently rejuvenated the historic city center, anchored by the courthouse. Built in 1825, it is the oldest surviving courthouse in the state, and for those who love things like giant balls of twine, it holds the world's longest courthouse bench (fifty-eight feet). Hip cafés and restaurants have sprouted nearby, and the population has grown by 49 percent since I lived here.

While the Iron Sheik has resided in Fayetteville since 1984, the influx of a new breed of superheroes has done more than anything else to boost the town, this of the comic book variety. Pinewood Studios, renamed Trilith, took advantage of the state's tax breaks and set up shop here in 2013. Since then, Marvel has called Trilith home, filming such movies as *Ant-Man* and much of the Marvel Cinematic Universe on its eighteen sound stages. The complex has become a veritable village unto itself, with three hundred homes and a thousand residents.

I head out and drop by the Fayette County Historical Society, located in a modest white house downtown. Their president, Deborah, greets me in a musty room full of old bound newspapers and walks me through the town's history, from its naming in honor of Revolutionary War hero Marquis de Lafayette to the fallout from the "War Between the States," as she calls it.

Oh yes. I am back in the South.

A few minutes later, I grab a seat at the bar at the nearby Old Courthouse Tavern for a late lunch, part of the downtown renaissance, where the Georgia state flag and Confederate flag fly side by side. Many of the local businesses are struggling with supply chain issues and staffing due to COVID, and a recent surge in Georgia has complicated matters.

"They can't find anyone to pick the tomatoes," I overhear one of the bartenders say.

"Can't we get some fourteen-year-old kid to pick tomatoes for ten dollars an hour?" asks another one.

My neighbor sips a glass of vodka and tells me she is a fire department medic who is off for the month, waiting for the next movie to start production at Trilith. She's wearing a tight and skimpy white tank top and shorts that reveal a massive lower back tattoo. Her baseball hat is from a brewery she visited in Chicago.

"I want to know if Hulk Hogan's hair is stitched in," she says when I explain my project.

I laugh and tell her I didn't have the opportunity to yank on the Hulkster's bone-straight doll hair when I saw him at his karaoke bar, but that yes, it probably is not real.

Tomorrow I will see Khos's daughter, Nikki, and shortly after that, Khos himself. I sip my beer and cradle a bag of pistachios I bought at a Persian market on my drive into town. Khos's family back in Iran sent him tubs of the nuts when he was homesick during those first few years in Minnesota. His wrestling students, Pat Marcy and Dan Chandler, recall always seeing him with a handful of pistachios or popcorn, watching amateur wrestling matches from the stands.

I'm anxious about how Khos will receive me after all these years. Has he truly cleaned up? How much of the Iron Sheik still remains, and how much has he returned to being Khosrow Vaziri? Nikki has assured me that he is a completely different person, but I can't shake the memory of his beet-faced death threats in his living room.

I tip my glass back and take a long swig.

My life is likely halfway over. A ring of gray runs along the sides of my head. I never wrote the Iron Sheik's biography, and my life has taken a much different course than what I expected when last I was here. The invincibility of youth has been replaced by something less exciting, perhaps, but more durable and, dare I say, healthy.

And yet if I looked in the mirror right now I would see a nervous six-year-old boy with buck teeth and a squeaky voice, holding his Iron Sheik action figure, waiting to see his hero emerge from behind the curtain.

*   *   *

"Do you want to see the shrine?" Nikki asks, welcoming me to her gorgeous home in the suburb of Peachtree Corners on the other side of Atlanta. The two-story white-brick house sits at the end of a quiet cul-de-sac, the entrance a high archway of glass spanning both stories.

She greets me with a warm hug. Her dark brown eyes and tall figure instantly remind me of her father. High cheekbones and a dimpled chin give her a striking appearance, a kind of regal countenance. Nikki is closest in age to me of Khos's three daughters, and we hit it off during my time in Fayetteville. She understood my frustration perhaps better than anyone—she was there with me and Caryl when we sat down to celebrate Khos's birthday dinner and he excused himself from the table after hardly eating, disappearing into the night to sate his addiction.

A lot has changed for her since I last saw her. This enormous house for one, the result of a successful career working for Ritz-Carlton's corporate office followed by a stint with Bain & Company. She now handles all the finances for a major commercial real estate firm. A marriage has come and gone, but the legacy of that marriage, two spunky daughters named Alexis and Chloe, immediately make me feel at home—I find a stuffed animal on the bed in the guest bedroom with a note that reads, "Hi I'm Bella the Bunny (you may not keep me), -Chloe and Bella."

The shrine that Nikki speaks of is her living room, a carpeted space with a sofa and piano and walls covered with framed Iron Sheik memorabilia.

There's a photo of the 1971 AAU National Championship team, Alan Rice all smiles hoisting a large trophy, Khos to his left wearing a National Iranian Television shirt. His hairline is in slight retreat, his face unsmiling but peaceful. A giant poster of the 2014 documentary *The Sheik*, produced by his agents the Magen Brothers (the successors to Eric Simms and the people behind his infamous Twitter account) hangs nearby, and opposite that is a yellowed family portrait of his three daughters, Nikki in the middle with a bow tied on the top of her head. Several Iron Sheik action figures, still in their packages, cover the top of a wooden bookshelf. Five thumb wrestlers—the Junkyard Dog, Nikolai Volkoff, the Iron Sheik, Big John Studd, and Hulk Hogan—are lined up on the edge of the bookshelf looking like they are dipping their toes in a pool together, the Boys getting a rare moment of R&R.

"Take a look at this," Nikki says, handing me a stack of letters and cards, some of the envelopes addressed "To Mr. Iron Sheik" along with his address.

There are plenty of parcels from fellow Gen Xers, but one note written in big bubbly letters and full of hearts catches my eye:

Hi Mr. Sheik,

How are you sir? My name is Vicky. I am an 11-year-old honors student. I love my great-grandma, she is your number one best fan ever. Could you please write her a nice letter for her one hundredth birthday. Thank you.

I love you,
Vicky

I picture the great-grandma forty years ago, already well on in years, tuning in on Saturday mornings during the Iron Sheik's prime, so excited to boo her favorite bad guy, and how this cartoonish villain has now helped span an eighty-nine-year gap between great-grandmother and great-granddaughter.

"He literally gets like seventy letters a month. So that's just a small sample of the stuff. But he'll actually do the autographs, he'll respond to every single person," Nikki says.

We move into the office to talk some more, shooing out Charlotte, a ninety-pound Bernese mountain dog with plaintive eyes.

"Mom, can we play Clue?" asks Chloe, Nikki's eleven-year-old daughter. She's still tiny, not having sprouted yet like her sister.

"Not now, Coco, I have to talk to Mr. Brad," she replies. I've already refereed one Battleship game between the two of them.

"What was your dad like when you were really little?" I ask Nikki.

"He was always very, very big on manners. Even though he traveled so much, he would always come home and tell us, 'Always say good morning to your bus driver and your teachers, always look people in the eye and shake their hand firmly and show respect to everyone.'"

Javanmardi, that ancient Persian word for chivalry and respect.

Every night, no matter where he was in the world, Khos would find a phone and call Caryl and his girls to tell them he loved them.

As soon as she could walk, Khos had Nikki and her sisters out on the local school track, running laps, training just as he had in the mountains north of Tehran. It's no secret Khos always wanted a son, but if that wasn't meant to be, his daughters could still learn to handle themselves.

When free will kicked in, the girls went their own way.

"Marissa was always the stylish, fashionable, prettiest one. And Tanya was a tomboy who would go to the gym and lift weights with my dad. I was the academic one. I always knew I would go to college."

Khos, of course, didn't smarten them up to the worked nature of the wrestling business, but reassured them that he was strong enough to not get hurt, even if it looked like it on TV.

"With him being a bad guy in wrestling, did you ever worry or wonder why he was a bad guy?" I ask.

"No, we knew how much he loves America. So we know all that stuff was a gimmick and just for fun and show," she replies.

"Kids never did tease us or make fun of us. But it's funny, we'd ride the bus home, and he'd be out there in the driveway sweeping in just his wrestling trunks. And like, maybe even his wrestling boots."

Now that is a visual.

Still, Khos worried about his girls, wanted to make sure that they were kept safe. He had seen atrocities committed in the streets of Tehran and knew what human beings were capable of. When she was a teenager, Khos gave Tanya a Bowie knife, which she hid under her mattress.

"I guess my dad told her it was her job to protect us," Nikki says.

Caryl was furious when she found it.

All three girls were beautiful. While Nikki was more studious and shy, Marissa and Tanya started bringing guys around in high school. At the time they lived in a gorgeous four-bedroom house on Sycamore Bend, the house they bought in 1984 and that Caryl decorated all by herself while Khos was off on the Road. Caryl put in a huge custom patio with stamped cement, only to see Khos move in all of his weight racks and dumbbells, turning the aesthetic from Southern idyllic to Clubber Lang.

"I'd be inside watching the *Brady Bunch* and eating Doritos and was like, oh, one of their boyfriends is over," Nikki recalls.

As soon as a guy showed up at the house, Khos would invite him on to the patio.

"I'm her father. Who are you? What do you want? Let me show you my gym," Khos would say, tensing his jaw.

Just as he had challenged anyone in the audience to do his *meels* back in the late seventies and early eighties, he forced his daughters' suitors to get under the bench press. However many reps they did, he would do double.

As much as she loves her dad, Nikki is acutely aware that it was Caryl who kept it all together.

"She was a saint. I think without her, he never would have survived that life," she says.

When Khos came off the Road, Caryl got two jobs, as a bank teller and a travel agent, to support the family.

"She would work from seven a.m. until like eleven at night. She was working so hard to just keep the house and things afloat. He never drove us to school or practices or cheer or any of that stuff. She did everything. He never cooked or cleaned—he really didn't do anything but wrestle and go to the gym."

There may be no shrine to Caryl, but she deserves one.

* * *

IN 1984, THE IRON SHEIK PEAKED. HE EARNED MORE THAN $400,000, THE most he would ever make in a year, and main-evented several times with Hulk Hogan in rematches for the WWF title. Growing up in Iran, he didn't even know that professional wresting existed—now he was one of its most recognizable faces, his face on lunch boxes (I had one). The WWF invaded every territory that it could, becoming so popular that it returned to network TV for the first time in thirty years, preempting NBC's *Saturday Night Live* every couple of months for a special called *Saturday Night's Main Event*.

The Sheik was a bona fide celebrity. He appeared on Regis's *Morning Show* to promote WrestleMania, where he and Nikolai Volkoff became the world tag-team champions. America's real-life fear that Iran and the Soviet Union would team up became reality in a WWF ring, with Volkoff singing the Russian national anthem while the Sheik stood nearby saluting. Ironically in real life, Volkoff was, like Khos, a true American patriot—born Josip Peruzovic in what is now Croatia, he escaped communism in 1968 and defected to Canada and later the US.

The Sheik's 1984 feud with Sgt. Slaughter drew headlines and sellouts, arguably the second-most-popular attraction after whatever feud Hulk Hogan was involved in. After all those peripatetic years, bouncing from territory to territory, sending money home to Caryl to feed the growing family, it was finally paying off. Vince McMahon's merchandise machine also stuffed the Sheik's pockets—his first action figure made him almost

$100,000 before Vince slashed his wrestlers' share of royalties for fear they would forget who was really in charge (and in case you're wondering why a heel's action figure would sell so well, kids needed someone for the baby-faces to beat up). The lithe 190-pounder from Iran now packed 250 pounds onto his frame; the Junkyard Dog had introduced him to steroids in the Mid-South territory, and the Sheik was suddenly swole.

But for all his popularity as the guy you loved to hate here in the US, back in Iran he was persona non grata. To the ayatollah's ruling class, he was making a mockery of serious business, a defector to the Great Satan who was now using his heritage to make money in a sham profession. After struggling to get out of the country during his one visit back (only a few years after leaving in 1969), he never again returned to Iran. His parents passed away in the 1990s, but he did not attend their funerals.

The masses in Iran knew nothing of the Iron Sheik character during its peak in the 1980s. The ayatollah forbade access to any outside TV or media, and professional wrestling did not exist in Iran. Even as the internet emerged in the 1990s and Iranians became more globalized thanks to workaround access (VPNs, etc.), the Iron Sheik was not beloved in his home country.

"In general Khosrow Vaziri's character in the ring was considered an insult to Iranians and to the government of Iran at that time. Look at the anti-Iranian sentiments of those 444 days [of the hostage crisis]. It caused the displacement of many Iranians in the US during that period. A Farsi podcast some time ago listed the music that was made in America about the hostage situation. Bomb, bomb, bomb Iran. In such an atmosphere, the Iron Sheik was one of the things that fueled those anti-Iranian sentiments," an Iranian journalist based in Tehran tells me over email. He did not want to be identified, fearing for his safety (Iran is still far from a free country).

Khos was now unquestionably an American, embraced more here, even by the people booing him, than by his fellow patriots in Iran.

It's a lot harder to stay on top than to get to the top, an adage that is especially true in wrestling, where promoters control the outcomes. A steroid regimen gave Khos an extra boost to his already impressive physique, but his behavior out of the ring was becoming unsustainable. Khos was on a collision course with himself, the self-medicating and partying changing his very nature. He was still highly functioning, but the spirit of *Javanmardi* that he held in such high esteem began to vanish. During his time in the Mid-Atlantic promotion in 1980–1981, he ran across some of the industry's most notorious hellraisers and got heavy into the drugs.

Now in his midforties, his body couldn't keep up with the rigors of the Road—he gained weight and started breaking down. While most remember his brush with the law in 1987 with Hacksaw Jim Duggan (we'll get to that momentarily), the harbinger of trouble was his arrest at a gas station in Fairfield, Connecticut, in August 1985, an episode entirely forgotten in the annals of wrestling history (and perhaps never remembered to begin with).

What happened is still a matter of much dispute, other than the fact that Khos was arrested and charged with third-degree assault. According to Khos's lawyer Mickey Sherman (the same celebrity defense attorney who served one and a half years for federal income tax evasion and who defended Michael Skakel in the Martha Moxley case), who I tracked down in an assisted living facility in Connecticut, the incident began when Khos stopped for gas, and seventeen-year-old station attendant Antonio Torres allegedly told him, "I don't serve gas to Iranian motherfuckers."

"Sheik tried to just calm him down. The guy kept on hollering at him. So finally Sheik took the money out of his pants and spit on it," Sherman recalls over the phone.

While I am unable to find Torres, I dig up an article from the October 4, 1985, issue of the *Stamford Advocate* covering the incident.

"The attendant's attorney, Eddie Rodriguez of Bridgeport, said Vaziri attacked his client, swearing at him and hitting him so hard in the mouth that he needed hospital treatment," the article reads.

Rodriguez is further quoted as saying Torres was a wrestling fan, and "Tony liked the Sheik, until the Sheik proved that he's the beast in real life that he is on TV."

These were pretty divergent accounts—something Torres said or did likely provoked Khos, who reacted to the extent that the police put him under arrest. When I ask Sherman if there was any evidence of Torres's alleged injury, he dismisses it, saying, "It is 100 percent common for somebody to make a claim like that."

Following the incident, Vince and Linda McMahon immediately set Khos up with Sherman, a well-known personality around Greenwich, and he set to work using Khos's fame to his advantage. He had Khos sign eight-by-ten glossies, which he brought to the hearing for the prosecution and for the judge. He says the police report was written very much in Khos's defense.

"Cops loved the Sheik," he says.

And then, in the ultimate blending of myth and reality, Sherman visited WWF headquarters to film a seven-minute video directed to the judge in which various wrestling personalities acted as, get this—*character witnesses* for the Iron Sheik. Sherman stood next to a stone-faced Sheik, in full wrestling regalia, while asking "Classy" Freddie Blassie, Bobby "The Brain" Heenan, pop star Cyndi Lauper, and others to vouch for Khos being an upstanding member of society.

In this presentation intended to address the serious matter of criminal assault, Blassie was in full character, calling the judge a "pencil-neck geek" before promising to vote for him "ten to fifteen times if necessary"; Captain Lou Albano descended into a madcap rant in which he called Khos "Cosgrove" (to this day, many of the Boys who spent decades with Khos on the Road don't know his true first name) and claimed that whatever trouble he was in, it was because he didn't speak English. "Mean" Gene Okerlund flat-out lied, saying he first met Khos while covering the Olympics for NBC in 1968 (Khos wasn't at the Olympics and at the time Okerlund was a radio DJ in the Midwest).

But as is so often the case in the world of wrestling, the truth didn't matter. Even in a court of law, perception was reality. Sherman showed the tape to the judge in his quarters, and he loved it so much that he asked Sherman for twenty-five copies.

According to Sherman, the prosecution offered a probation deal, and sensing his momentum, Sherman declined. The case was transferred to another judge and subsequently dropped.

Two years later, Sherman had to work his magic once again.

WrestleMania III was arguably the peak of the WWF's 1980s boom. On March 29, 1987, more than seventy-eight thousand people packed the Pontiac Silverdome outside of Detroit for what had become the WWF's version of the Super Bowl.

The Iron Sheik, who at forty-five was the oldest wrestler on the card, and his partner, Nikolai Volkoff, took on the Killer Bees in the penultimate match of the evening, right before Hulk Hogan and André the Giant took center stage. The match ended when "Hacksaw" Jim Duggan, a babyface with a patriotism gimmick, came in the ring and attacked the Sheik (not a very babyface thing to do, by the way), resulting in the Killer Bees getting disqualified. Duggan was a newcomer to the WWF, hot off a successful run in the Mid-South territory and primed for a lengthy USA vs. Iran feud with the Sheik, recycling the same old tried-and-true formula once again.

A couple months later, on May 26, 1987, several WWF wrestlers flew into Newark, New Jersey, their usual hub in the New York City area. Sheik and Duggan were scheduled to wrestle each other as part of a tag-team match that night at the Asbury Park Convention Hall. The drive from the airport to Asbury Park is less than an hour.

Sheik approached Duggan at the baggage claim, saying that he didn't have a credit card to rent a car and asking if he might ride with Duggan. Although Kayfabe discouraged babyfaces and heels from riding together (especially if they were in the midst of a program with one another), the code had become a bit lax as the McMahons emphasized the entertainment part of sports entertainment. Sheik was a veteran who Duggan respected, and still being new to the company, Duggan wanted to make a good impression.

Sure, why not? Duggan figured.

At this stage in his career, Sheik couldn't even go an hour without his medicine. He implored Duggan, who was driving, to stop for a six pack of St. Pauli Girl beer. Back on the road, Duggan rolled a joint and he and Sheik cracked open beers, standard practice for Road life at the time.

Then the flashing lights appeared in the rearview mirror. One type of six pack got the Sheik to the mountaintop, and now another was about to knock him off it.

State trooper Peter Bruncati had seen Duggan swigging his beer, and now he smelled marijuana wafting out of the car.

Bruncati smelled something funny in the car, and decided to search the vehicle. (I was able to track down Bruncati, but alas, he was unwilling to talk.)

At first, the Sheik wasn't too worried. He had been pulled over many times before, and always got off because, as Sherman said, the cops loved wrestlers; the autographed eight-by-ten glossy can go a long way in these situations.

But Officer Bruncati was not impressed by these cartoon characters. He called for backup, and a search of the car turned up three grams of cocaine in the Sheik's shaving kit, open containers of beer, and marijuana. Since the Sheik had the more serious charge, a felony (with a maximum penalty of five years in prison and a $15,000 fine), he had to appear before a judge before being released on $5,000 bail. Duggan waited while the Sheik had his arraignment, quietly hoping this would all just go away. They returned to their car, drove to Asbury Park for their match, and didn't tell a soul.

For about twelve hours, Sheik and Duggan thought they may just get away without the media finding out. But then the story broke on the AP wire, and two days later, the incident made page two of the *New York Daily News* with the photo caption "Brawny Bozos." At the height of Reagan's War on Drugs, working for a promotion catering to kids, Duggan and Sheik, mortal enemies in the ring, had been caught together *just saying yes.*

Both were immediately fired, with Vince calling an all-hands meeting to announce that Sheik and Duggan would never work for this company again (Duggan would be back by August and the Sheik by the following February). Duggan returned home to Louisiana fearing he had wrecked his career (he was slated for a major push) and spent the next several weeks shooting rabbits in his backyard while pounding whiskey. The Sheik returned to Fayetteville with his tail between his legs. Caryl was beside herself. Khos had been making good money for the past four years, and they were just about to put a swimming pool in the backyard.

With a PR crisis on his hands, Vince immediately implemented drug testing (for cocaine, a test Khos would fail when he returned to the company the following year, leading to another firing) and called attorney Mickey Sherman back into duty.

Khos was charged with cocaine and marijuana possession. Fans flocked to his court appearance on June 1, where he appeared flanked by Sherman wearing a polo shirt and plaid sports jacket. He signed an autograph for four-year-old Matthew Viaud, a moment captured in the next day's paper. When the press began asking questions following Khos's "not guilty" plea, Sherman cringed as he watched Khos lapse into Kayfabe in real life.

"I don't like him. I never have. I hate him. I think maybe he did it on purpose," Khos said when asked about Jim Duggan.

"Some way, somehow, I'll get him, whether it's in a ring or not," he added.

It was time for Sherman to intervene.

"This is a court of law. Let's not associate the charges and wrestling. It's an insult to the court," he interjected.

Sherman worked his magic—a couple weeks later, Khos accepted one year of probation without any admission of guilt.

This was the beginning of the end for Khos's run as a wrestling superstar. While Vince continued to give him breaks and chances, recasting him as Colonel Mustafa during the Persian Gulf Crisis, having him manage a wrestler named The Sultan when he could no longer work in the ring, Khos was his own worst enemy, failing drug tests and spiraling further downward. The WWF paid $33,000 to send him to the Ridgeview Institute for rehab, but none of it took. Addiction had its talons in deep.

Caryl urged him to find another job outside of wrestling, anything to keep him busy and provide some structure—he could drive a bus or go back to welding like he had done when he first came to the US. But Khos had no interest in anything that wasn't wrestling.

"He got grumpier, harder to be around. He was just getting really depressed because of the way his life went. We saw the real him in small bursts but then there'd be the angry, drug-fueled, bad him," Nikki says.

*   *   *

NIKKI DOESN'T LIKE TACO BELL. SO WHY DID SHE FIND HERSELF IN A drive-through late on a Friday night with the weirdest craving for Mexican fast food?

She had felt off all night, thinking about her sister Marissa (who loves Taco Bell). There was an inexplicable feeling of dread sitting like lead in the pit of her stomach. She had been at an art gallery opening with her friends but couldn't shake that miserable feeling. The night before she had been out with Marissa and a new guy she was seeing named Charles, and she asked her sister if she wanted to go to an upcoming party. Marissa, always outgoing and fun-loving, said sure. Charles shot her a look, and Marissa immediately changed her mind. Nikki was appalled.

"I remember yelling at him, like, 'You don't tell my sister what she can do,'" Nikki says.

Although Charles had seemed nice enough at first (they had only met a few weeks prior), he quickly showed his true colors—controlling, possessive. Scary. Marissa was nice, too nice, but even she began realizing that Charles was not right for her. The day of the art gallery opening, she instant messaged (remember that precursor to texting?) Nikki: "I'm gonna break up with him tonight," it read.

The next day, Nikki tried to reach Marissa all day, but she wouldn't pick up, wouldn't answer her IMs. Sunday morning, Nikki was by the pool when her phone rang. It was her sister Tanya's mother-in-law.

Marissa was dead.

Nikki was hysterical. Her roommate, Edith, drove her over to Fayetteville, where Khos was hanging out in the garage.

"Daddy, Marissa is dead," she said.

"No no no no no no, that's not true, that can't be true," Khos said, laboring to his feet. Despite just having had both knees replaced, he charged into the yard, bellowing a cry that originated somewhere in the deepest recesses of his soul, his insides splitting apart. This man who had endured unimaginable pain in his life had never felt anything quite so excruciating.

Nikki's memory of that day is mostly darkness. A nauseous feeling of emptiness. They called Caryl home from work, and she held it together as Khos completely unraveled. The next several days were a blur.

Khos had had a bad feeling about Charles Reynolds from the start, and Khos's intuition was usually right. The feeling was so strong that when he met him, he said, "If you ever hurt my daughter, I'll slit your throat like a sheep and leave you in a ditch for dead." Now his worst fears had been confirmed.

According to the investigation, Marissa and Charles had had friends over to her apartment for drinks on Friday night. An argument between them broke out, possibly because Marissa was wanting to break up, and the friends left. On Sunday morning at around eight, Reynolds called his pastor and asked if he could come by to pray with him. When his pastor arrived, Reynolds showed him Marissa's body, her face discolored from strangulation, tucked in to the bed. The pastor called the authorities, and soon afterward Reynolds was put under arrest.

"She wouldn't calm down. What was I thinking? I don't want to live. I want to lay down. It was those fucking pills. I was wrong. Now I must die," Reynolds said in "spontaneous statements" recorded in the police report.

Marissa had had no idea quite how checkered Reynolds's past was. A search of the Clayton County Criminal Court archives reveals nine criminal violations before the murder charge, beginning in 1986 when he was twenty-one, and including harassing phone calls, public drunkenness, and aggravated assault. In 1990, he was convicted of aggravated assault and served nine years in prison. Apparently Marissa was not his first victim—he had strangled another woman nearly to death, leaving the scene; luckily, her roommate found her in time for her to be revived.

Reynolds was charged with Marissa's murder, and the case was bumped up to Superior Court.

On April 9, 2004, Nikki, Khos, and Caryl rode together to the courthouse. Reynolds had pleaded guilty, and Judge Stephen Boswell would be presiding over his sentencing. As they walked in through security, Khos set off the metal detector. Everyone recognized him as the Iron Sheik, so they weren't going to give him much trouble.

"I had dental work done," Khos explained.

They sat in the courtroom as Judge Boswell walked Reynolds through the proceedings.

"Will the assistant district attorney state the terms of the negotiated plea?" Boswell said.

"Life in prison," replied B.J. Dixon.

"How do you want to plead to this offense, guilty or not guilty?" Boswell asked Reynolds.

"Guilty," Reynolds replied.

In the courthouse pews, Khos shifted in his seat. Tanya, seated next to him, grabbed his leg tight and whispered something to him.

With the sentencing wrapping up, Dixon said to the judge: "Your honor, the victim's family is here, and Caryl Vaziri, the mother, would like to address the court, as well as the defendant."

Caryl, who had kept her feelings in check all this time, wasn't about to break down now:

First of all, I want to say that life in prison is just too good. Only the death penalty would have satisfied us. Marissa never loved you, Charles. She pitied you. And she never considered you her boyfriend. You have devastated our entire family and all the people who care about Marissa.

Over 500 people. More than any amount of people that have ever filled our church were there for her funeral. The worst part was that Marissa was so discolored—she was totally black. We couldn't even see her before we buried her. And that just kills us. No one here today more than me wanted to see you get what you deserve. Unfortunately we didn't get it. When your judgement day comes, I think you need to be very afraid. We have hundreds and hundreds of people standing ready to testify at any parole hearing that comes up in the future to make sure that the monster you are never, ever hurts another human being. We can never forgive you for taking away our oldest daughter and the love of our lives. But her beauty will live on in our hearts forever.

Reynolds died of a heart attack in prison in 2016.

Back outside the courthouse, Caryl, Khos, and Nikki got back in the car to drive home.

Khos opened his mouth and spat out a razor blade.

"I was going to slit his throat just like I told him I would," Khos confessed.

"Even if I'm crippled, I can still kill that motherfucker," he added.

Khos had fashioned a piece of razor blade to conceal in his mouth, just as he had hundreds of times in wrestling when he needed to blade during a match. He woke up that morning planning to rush Reynolds in the courtroom and slice his throat. It was Tanya, when she got wind of the plan, who talked him out of it through her courtroom whispers.

If you kill him, we'll lose you just like we lost Marissa, she told him.

He was a killer on the wrestling mat, but not in real life. Nothing hurt him worse than knowing that he had not been there to protect his Marissa, his firstborn, that his absolute worst fears had actually come true.

The only salve for his wounds came in a crack pipe. Marissa's death put him over the edge.

It's no wonder that when I came calling less than a year later, Khos was in no state to collaborate on his biography. I understand now what I did not know then—the *why* of Khos's addiction and not just the existence of the addiction itself.

"I was not the same person I was before," he had told me.

In a truth-is-stranger-than-fiction event (of which there are many in this book), just a year or two after I left Fayetteville and retreated to California, Jian and Page Magen, identical twins from Toronto who are around my age, traveled to Fayetteville to try and film a documentary about Khos's life. Like me, the Magens were lifelong Iron Sheik fans, but had a more personal connection—their father, Bijan, was a friend of Khos's back in Tehran and went on to compete internationally in ping-pong. Bijan and Khos had fallen out of touch for years, only to be reunited when Bijan's wife heard a voice ranting on TV in Farsi in the early 1980s.

"Bijan, that's your friend!" she said, recognizing Khos behind the handle-bar mustache and bald head of the Iron Sheik.

The next time Khos came to Toronto and from then on whenever he was in town to wrestle, he came by the Magen household for dinner, much to the delight of Jian and Page, who were little kids at the time.

Jian and Page ran into the same wall of addiction that stymied my book attempt when they tried collaborating with Khos on the documentary. But unlike me, they persisted, creating a Twitter account for the Iron Sheik that went viral, which led to a surprising resurgence in his popularity. When Khos finally cleaned up in recent years, they were able to complete the documentary (the aforementioned film *The Sheik*) in which they recounted their own up-and-down journey with their childhood hero. The film garnered praise and a screening at the Hot Docs Canadian International Documentary Festival. The pop was huge.

*   *   *

It's family dinner night at the Vaziri house and I'm invited.

I pile into Nikki's car with her kids. We stop at Rumi's Kitchen in Atlanta to load up on Persian food—falafel and hummus and chicken kabob and pita and rice and Khos's favorite, the koobideh kabob.

My mouth waters from the smell of all the spices blended together. I'm clutching the bag of pistachios and dried apricots that I bought for Khos at the Persian market; I also picked up some white wine and baklava.

"Here," Nikki says, handing me a bouquet of flowers after another quick stop.

"Give these to Caryl. You've got to make Caryl happy," she says.

The last time we were all together, seventeen years ago, Nikki's kids didn't exist. Between her two daughters and Tanya's three kids, Khos and Caryl now have a flock of grandchildren.

I think back to the months after I left Fayetteville in 2005, when I would lie in bed in California with my mind racing, trying to find a way that I could still make his biography work. I didn't want to accept that things were beyond my control, that my passion wouldn't be enough. A couple of years after my failed attempt, the WWE hired a writer, Keith Elliot Greenberg, to pen the Sheik's biography. Seeking closure, I got in touch with Keith and sent him my research material, wishing him luck. (The book to this day has never been released, despite several false starts.)

We pull up to a ranch-style house with a sloping backyard and a trailer for transporting cars parked in the driveway. There isn't anything left for me to learn about my hero's life. All that's left is to close the circle.

Caryl opens the garage door and it's a melee of hellos and hugs as the grandkids bound in and I present Caryl with the flowers. She looks the same, greeting me with a big hug and an even bigger smile. A flood of memories rushes in—walking with her around Universal Studios during WWE Hall of Fame weekend after Khos threw a fit in the hotel room, countless conversations in the dining room of their old house about how to get Khos to cooperate. It's all led back here.

As everyone files inside, something in the garage catches my eye. I hang back for a moment. On the back of a door, in an oversize gold frame, is an eight-by-ten glossy of the Iron Sheik pinning Hulk Hogan against the ropes. Sheik's expression is maximum effort, doing his pretend all to hold the much-larger Hulkster in place. To think, after all the thousands of miles I've traveled on this journey, all the characters I've come across, it really all started with this. A good guy and a bad guy, the US and Iran, Terry Bollea and Khosrow Vaziri pretending to hate each other to put a smile on my face and the faces of millions of others.

I walk inside, through the kitchen and into the living room, where A&E's series *WWE Legends* is playing on the TV. Of course it is.

One such legend is sitting in a blue recliner, a facecloth on one armrest, his cell phone on the other.

The Iron Sheik, eighty years old, turns to look at me.

He's physically diminished, showing the added years in the creases around his eyes. His mustache is grayish white, the days of dyeing long gone. He's wearing a blue polo shirt tucked into black pants and a Wrestle-Mania baseball hat. But the biggest difference is in his eyes. They are tired but kind, content. At peace. There's no sign of the aggression and vitriol that I remember so vividly from the past.

With great labor, he pushes himself up to his feet, and I move closer to help him. It's the only time he'll stand during my visit.

I lean in close and give him a hug.

"Brad Belushi baba, good to see you. Wow. You look good. Thanks to the God I see you again," he says, his lips parting to reveal a gummy smile. He had teeth extracted for permanent dentures, but the procedure caused such inflammation that he is putting off the implants for now.

I take a seat on the couch next to him and take out my phone, excited to show him pictures and videos from my road trip. I've collected short video tributes from Tony Atlas and Alan Rice and Pat Marcy and others as I've gone, which I now play for him.

I'm the twenty-year-old again in the Holiday Inn in Secaucus, New Jersey, showing him the tribute book I put together.

Behind him, the dining room is set up much the same way it was at their old house, with the china cabinet and oil paintings of flowers.

Nikki puts out a spread of pita and hummus on the table in front of us and Caryl hands me a cocktail.

"What would you like, Khos?" she asks. He has been clean for several years, just having the occasional drink.

"I imagine whatever the Brad is having," he says. Caryl makes him a smaller version of my screwdriver.

"Nikki baba, turn down those lights please," he says, motioning to the chandelier in the dining area. Caryl tells me that Khos is struggling with some health issues—chronic obstructive pulmonary disease (COPD), congestive heart failure, arthritis, and other maladies.

"How are you feeling, Khos?" I ask.

"Not too bad, hang in there. Back, knees, ankle." He pulls up his right pant leg to show me a scar. Since I was last here, he finally had his troublesome left ankle fused and the right one "fused on its own," Caryl says. He also had to have surgery to realign the bones of his legs. Walking for any great distance is out of the question. A giant staff leans next to him on the couch.

Nikki brings over some more mementos from his archive, old photos and documents, even his report cards from elementary school in Iran. I ask Khos to identify some of the people in the pictures and he struggles with some names and specifics. When I share the video tributes with Caryl, she turns to Khos and says, "Everyone loved you, Khos. You were the most popular."

He grins shyly and says, "I don't know, I guess." His breath is labored.

I about hit the floor. The Khos I remember would have taken Caryl's comment as the opening to launch into a self-indulgent promo about how nobody beat Bob Backlund for six years, and then how, in the greatest arena in the world, Madison Square Garden, he prevailed.

Caryl sits in the recliner next to him.

"So what is this you're working on?" she asks me.

"After my first book, I wanted to do something on wrestling. Why do people like wrestling, why is it popular? I'm gonna write about the guys I grew up watching. And wrestling really changed with the Iron Sheik and Hulk Hogan and all that, when the WWF blew up," I reply.

I fill them in on the last couple decades of my life, leaving *Islands* magazine and breaking up with Melissa and getting my PhD. Khos used to tell me that his PhD was earned on the Road, learning all of the hard lessons that it forces on you. I describe the process of writing *The Wax Pack* and what a different breed wrestlers are from baseball players.

"So, Caryl, you moved out a couple years after I was here, around 2007?" I ask.

"I left. I had to take a stand and shock him and make him realize I'm not going to live this life," she says matter-of-factly of her decision to separate from Khos.

Her sister came down and helped her find an apartment near her job and closer to Nikki in the Buckhead area of Atlanta. It was hard, so hard, but Caryl knew it was what she had to do, for herself and for Khos. For the next two years, Khos lived in a small, simple apartment by himself, surrounded by his wrestling mementos. Tanya kept a close eye on him, making sure he had the essentials.

"Khos, when Caryl moved out and you were on your own, that's when you quit the drugs, right?"

"Right."

"How did you do that? Tell me how that happened," I say.

He doesn't shy away from my question, doesn't shut down.

"Just better I change my life. I just say I'm gonna change, I hope Caryl come back to me. Be a new person. It was a little bit hard but I did it."

Short, simple, and to the point. *I needed to change and so I did.* Quitting hard drugs after decades of addiction must have been incredibly difficult; the physical withdrawal alone is too much for many to bear. But, as Nikki tells me, no one has more willpower than Khos, and seeing his life ending all alone in a tiny apartment, he knew what he had to do.

Caryl found this house in Fayetteville and hearing that Khos had finally cleaned up, agreed to let him move in. It's been night and day.

"He's so cool. We've been married forty-seven years. Every night, he thanks me profusely for everything I've done for him that day," she says.

When the pandemic hit, she decided to retire from her job as a travel agent at Carlson Wagonlit. She had paid her dues. Time to ride off into the sunset, next to her companion for life.

Every day, they sit side by side in their recliners, watching TV and visiting. The girls stop by to say hi, but it's mostly just the two of them, just as it was in 1975 when Khos had a full head of hair and the Iron Sheik had not yet been conjured.

"He's very, very accommodating. He's like, 'We'll watch whatever you want to.' And he doesn't want me to go in the bedroom, he wants me right here where he can see me. He wants company. So we're gonna buy a new couch with the recliner on the ends, and that way, we could even hold hands or something," she says.

Khos stopped making public appearances about seven years ago. He's been offered big money for all kinds of deals, but the Iron Sheik is gone. He feels the legacy of that character every day when he gets out of bed, feels every bump in his inflamed joints and brittle bones.

There's nothing left to prove, no promos left to cut. Even as his agents write unhinged tweets in his name (while we're sitting here, the "Iron Sheik" on Twitter writes, "IT'S ABOUT TIME FOR EVERYONE TO GO FUCK YOURSELF"— Khos doesn't know how to turn on a computer, let alone tweet), Khos is content to be himself, his real self, with Caryl at his side.

I'm curious how he feels about Hulk Hogan after all these years. If his Twitter account is to be believed, he still despises the Hulkster.

"Do you still not like Terry?" I ask.

"I don't call him, he doesn't call me. We don't bother each other," he replies.

"But you don't have bad feelings toward him?"

"No."

The Iron Sheik may hate Hulk Hogan, but for all the hype and internet gossip, Khosrow Vaziri has no animosity toward Terry Bollea.

Throughout the night, Khos keeps his eyes on me, watching me like a hawk as I go through his archive of old material, making sure I handle everything with care. He checks in and makes sure I have enough to eat, that I am comfortable in his home. I am his guest, and he makes sure I am well taken care of.

Javanmardi.

Welcome back, Khos.

THE END

PART V
THE FINAL BELL

EPILOGUE

I learned that every mortal will taste death.
But only some will taste life.

—Rumi, as quoted in the program for Khosrow
Vaziri's funeral, June 17, 2023

LESS THAN A WEEK AFTER I FINISHED WRITING THIS BOOK, KHOSROW Vaziri died.

My phone chimed with a text message at 5:10 a.m. on June 7, 2023. No good texts arrive at 5:10 a.m.

"My dad went in his sleep last night. Thankfully we were all here," it said.

It was from Nikki, Khos's youngest daughter who less than a year prior had been such a gracious host during my return visit to Fayetteville.

I cleared the sleep from my eyes and sat on the edge of my bed, processing. In some ways, given how hard Khos had lived his life, I realized I had been expecting this day for years; in other ways, given how many comebacks he'd made when things seemed impossibly bleak, he had seemed immortal.

I didn't know exactly what Khos's cause of death was, and I didn't ask. Knowing that he passed in his sleep was all I needed to know. Nikki asked me to help her write his obituary for the Islamic funeral that would happen within forty-eight hours of his passing.

Only a couple of hours later, the whole world knew. Social media blew up with tributes and remembrances. My phone began chirping and chiming, messages from childhood friends, long-lost college buddies, colleagues, and people I met for this book, all expressing their condolences. That felt both heartwarming and a bit awkward. At first, I resisted the attention—it felt weird to receive condolences for a man who was not family or a peer. But I sat with it, and soon that awkwardness melted into appreciation. Because what all those text messages meant is that the people in my life, some of whom I hadn't seen in years, saw "Iron Sheik passes away" in the headlines and thought of me. The range of people who reached out represented the entire breadth of my life, from those who accompanied me to watch the WWF at the Providence Civic Center when I was a kid to the people I met on last year's road trip. If a life could be expressed through a series of mathematical equations, then the Iron Sheik had been a constant.

About a week later, I got a text from Khos's other daughter, Tanya: "Hi Brad, we are having a service for my father this Saturday, and would be honored if you are able to attend," it read.

I thanked her for the invite and immediately scuttled all of my weekend plans, making last-minute arrangements for a flight, lodging, and rental car. I was honored to be invited to the private service. When I had left Fayetteville last July, I had no idea I would be back so soon.

*　　*　　*

THE SKY IS A BRIGHT WHITE THE MORNING OF THE FUNERAL, THE AIR WARM and pleasant. I arrive early at Prince of Peace Lutheran Church, a brick building topped by a narrow white steeple, with rows of pear trees outside.

Just inside the lobby is a large photo of a young Khosrow Vaziri in his military uniform, square-jawed with matinee idol looks. A TV screen flashes a rotation of pictures from his life and career, and two gorgeous floral arrangements, one in white, another in red, flank the entrance to the sanctuary. I peer down to look at the attached cards:

"*You'll Always Be Loved and Respected*" –Vince & The WWE Family, reads one; "*Our thoughts and prayers are with you and your family. With deepest sympathy*" WWE, reads the other. Next to the flowers, on either side of the doors, enlarged photos signify the two men being laid to rest today: to the left, Khosrow Vaziri, receiving a trophy in Iran for one of his many amateur wrestling championships; to the right, the Iron Sheik, standing in the locker room next to Ayatollah Blassie moments after winning the WWF title on that fateful night after Christmas, 1983.

I take a seat in the back of the church, and for the next three hours, I remember what it feels like to believe. The wood-paneled vaulted ceiling and stained-glass windows evoke the experience of attending my childhood Methodist church, countless Sundays spent in a similar room with similar-looking people. The pastor's voice follows the template of seemingly every Protestant pastor—a soothing cadence that rises and falls like a piece of music, peppered with extended pauses and clusters of words suddenly imbued with force, crescendos pleading for meaning. I close my eyes to disorient myself to space and time, conjuring the presence of my parents to either side of me during all those Sunday sermons, wondering if they were actually paying attention or just nodding to keep up the act, their own form of Kayfabe. I remember wanting the services to be over so badly so I could eat the Vienna fingers waiting at coffee hour and then get home to plug in my VHS tapes to watch the Iron Sheik in action. That version of me unequivocally believed in God. I would say little prayers to Him throughout the day, petty little prayers like "Jesus, please help me to get all my homework done so I can have time to watch wrestling tonight," or "God, please make the Iron Sheik the WWF champion again." That version of me, so impressionable, saw this muscly Iranian with a handlebar mustache and funny boots and for just a few minutes, believed in something bigger than whatever surrounded me. I knew even then that the matches weren't real, but that the feelings they evoked were.

The more cynical, agnostic, adult version of me, the me sitting here in Fayetteville, Georgia, on Father's Day Eve, 2023, lets those feelings slip back in as those who knew and loved my hero best now eulogize him. It is a beautiful ceremony in front of about a hundred people, a series of tributes that acknowledge both Khos and his alter ego. It's private (a public announcement would likely have overrun the church with wrestling fans), but only so much so—the pastors delay the service fifteen minutes because the internet live stream is experiencing technical difficulties.

The two lead eulogies come from Jian and Page Magen, the identical twins from Toronto who are largely responsible for the Sheik's pop culture renaissance of the past fifteen years. Page is the mastermind behind the Sheik's infamous Twitter account, channeling his outlandish rants to titillate the masses. Their speeches reflect their affection for the man, recounting numerous brushes with other celebrity icons (the time at the Grammys when Tony Bennett and Mick Jagger invited the Sheik to sit in their dressing room to visit; the time his presence caused Beyoncé [accompanied by Jay-Z] to double back to tell him, "I used to sit on my grandma's lap and she would curse you on the TV!"). But what stands out most for me is an anecdote from Jian, who talks about the time a gang of Hulk Hogan fans tied him and Page to a tree and "roughed us up" for cheering the Iron Sheik. Jian and Page idolized the Sheik just as I did, but they had even more reason to than me—he, like them, was Iranian. Costume or not, real or not, they believed in him.

"He was the man that gave young Iranians a voice of strength and confidence. While everyone saw him as the bad guy, we saw him as the hero," Jian says.

The Sheik's reach went well beyond Iranians. At the reception afterward, I meet Ray, also about my age, who grew up in the United Arab Emirates. Although UAE is an Arab nation with a completely different culture than Iran, for young kids like Ray, the Iron Sheik represented all of them. He tells me how he and his friends would modify the tips of their shoes to resemble the curved toes of the Sheik's wrestling boots.

Following the Sheik-centric eulogies, the memory of Khosrow Vaziri takes center stage. His oldest granddaughter, Marissa, named for Khos's late eldest daughter, takes the lectern and in a soft, sweet voice details the mundane joys of daily life with her Papa Sheik—fetching him his favorite doughnuts (chocolate-covered and yellow), watching John Wayne movies, helping him respond to fan mail. Then Joni Moore Kanazawa, who grew up across the street from the Vaziris, shares her memories of Khos leading the neighborhood kids in calisthenic drills.

"The Iron Sheik was his title at work, but to us, Mr. Vaziri's real-life calling was as a motivational speaker and coach. He had us running endless laps around the house over and over again, and I will forever hear his voice yelling, 'Faster, baba, faster!' He was a man of his word. If he loved you, he kept wanting to teach you and push you to be the best version of yourself," she says.

Finally, we get word from one of Khos's peers. His only contemporary to show up is not Hulk Hogan, nor Vince McMahon (but he sent flowers!) nor Bob Backlund; it's the one Six Packer who eluded me on my journey: Sgt. Slaughter.

"My name is Bob Remus," he says from the pulpit in his signature gravelly voice. He looms over the congregation, recounting his deep and long-time friendship with his greatest onstage adversary. He speaks with a distinctly Midwestern cadence, deliberate, the words clearly enunciated. He describes the first time he met Khos at Verne Gagne's training camp in that creaky barn, his counsel to turn down Gagne's offer to break Hulk Hogan's leg, and other greatest hits of their time together.

He closes with a reminder of both the cost of their profession and the reason why Khos excelled in it:

"Because of always being away for birthdays and anniversaries, Christmas and Thanksgiving, he [Khos] was very fond, as I am, of young children. We didn't have ours with us so we would take other people's children and put them on our laps and act as if they were our children because we missed ours so much. And so that's the one thing I always remember about Khos is not only his love for family, but for children. He loved everyone," he says.

Following the service, I walk up to Bob, wondering if I should tell him the extreme lengths that I went to trying to find him, only to end up with him here.

But no, this isn't the time, or the place. This day is about Khos.

"Bob, I'm Brad," I say, extending my hand across the pew.

"Brad, it's nice to meet you," he says with a firm handshake. His eyes are golden, shining behind a pair of glasses. His bald head is exposed, his pencil mustache dyed brown. There's no sign of Sgt. Slaughter, and yet in his remarks he couldn't help but refer to Hulk Hogan as the "immortal slime," a momentary lapse that he immediately followed with "I'll try not to get into character here."

"I enjoyed your words," I tell him.

"Thank you. That's the thing, when you ad lib, you end up forgetting some of the things you were going to say," he replies.

Bob and Khos never needed a script anyway.

The next morning, Father's Day, I have some time to kill before heading to the airport. I head to the plaza in Fayetteville where I did my grocery shopping when I lived here back in 2005, vaguely recalling a café where I might be able to grab some breakfast.

I walk through the doors to discover a hive of activity, the restaurant staff hustling to set up special black-and-blue tablecloths for Father's Day. I grab a table for one, order a breakfast sandwich, and open a blank page of my notebook, trying to figure out what exactly I want to say in this epilogue.

Two women sit at a table diagonally opposite from me, wearing yoga pants and T-shirts. One of them glances over at me with a big smile and reminds me of a cardinal difference between where I live in California and here: how friendly everyone is.

"Excuse me, are you a father?" the one in purple pants asks me.

"No, I'm not," I say, returning the smile.

And then she says something delightful and wholly unexpected.

"Well, I'm sure at some point you brought light into some young person's life. So happy Father's Day."

I thank her, surprised by the way she makes me feel like I belong on a day that generally carries little personal meaning (other than thinking of my own dad).

I shovel warm buttery eggs into my mouth and clamp down on crispy bacon, savoring the tastes of the South. Somewhere down the road, Nikki and Tanya are silently wishing Khos a happy Father's Day. Like Jian and Page and so many other now-grown kids of the 1980s, I am grateful to Khos for having been that figure for us all to believe in.

On the way out the door, I turn to look at the sign above the café. I hadn't even looked on the way in to see its name, but want to remember it on the odd chance I ever come back again to Fayetteville.

"Truth Breakfast Bar & Grill," it reads.

THE END (really this time)

ACKNOWLEDGMENTS

HOLY CRAP, IS IT HARD TO WRITE A BOOK. IT IS BOTH THE MOST JOYFUL AND painful of experiences, exquisite torture that produces anguish and bliss in equal parts. Writing is a very solitary endeavor, and yet it can't be done entirely alone.

First and foremost I want to put over Khosrow Vaziri and his family for being so generous and gracious with their time. I had no idea as a little kid watching the Iron Sheik on TV just how well I would one day get to know him, but with all the heat and the highspots that I experienced, he's still my hero.

I also want to thank the other Six Packers and wrestlers who agreed to give me a push and relive their journey in the bizarro world of pro wrestling. They deserve a Road Warriors pop.

I'd like to make the hot tag to the following babyfaces for agreeing to be interviewed for the book or for providing helpful information: Mike Chapman, Alan Rice, Bob Buzzard, Jim Duschen, Ali Dehestani, Amir Dehestani, Bijan Magen, Matt Turk, Dave Meltzer, Abraham Josephine Riesman, Gerry Brisco, Curt Connaughty, Mark Adzick, George Adzick, Pat Marcy, Brad Rheingans, Dan Chandler, Tunisha Singleton, CarrieLynn Reinhard, José Mario Cavazos, Mike Mooneyham, Bob McMullan, Graham Cawthon, Tim Hornbaker, Richard Land, Rob Miller, Jim Troy, Mark Solis, Michael Solis, Tom Emmanuel, Nelson Sweglar, Mike Breen, Ed Helinski, Jean Manning, Tony Garea, Jim Brunzell, Ken Patera, Brian Blair, Eddie Sharkey, Kathie

Case, Tim Wilhelm, Gino Caruso, Mickey Sherman, Konstantine Kyros, Jack Edmonds, Johanna Rivera, Ed Ricciuti, Steve Olsonoski, Steve Taylor, Allan Barrie, and Keith Elliott Greenberg.

Thanks to the *Wrestling Observer* archive, thehistoryofwwe.com, the wrestlingclassics.com message board, kayfabememories.com, and wrestlingdata.com for providing abundant reference material.

I can't put over Eric Bischoff enough. We first got in touch a few years ago when I was working on *The Wax Pack*, and Eric didn't know me from Adam. He generously gave me his time, and then helped me enormously with setting up contacts for this book. Thank you, Eric, for all that you have done to help me.

The rough cuts of this book were, well, rough, and so I'd like to thank the following readers for shooting with their honest feedback and helping to clean up my prose: Terry Shames, Laird Harrison, Karen Laws, Sandy Char, Robert Luhn, Chris Cataldo, Monica Ambalal, Hana Hayashi, Adoria Williams, Jesse Brouillard, David Munro, Mark Wallace, and Jeff Bailey. Phil Marino has been wonderfully generous with his time helping me with my website.

The group of professionals at Hachette who shepherded this program from conception to execution rival the nWo, D-Generation X, or any other wrestling faction for their performance, able to take all kinds of bumps on the way to a five-star finish. Thank you to Mary Ann Naples, Michelle Aielli, Michael Barrs, Amanda Kain, Michael Giarratano, Kara Brammer, Terri Sirma, Fred Francis, Mollie Weisenfeld, and Monica Oluwek.

I want to thank my tag-team partners, my agent Farley "The Great" Chase, and my editor, Brant "Ready to" Rumble, who made this whole process fun. I've heard so many horror stories of agents and editors who are nonresponsive and checked out, so every day I consider myself lucky to work with two people at the top of their game and who on a personal level, I truly like. Life's too short to spend time working with heels. Brant, thank you for always taking that extra minute to make your communications thoughtful.

Speaking of personal, every writer needs a support system in order to stay sane. I'm grateful for mine, consisting of my hockey buddies on the Sofa/BeaverKings (Derek Godfrey, Jeff Bailey, Nick Wirz, David Granzotto, Jake Stanello); my colleagues in the Merritt College Natural History and

Sustainability program (Ben Nelson, Greg Vose, and Elizabeth Boegel); the Team (Adam and Jesse Brouillard); Marilyn Clerkin, my aunt, who inspired me to read from a young age and brought her eagle eye to each of my chapters; my parents, Jim and Nikki Balukjian (thanks, Mom, for buying me the figures that appear on the cover of this book!); and my sister, Lauren Balukjian, and her flock (Chase, Stacia, Olivia, and Bianca). Also a special thank-you to my cousin Romulo "Nic" Valdez for talking me through the finer points of our legal system as I researched Chapter 8. I would job for all of you any time.

Finally, the biggest thanks of all go to you, the reader (and if you're still reading the acknowledgments, thank you, I must have done something right). In our modern society, few things get our attention for very long as emphasis is placed on everything being shorter and snappier. So in that context, it is truly an honor for you to sit and read (or listen to) me for eight or nine hours. I am flattered that you would spend the length of an entire workday with me.

Thank you.

NOTES ON SOURCES

Prologue

Interviews: Caryl Vaziri, Khosrow Vaziri

Opening Match: Back on the Road

21   **"In the early eighties":** Kevin Cook, "Playboy Interview: Vince McMahon," *Playboy*, February 2001.

24   **The 24,592 fans:** Graham Cawthon, *Holy Ground: 50 Years of WWE at Madison Square Garden* (self-pub., CreateSpace, 2014), 163.

24   **more than nine hundred live events:** "Professional Wrestling Merchandise Takes Off," *Daily Press*, October 12, 1986.

Match 2: The Iron Sheik vs. Khosrow Vaziri

Interviews: Caryl Vaziri, Khosrow Vaziri, Tony Atlas, Alan Rice, Jim Duschen, Ali Dehestani, Amir Dehestani, Bijan Magen, Pat Marcy, Dan Chandler, and Jim Brunzell

32   **an independent country for the past three thousand years:** John Ghazvinian, *America and Iran: A History 1720 to the Present* (New York: Knopf, 2021), xv.

32   **home to sixty million:** Ibid., 3.

32   **Europeans named it "Persia":** Ibid., xiii.

32   **greater than 90 percent:** Ibid., xv.

32   **fifty thousand Americans were living in Iran:** Ibid., 8.

32   **"an island of stability":** Ibid., 9.

33   **Iran went to war:** Ibid., 28.

33   **again in 1856:** Ibid., 31.

33   **Shah Muzaffar al-Din's decision:** Ibid., 55.

33   **world's first Muslim democracy:** Ibid., 61.

34   **five hundred such buildings:** "Iran's House of Strength," *World Policy Journal*, Summer 2015.

34   **seventy-five to one hundred centimeters deep:** Mohammad-Ghorban Kiani and Hassan Faraji, "Zoorkhaneh: Historic Training in Iranian Culture," *World Applied Sciences Journal*, 2011.

35   **an Iranian king who ruled:** "Khosrow I," Britannica.com.

35   **Takhti's family had been:** H. E. Chehabi, "Sport and Politics in Iran: the Legend of Gholamreza Takhti," *International Journal of the History of Sport* 12, no. 3 (1995): 48–60.

36   **he was named *Time* magazine's:** "Man of the Year: Challenge of the East," *Time*, January 7, 1952.

36   **In 1951 he took back control:** Ghazvinian, *America and Iran*, 169.

36   **The CIA funded strongmen:** Ibid., 198.

36   **He imposed martial law:** Ibid., 209.

36   **Iran was spending as much:** Ibid., 253.

36   **the Buin Zahra earthquake killed:** "Gholamreza Takhti," documentary film, 2019.

36   **When he refused to attend:** Chehabi, "Sport and Politics in Iran."

37   **At the age of twenty:** Report card from the Iranian Ministry of Education, Farahmand Secondary School, 1961–1962.

37   **placing second in the:** Memo from the Iranian Amateur Wrestling Federation, January 1967.

37   **who can be seen in archival footage:** "Gholamreza Takhti," documentary film, 2019.

38   **In late fall of 1969:** Receipt from the Department of State, United States of America, September 27, 1969.

48   **the US admitted the Shah:** Ghazvinian, *America and Iran*, 324.

MATCH 3: EXCITING BALUKJIAN VS. BRAD BALUKJIAN

Interviews: CarrieLynn Reinhard, Tunisha Singleton, Gino Caruso

55   **when asked what she would miss most:** "Profiles in Carnage," *Hartford (CT) Courant*, September 26, 1982.

55   ***The Epic of Gilgamesh:*** "Gilgamesh," World History Encyclopedia. Web.

55   **The Irish brought their:** Scott M. Beekman, *Ringside: A History of Professional Wrestling in America* (Westport, CT: Praeger, 2006), 10.

55   **The less-restrained "catch" style:** Jake Shannon, *Say Uncle: Catch-as-Catch-Can Wrestling and the Roots of Ultimate Fighting, Pro Wrestling, and Modern Grappling* (Toronto, Canada: ECW Press, 2011), 6; Beekman, *Ringside*, 19.

55   **which arrived in the US in:** "Folk Wrestling from the Circus to the Stadium: The Birth of Greco-Roman and Freestyle," in *Routledge Handbook of Global Sport* (January 2020). Web.

55   **practiced at the first Olympic:** "What Is Greco Roman Wrestling: From Rules to Olympic History," Olympics.com.

56   **Newspaper accounts of a November:** "Karl Stern's Longform History of Pro Wrestling," When It Was Cool platform on Patreon.com.

56   **matches began taking place:** Beekman, *Ringside*, 36; Gerald W. Morton and George M. O'Brien, *Wrestling to Rasslin: Ancient Sport to American Spectacle* (Bowling Green, OH: Bowling Green State University Popular Press, 1985), 39.

56   **An estimated 90 percent of all:** Beekman, *Ringside*, 40.

56 **an eight-hour draw:** "Karl Stern's Longform History of Pro Wrestling," When It Was Cool platform on Patreon.com.

56 **the longest match on record:** Graeme Kent, *A Pictorial History of Wrestling* (n.p.: Spring Books, 1968), 138.

56 **a 1920 bout that drew ten thousand:** Beekman, *Ringside*, 56.

57 **After winning the belt from:** Ibid., 59.

58 **"It's possible that the illusion":** Abraham Josephine Riesman, *Ringmaster: Vince McMahon and the Unmaking of America* (New York: Atria, 2023), 85–86.

58 **"Every one of them":** Riesman, *Ringmaster*, 86.

64 **"When the WWF's Linda McMahon":** Testimony of Linda McMahon to Commonwealth of Pennsylvania State Government Ad Hoc Committee House of Representatives, "Stenographic report of hearing held in majority caucus room, Harrisburg, PA," June 11, 1987.

MATCH 4: MR. USA TONY ATLAS VS. ANTHONY WHITE

Interviews: Anthony White, Reggie Dean, Jim Troy, Monika White

70 **Hydro-powered textile mills:** John A. Rand, *The Peoples Lewiston-Auburn Maine 1875–1975* (Freeport, ME: Bond Wheelwright, 1975), 2–5.

70 **by 1865 Auburn was producing:** Richard H. Condon, "Bayonets at the North Bridge: The Lewiston-Auburn Shoe Strike, 1937," *Maine Historical Quarterly* 21, no. 2 (Fall 1981).

70 **earning it the title of:** "Auburn, Maine," The Historical Markers Database. Web.

85 **"I was the one who killed":** 2006 WWE Hall of Fame Induction Ceremony, April 6, 2005. Viewed on streaming platform Peacock.

87 **"Saba Simba, who went":** "Roaring for Action," *WWF Magazine*, 1990.

93 **In the US's infancy:** Thomas W. Dixon Jr., *Chesapeake and Ohio: Alleghany Subdivision* (Clifton Forge, VA: Chesapeake and Ohio Historical Society, 1985), 1.

93 **Rivers and railroads drove:** Ibid., 24.

93 **spurring an iron boom:** "Our History," Alleghany Historical Society. Web.

MATCH 5: MR. MCMAHON VS. VINCE MCMAHON

Interviews: Nelson Sweglar, Jim Troy, Ed Helinski, Rob Miller, Eric Bischoff, Dave Meltzer, Abraham Josephine Riesman, Mike Breen, Brad Rheingans, Bob McMullan, Tom Emanuel, Ed Ricciuti

97 **Epigraph, definitions of "sport" and "entertainment":** *American Heritage Dictionary of the English Language*, 3rd ed., 614, 1742.

97 **The facility includes 105,000:** "Greenwich Library," Apicella + Bunton Architects. Web.

97 **Fresh from an $18 million:** Ibid.

98 **it's been reported that:** Riesman, *Ringmaster*, 6.

99 **"I lived with her and":** Cook, "Playboy Interview: Vince McMahon."

99 **"Was the abuse all":** Ibid.

99 **"That's not anything I":** Ibid.

99 **"Did it come from":** Ibid.

100 **"No. It wasn't . . . it wasn't":** Ibid.

100 **"I'm not big on excuses":** Ibid.

100 **Jess was part of the New York:** Tim Hornbaker, *Capitol Revolution: The Rise of the McMahon Wrestling Empire* (Toronto, Canada: ECW Press, 2015), 39.

100 **In 1925 he was named head:** Ibid., 51.

101   **Jess helped set him up as:** Ibid., 107.

101   **By 1953, Vince Senior:** Ibid., 117.

101   **"In a game of misinformation":** "Wrestling with Success," *Sports Illustrated*, March 25, 1991.

101   **"My dad was a fabulous":** Ibid.

101   **"I would say that I idolized":** "Wrestling Mogul Knows the Ropes," *Durham Sun*, July 22, 1986.

102   **"He was a persona non grata":** Ibid.

102   **founded in Iowa in 1948 by:** Tim Hornbaker, *National Wrestling Alliance: The Untold Story of the Monopoly that Strangled Pro Wrestling* (Toronto, Canada: ECW Press, 2007), 8.

102   **strained by a 1956 anti-trust lawsuit:** Hornbaker, *Capitol Revolution*, 137.

103   **worth upward of $800 million:** United States Securities and Exchange Commission Form 10-Q, filed December 10, 2001.

103   **his partners for $1 million:** Tim Hornbaker, *Death of the Territories: Expansion, Betrayal, and the War that Changed Pro Wrestling Forever* (Toronto, Canada: ECW Press, 2018), 22.

104   **which drew some seventy-eight thousand fans:** *Wrestling Observer Newsletter*, April 21, 2003, 8.

104   **the company sold $498,270:** Memo from Elias Brothers Restaurants to Edward Helinski, dated March 30, 1987, WrestleMania 3 Merchandise Report.

104   **more than thirty million people would tune in:** Jim Smallman, *I'm Sorry, I Love You: A History of Professional Wrestling* (London: Headline, 2018), 161.

105   **On February 21, 1980, the power couple:** "Titan Sports Inc.," Open Corporates Profile. Web.

107   **On June 5, 1982, the trio:** Hornbaker, *Death of the Territories*, 22.

107   **Troy and Vince each carried:** Ibid.

107   **Although other lords had tried:** Ibid., 62, 66.

108   **according to internal WWF documents:** "Wrestling Television Play Dates as of October 15, 1983," internal WWF document.

108   **up from just twenty-four in September:** "Profiles in Carnage," *Hartford Courant*, September 26, 1982.

108   **they were in 201 markets:** "It's Rough, It's Tough, It's Wrestling," *Hartford Courant*, August 21, 1986.

108   **With the US market growing from:** "The Cable History Timeline," The Cable Center, 2014. Web.

108   **most-watched cable show in the nation:** *Wrestling Observer Newsletter*, 1982 Yearbook.

111   **$63.125 million in 1985:** "Damage Determination Report for United Wrestling Association Inc. vs. Titan Sports Inc," submitted by Ellis G. Godwin, November 19, 1992.

118   **"If you leave to do the *Rocky* movie":** Hulk Hogan, *Hollywood Hulk Hogan* (Stamford, CT: World Wrestling Entertainment, 2002), 112.

120   **"I'm not coming back":** Riesman, *Ringmaster*, 79.

122   **worth an estimated $8.3 billion:** *Wrestling Observer Newsletter*, September 11, 2023.

122   **broadcasted in thirty languages and 180 countries:** "Company Information," World Wrestling Entertainment. Web.

123 **"WWE board probes secret \$3 million":** "WWE Board Probes Secret \$3 Million Hush Pact by CEO Vince McMahon, Sources Say," *Wall Street Journal,* June 15, 2022.

124 **The show earned its highest ratings:** *Wrestling Observer Newsletter,* June 27, 2022.

MATCH 6: TITO SANTANA VS. MERCED SOLIS

Interviews: Merced Solis, Michael Solis, José Mario Cavazos

129 **Prickly pear cactus pads and mesquite:** Placards on public display at the Mission Historical Museum, visited by the author on July 29, 2022.

129 **in 1861 Catholic French missionaries:** Ibid.

129 **spurred the founding of the city:** Ibid.

129 **The town's first census:** Ibid.

129 **fresh from the redwood lumber:** Ibid.

130 **acquired 49,000 acres of land:** Ibid.

142 **"One of the most impressive things":** WWE 2004 Hall of Fame Induction Ceremony, DVD.

145 **"When you get into wrestling":** Ibid.

146 **Randy Colley, a typical mid-card:** "Talent Earnings Analysis: Randy Colley," part of discovery file in William R. Eadie vs. Vincent K. McMahon and Titan Sports, Inc.

MATCH 7: SGT. SLAUGHTER VS. BOB REMUS

Interviews: Kathie Case, Curt Connaughty, Mark Adzick, George Adzick

153 **Director of marketing and development Don Levine:** "Now You Know the History of G.I. Joe. And Knowing Is Half the Battle," Smithsonian.com.

158 **In a 1991 survey of 114:** *Wrestling Observer Newsletter,* September 22, 2003, 2.

160 **East Coast writer Elizabeth Fries Ellet:** "Eden Prairie History," Eden Prairie Minnesota. Web.

160 **In 1962, Eden Prairie graduated:** Ibid.

160 **By the year 2000, the population:** Ibid.

160 **In 2010, *Money* magazine named:** "Eden Prairie, MN," Money.com.

163 **In newspaper articles from the 1980s:** "Officer Is No Gentleman; Serjeant Will Prove It," *Morning Call (Allentown, PA),* May 18, 1988; "Mom, Apple Pie, and Wrestling," *Baltimore Sun,* March 24, 1985.

163 **In a 2009 "shoot interview":** Sgt. Slaughter 2009 shoot interview, *Pro Wrestling Diary,* DVD.

164 **The *Marine Corps Times* ran an article:** "The Man Behind Pro Wrestling Legend Sgt. Slaughter Tells Stories of Combat Tours in Vietnam. But He Never Served," Marine Corps Times. Web.

164 **In a longer piece in *MEL Magazine*:** "The True History of Sgt. Slaughter's Stolen Valor," MEL Magazine. Web.

164 **reporter Steve Bryant filed a:** "U.S. Navy Responds to Reports that Sgt. Slaughter Never Served in the Military," Wrestlingnews.co.

169 **It was from the United States Patent:** Typed Drawing: Sgt. Slaughter, US Patent and Trademark Office Trademark Electronic Search System. Web.

169 **In his 2007 autobiography:** Bret Hart, *Hitman: My Real Life in the Cartoon World of Wrestling* (New York: Grand Central Publishing, 2007).

171 **In the basement:** "WWE's Most Wanted Treasures: Searching for Sgt. Slaughter's Iconic Swagger Stick," YouTube video.

MATCH 8: THE MASKED SUPERSTAR/
DEMOLITION AX VS. BILL EADIE

Interviews: Norma Ryan, Bill Eadie, Dottie Patton Melchiorre, Mike Smith, Pat Kostelnik Ward, Konstantine Kyros

176 **Bill will make $221,149 from the:** 1099-MISC form, 1990 Bill Eadie, Internal
Revenue Service.

176 **where Bill will earn $13,249:** 1099 Inquiry for Vendor Bill Eadie, 4/9/92, WWF
internal document.

178 **Incorporated in 1815, Brownsville:** Public exhibits at the Flatiron Building Heritage Center; visited June 16, 2022.

178 **Brownsville already served as:** Ibid.

179 **Brownsville peaked with about eight thousand people:** US Census, United
States Census Bureau. Web.

187 **"He was basically just an announcer":** Deposition of William R. Eadie, part of
Civil Action No. 5:91 CV 00423 (EBB), William R. Eadie vs. Vincent K. McMahon
and Titan Sports, Inc., July 21, 1992.

187 **"He told me when I would be starting":** Ibid.

187 **"I always called Vince McMahon's father":** Ibid.

188 **A glimpse at one such agreement signed:** Booking Agreement between Vince
McMahon and William Eadie, Titan Sports, signed January 6, 1984.

188 **"Although Talent Works for Promoter":** Ibid.

188 **"Talent grants to Promoter the unqualified":** Ibid.

189 **"consist of a percentage of the gross":** Ibid.

189 **"I don't like the mask":** Eadie deposition, July 21, 1992.

190 **According to Bill's deposition:** Ibid.

192 **On August 6, 1991, he filed:** Civil Docket for Case #:5:91-cv-00423-WWE, US
District Court, District of Connecticut (Bridgeport).

192 **According to those internal documents:** Royalty Report-Ax-Bill Eadie For
Period 1/1/85-12/31/96, Titan Sports Inc. internal document.

193 **"This letter will serve as an amendment":** Letter from Vince McMahon to Bill
Eadie, June 20, 1990.

193 **Bill began wrestling as Demolition Ax:** Graham Cawthon, *The History of Professional Wrestling, Volume 1: The Results WWF 1963–1989* (self-pub., CreateSpace,
2013), 614.

193 **the WWF should have paid Bill:** Damage Detail, December 3, 1997, attached to
letter from Howard B. Mintz to Theodore E. Dinsmoor.

194 **The docket alone for the case:** Civil Docket for Case #:5:91-cv-00423-WWE,
U.S. District Court, District of Connecticut (Bridgeport).

195 **On July 18, 2016, Bill and:** Plantiffs' Complaint, Joseph M. Laurinaitis et al. vs.
World Wrestling Entertainment and Vincent K. McMahon, United States District
Court, District of Connecticut.

195 **which was settled in 2013 with eighteen thousand:** Mark Fainaru-Wada and
Steve Fainaru, *League of Denial: The NFL, Concussions, and the Battle for Truth*
(New York: Crown, 2014), 357.

195 **Dr. Bennett Omalu's 2005 publication:** "Chronic Traumatic Encephelopathy in
a National Football League Player," *Neurosurgery*, July 2005.

195 **CTE was simply a new name:** "What to Know About CTE in Football," *New York Times*, July 5, 2022.

195 **A *USA Today* study of wrestler deaths:** "High Death Rate Lingers Behind Fun Façade of Pro Wrestling," *USA Today*, March 12, 2004.

196 **"After an injury the referee or":** Plaintiff Wrestlers' Second Amended Complaint, Russ McCullough et al. vs. World Wrestling Entertainment, November 3, 2017, Civil Action No. 3:15-cv-001074 (VLB).

196 **"You are not an independent contractor":** Independent Contractor Defined, Internal Revenue Service. Web.

197 **With an estimated median income:** Hingham, Massachusetts, City-Data.com.

198 **Eadie et al.'s case was dismissed:** Memorandum of Decision: Granting Defendants' Motions for Judgement on the Pleadings, Joseph Laurinaitis et al. vs. World Wrestling Entertainment, Civil Action No. 3:16-CV-1209.

199 **The Second Court of Appeals upheld:** "Former WWE Wrestlers' Lawsuit over Brain Damage Is Dismissed," *AP News*, September 9, 2020.

199 **fizzled in 2021 when they declined:** "Supreme Court Declines to Hear Appeal of Pro Wrestlers' Brain Damage Cases," *USA Today*, April 26, 2021.

200 **WWE has also implemented the:** WWE & ImPACT Concussion Management Program, WWE.com.

200 **"I called Chris Nowinski and said":** Konstantine Kyros, "The Cover-Up of CTE Science in Wrestling, Decades of Exploitation, and Violation of Employment Laws," May 18, 2019, wweconcussionlawsuitnews.com. Video.

201 **In 2016 the *Boston Globe* reported that:** "Ex-wrestlers Say One of Their Own Sells Them Short," *Boston Globe*, June 11, 2016.

MATCH 9: CONQUISTADOR #1/THE RED DEMON/ MAC RIVERA/JOSE LUIS RIVERA/THE BLACK DEMON/ SHADOW #2/JUAN LOPEZ/EL SULTAN VS. MARCELINO RIVERA

Interviews: Johanna Rivera, Marcelino Rivera, Jose Alberto Rivera

204 **Has its share of endemic creatures:** Puerto Rico, The Nature Conservancy. Web.

205 **while crops like coffee are still:** Puerto Rico Comprehensive Wildlife Conservation Strategy 2005, Puerto Rico Department of Natural and Environmental Resources.

207 **"The boys were very generous":** Tito Santana and Kenny Casanova, *Tito Santana: Don't Call Me Chico* (n.p.: WOHW Publishers, 2019), 259.

MATCH 10: HULK HOGAN VS. TERRY BOLLEA

Interviews: Anthony Barcelo, Danny Brower, Gerry Brisco, Eric Bischoff, Brian Blair

228 **Muchnick's disciple Larry Matysik fell out:** Larry Matysik, *Drawing Heat the Hard Way: How Wrestling Really Works* (Toronto, Canada: ECW Press, 2009), 251.

228 **In 1983, Matysik then made:** Ibid., 22.

228 **According to Matysik, a week:** Larry Matysik, *Wrestling at the Chase: The Inside Story of Sam Muchnick and the Legends of Professional Wrestling* (Toronto, Canada: ECW Press, 2005), 186.

228 **"Wrestling is a rotten business":** Ibid., 188.

229 **Bob Backlund had been told by:** Bob Backlund and Rob Miller, *Backlund: From All-American Boy to Professional Wrestling's World Champion* (New York: Sports Publishing, 2015), 442.

229 **Junior informed Backlund that:** Hogan, *Hollywood Hulk Hogan*, 152–153.

230 **"I'm just so glad it's here this Monday":** "Hulk Hogan MSG Promo #2 1-21-1984," YouTube.

232 **a survey by a University of Kansas:** "Which Wrestler Still Gets Named Most Often When the General Public Is Asked to Name a Wrestler?" PWTorch.com, December 26, 2022.

234 **Port Tampa was its own town:** "A History of the City of Port Tampa 1888–1961," Port Tampa City Woman's Club.

234 **In 1959, Black parents sued:** Andrew T. Huse, *From Saloons to Steak Houses: A History of Tampa* (Gainesville, FL: University Press of Florida, 2020), 232.

234 **Terry has claimed that he wrestled:** Hulk Hogan with Mark Dagostino, *My Life Outside the Ring* (New York: St. Martin's Press, 2009), 118.

234 **André the Giant weighed almost:** Ibid., 12.

236 **Terry was already six feet tall:** Ibid., 16.

236 **Terry says this is when he himself quit:** Ibid., 117.

237 **"When I say I was big":** Ibid., 16.

238 **Nick ended up spending 166 days in jail:** "Hulk at Twilight," *Rolling Stone*, April 30, 2009.

238 **Terry settled a civil suit with:** "Hulk Hogan's Son Arrested for DUI in Florida, Police Say," Fox59, November 19, 2023. Web.

238 **She filed for divorce in:** *Wrestling Observer Newsletter*, November 28, 2011.

238 **cost Terry about 70 percent of the:** Ibid.

239 **who published an excerpt along:** Ryan Holiday, *Conspiracy: Peter Thiel, Hulk Hogan, Gawker, and the Anatomy of Intrigue* (New York: Portfolio, 2018), 100.

239 **recovering $31 million of the $140.1 million:** "Gawker and Hulk Hogan Reach $31 Million Settlement," *New York Times*, November 2, 2016.

239 **tried to blackmail him with it:** Ibid., 116.

239 **While Terry cooperated with the FBI:** Ibid.

239 **According to a 2010 study:** "Sports Viewers Skew Republican—But NBA Fans Lean Blue," CBS News.com, April 2, 2010.

239 **"Are you a racist?":** "Hulk Hogan Asks Fans for Forgiveness Over Racial Slur Scandal," YouTube.

240 **a reported $10 million settlement for:** "Laser Spine Institute Shuts Down," Pain News Network. Web.

249 **his name was invoked multiple:** "Hulk Hogan's Testimony from the WWF's 1994 Steroid Trial," Angelfire.com.

251 **He was the most requested celebrity:** "WWE Superstar John Cena Grants 300th Make-A-Wish," ABC6 Action News Philadelphia. Web.

255 **"When it's time for me to go":** Cook, "Playboy Interview: Vince McMahon."

THE MAIN EVENT: *JAVANMARDI*

Interviews: Nikki Vaziri, Caryl Vaziri, Khosrow Vaziri, Mickey Sherman

258 **Marvel has called Trilith home:** "The Trilith Show," *Fayette County News Magazine*, 2021.

265 **"The attendant's attorney, Eddie Rodriguez":** "People," *Stamford Advocate*, October 4, 1985.

265   "Tony liked the Sheik": Ibid.

266   **Sherman visited WWF headquarters to film:** "Mickey Sherman with Iron Sheik and Friends," YouTube video.

267   **"I smell something in there":** "Wrestler Pleads Innocent," *Asbury Park Press*, June 2, 1987.

268   **before being released on $5,000 bail:** Ibid.

268   **the incident made page two:** "Thrown for Loss," *New York Daily News*, May 28, 1987.

268   **spent the next several weeks:** Hacksaw Jim Duggan with Scott E. Williams, *Hacksaw: The Jim Duggan Story* (Chicago: Triumph Books, 2016), 108.

268   **"I don't like him. I never have":** "'Sheik' Denies Drug Involvement," *Daily Register (Red Bank, NJ)*, June 2, 1987.

269   **"This is a court of law":** Ibid.

269   **Khos accepted one year:** "Iron Sheik to Enter Probation Program," *Asbury Park Press*, June 18, 1987.

270   **"She wouldn't calm down":** Clayton County Police Incident Report, May 4, 2003, Case Number 03022229.

271   **"Will the assistant district attorney":** State of Georgia vs. Charles Warren Reynolds, Case No. 03-CR-01468-7, Plea and Sentencing.

271   **"First of all, I want to say":** Ibid.

AND MUCH, MUCH MORE!

Where are the pictures? Is there more content?

If you're asking these questions, I've got good news—there's much, much more, just like the back of the wrestling VHS tapes in the video stores used to promise. You can unlock an entire multimedia experience of nostalgia and old-school wrestling content by scanning the QR code on the next page and joining The Brad Pack (on Instagram and X/Twitter: @bradpackbooks).

Among the bonus content available in this digital community:

- Hundreds of photos from my road trip and wrestlers' personal collections
- Internal memos from the WWF office during the 1983–1984 expansion
- Spreadsheets listing attendance figures and payoffs from various house shows in the 1980s
- Internal documents with pay-per-view revenues
- The Iron Sheik's report cards from Iran

The Brad Pack is a site dedicated to the untold stories and unsung heroes of Generation X, specializing in sports and entertainment (and, of course, sports entertainment). You know you're a member of the Brad Pack if the following resonates: The phrase "be kind, rewind" makes you smile. Mike Tyson, not Tyson Fury. The Angels play in California, not Los Angeles, and they're certainly not "of Anaheim." Music is actually on MTV. Han shot first. You have *a* Facebook, not Facebook. You know what it feels like to hold a recording device up to a radio. You know what a radio is . . . and a Shack that sells them. You know more than your own phone number from memory. It is and always will be the WWF. You read things longer than this paragraph.